THE MIGHTY ZODIAC

STARFALL

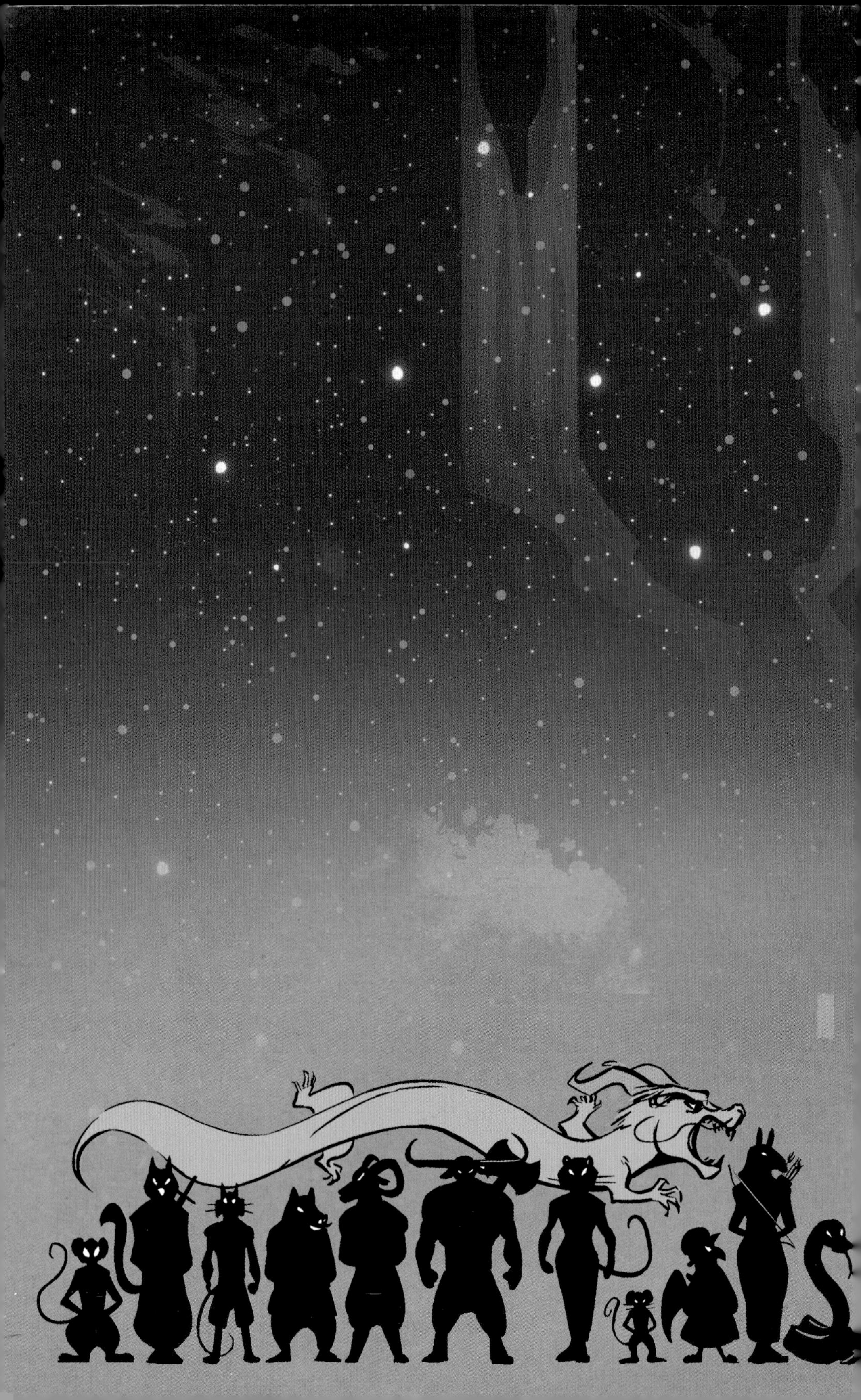

THE MIGHTY ZODIAC

STARFALL

WRITTEN BY J. Torres

ILLUSTRATED BY Corin Howell

COLORED BY Maarta Laiho

LETTERED BY Warren Wucinich

DESIGNED BY Hilary Thompson

EDITED BY Robin Herrera

PUBLISHED BY ONI PRESS, INC.

Joe Nozemack, **PUBLISHER**
James Lucas Jones, **EDITOR IN CHIEF**
Andrew McIntire, **V.P. OF MARKETING & SALES**
David Dissanayake, **SALES MANAGER**
Rachel Reed, **PUBLICITY COORDINATOR**
Troy Look, **DIRECTOR OF DESIGN & PRODUCTION**
Hilary Thompson, **GRAPHIC DESIGNER**
Angie Dobson, **DIGITAL PREPRESS TECHNICIAN**
Ari Yarwood, **MANAGING EDITOR**
Charlie Chu, **SENIOR EDITOR**
Robin Herrera, **EDITOR**
Bess Pallares, **EDITORIAL ASSISTANT**
Brad Rooks, **DIRECTOR OF LOGISTICS**
Jung Lee, **LOGISTICS ASSOCIATE**

ONIPRESS.COM
FACEBOOK.COM/ONIPRESS
TWITTER.COM/ONIPRESS
ONIPRESS.TUMBLR.COM
INSTAGRAM.COM/ONIPRESS

Originally published as issues 1-6
of the Oni Press comic series *The Mighty Zodiac*.

First Edition: March 2017
ISBN 978-1-62010-315-9
eISBN 978-1-62010-316-6

1 3 5 7 9 10 8 6 4 2

Library of Congress Control Number: 2016945265

Printed in China.

CHAPTER ONE

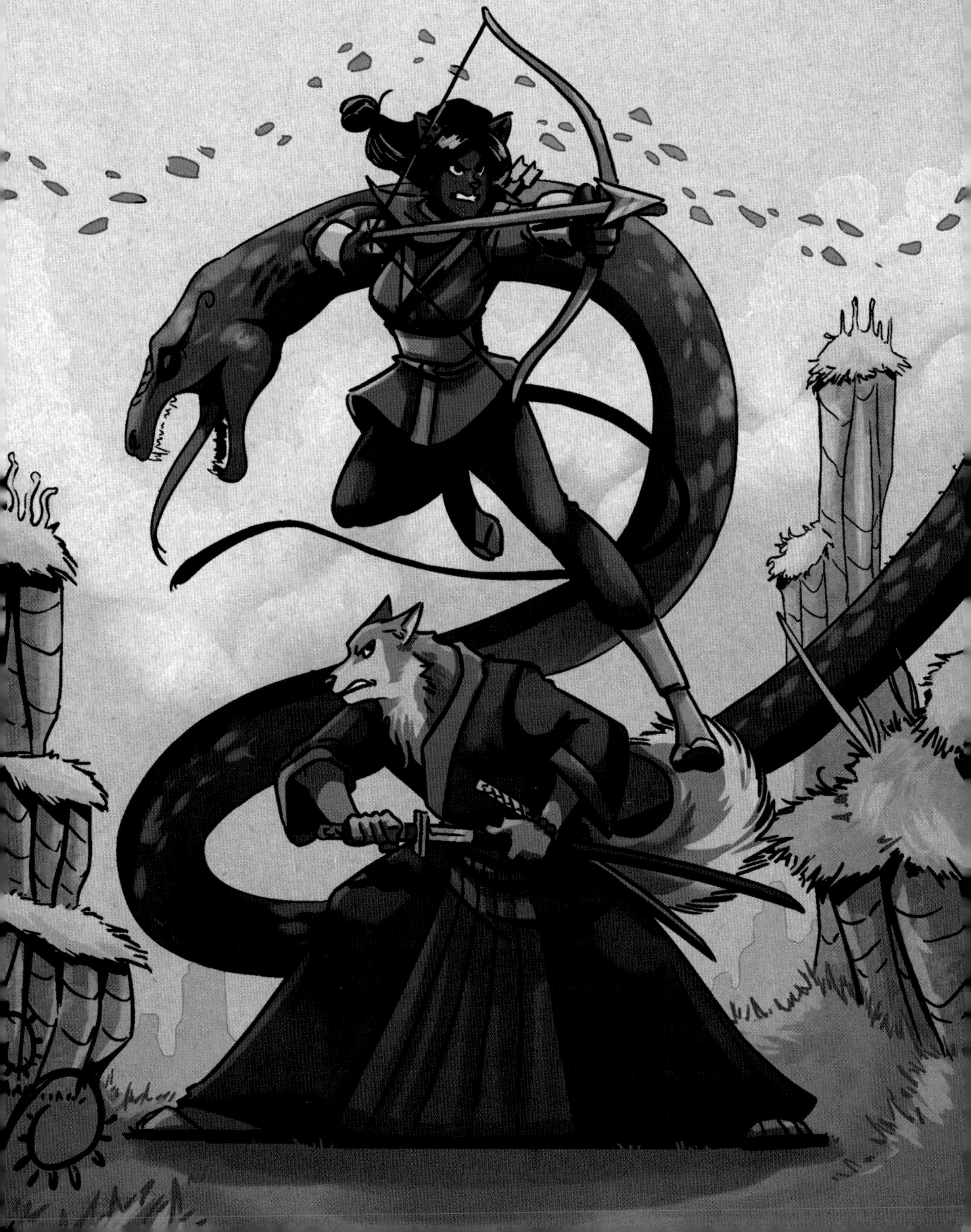

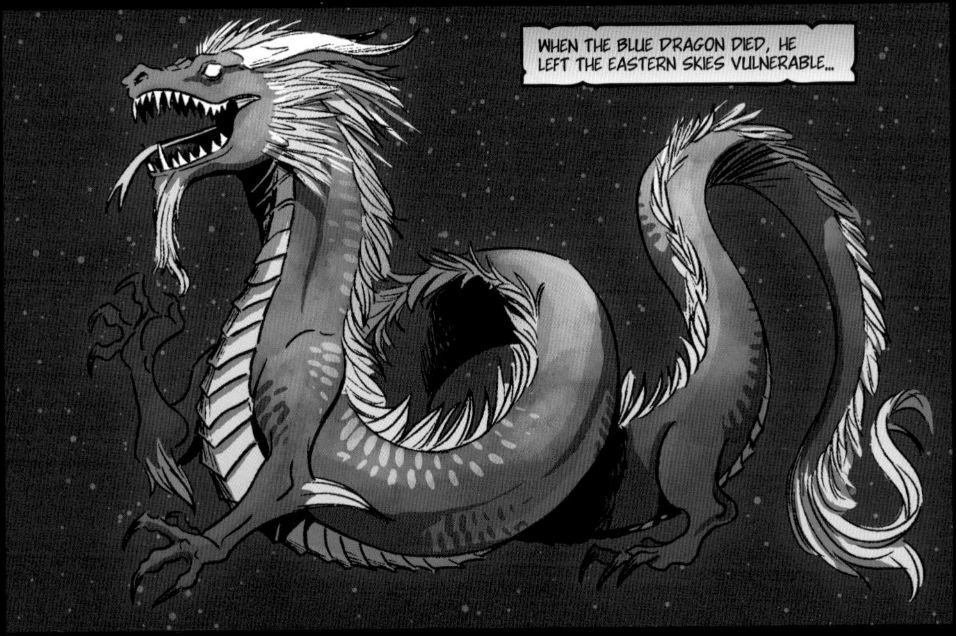
WHEN THE BLUE DRAGON DIED, HE LEFT THE EASTERN SKIES VULNERABLE...

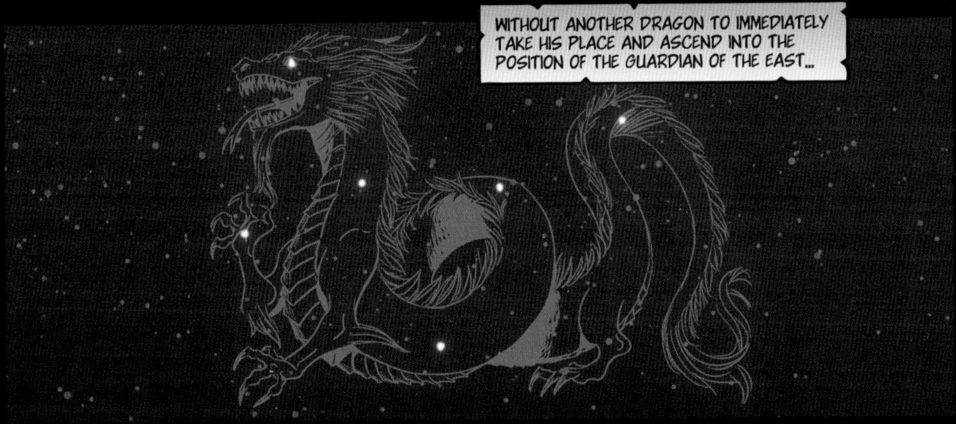
WITHOUT ANOTHER DRAGON TO IMMEDIATELY TAKE HIS PLACE AND ASCEND INTO THE POSITION OF THE GUARDIAN OF THE EAST...

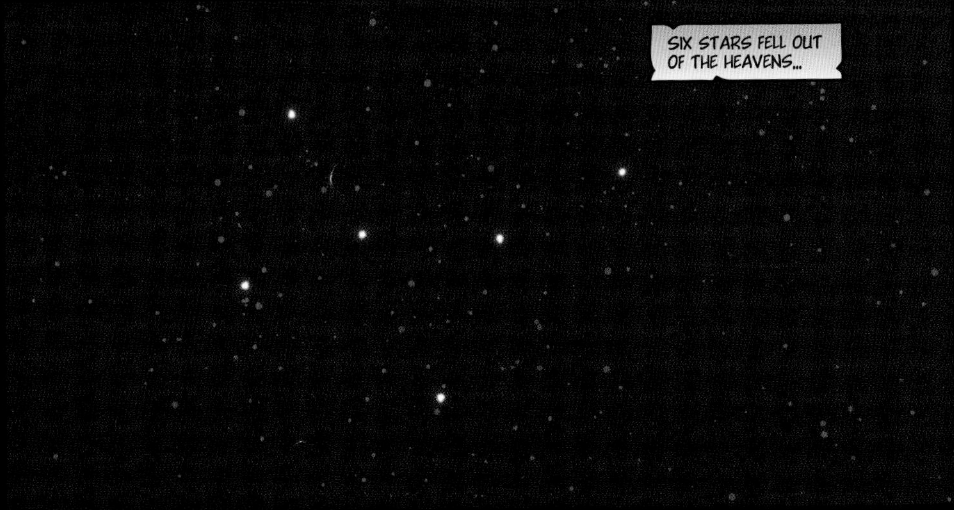
SIX STARS FELL OUT OF THE HEAVENS...

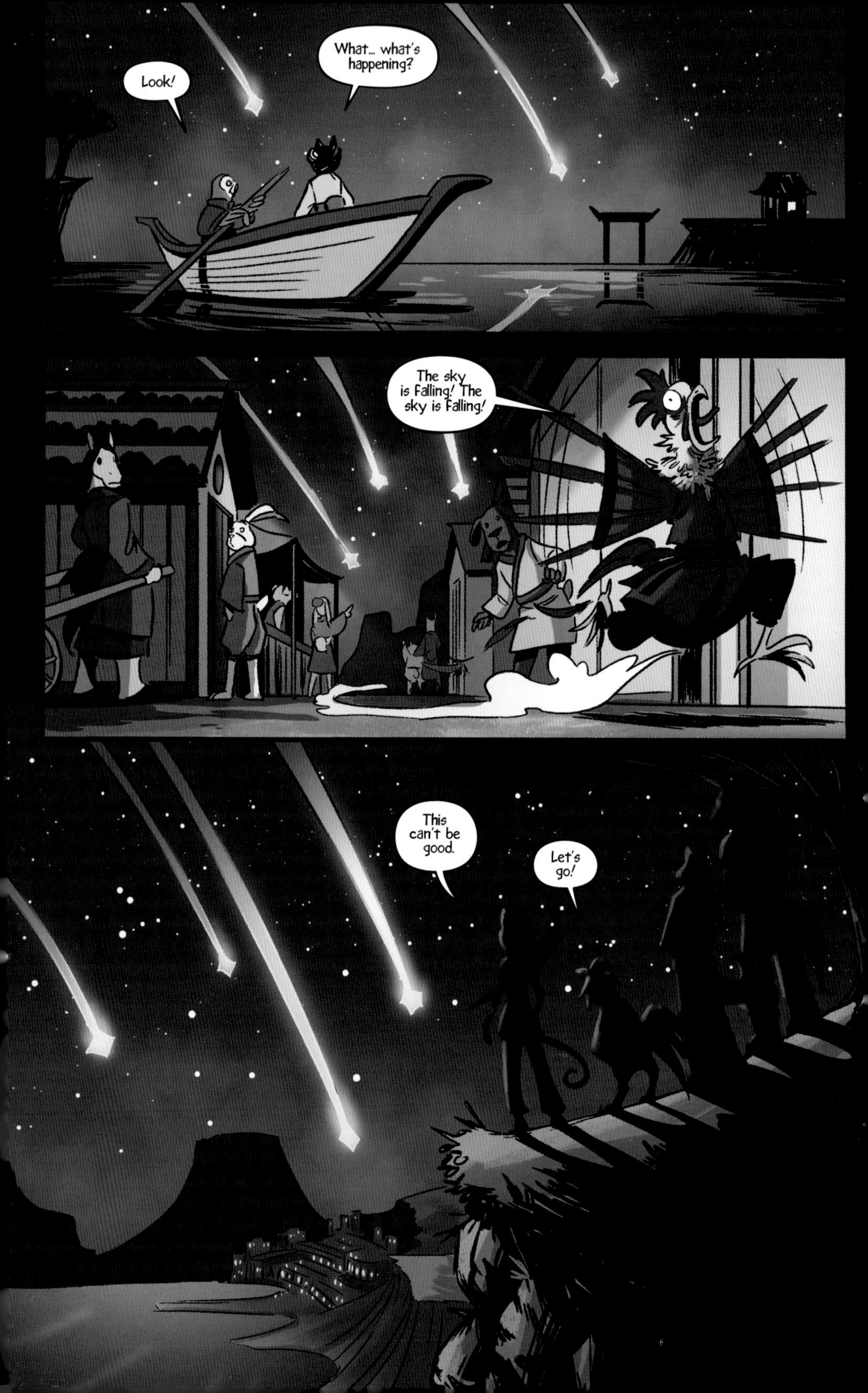
Look!
What... what's happening?
The sky is falling! The sky is falling!
This can't be good.
Let's go!

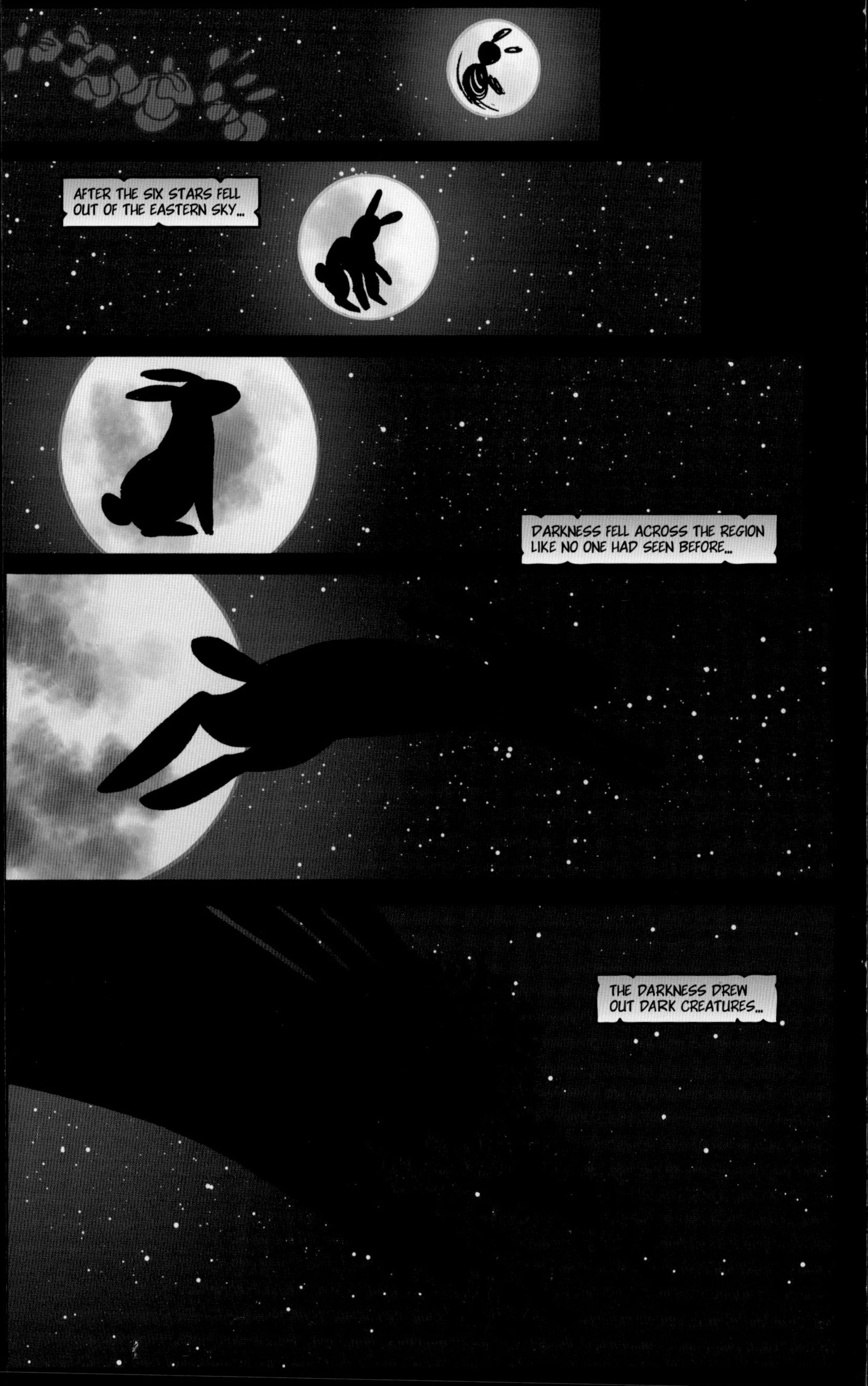
AFTER THE SIX STARS FELL OUT OF THE EASTERN SKY...
DARKNESS FELL ACROSS THE REGION LIKE NO ONE HAD SEEN BEFORE...
THE DARKNESS DREW OUT DARK CREATURES...

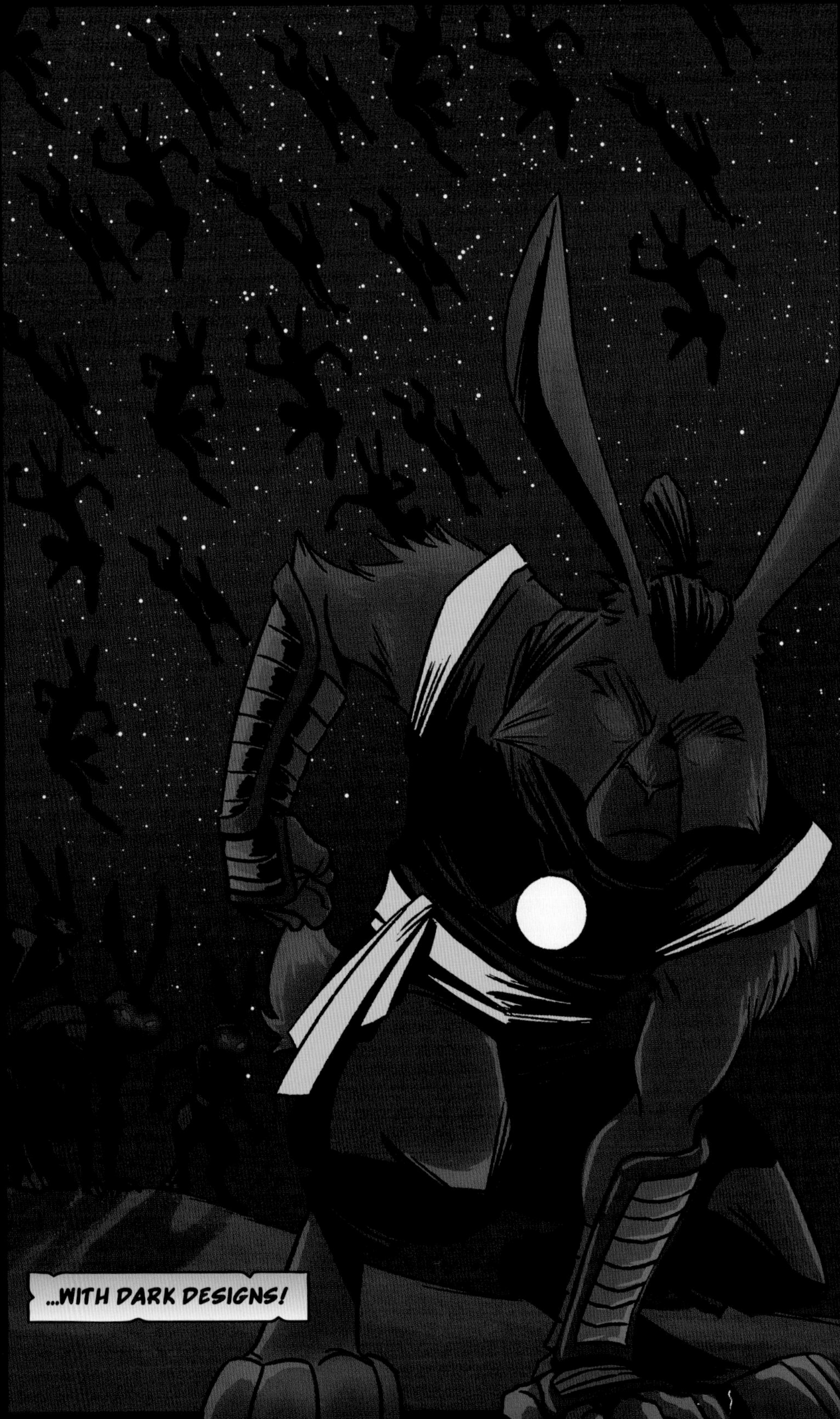
...WITH DARK DESIGNS!

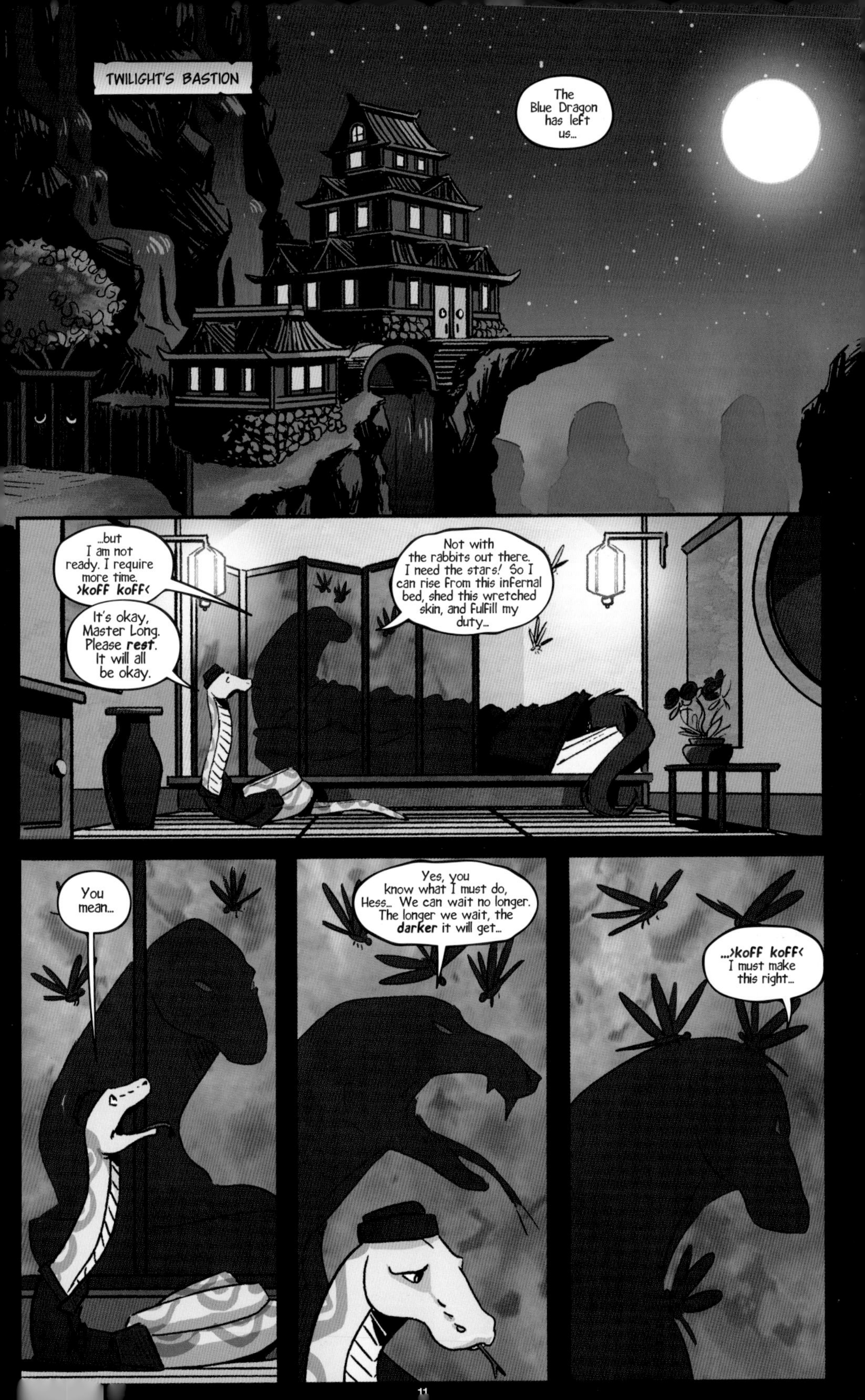
TWILIGHT'S BASTION
The Blue Dragon has left us...
...but I am not ready. I require more time. **>koff koff<**
It's okay, Master Long. Please **rest**. It will all be okay.
Not with the rabbits out there. I need the stars! So I can rise from this infernal bed, shed this wretched skin, and fulfill my duty...
You mean...
Yes, you know what I must do, Hess... We can wait no longer. The longer we wait, the **darker** it will get...
...>koff koff< I must make this right...

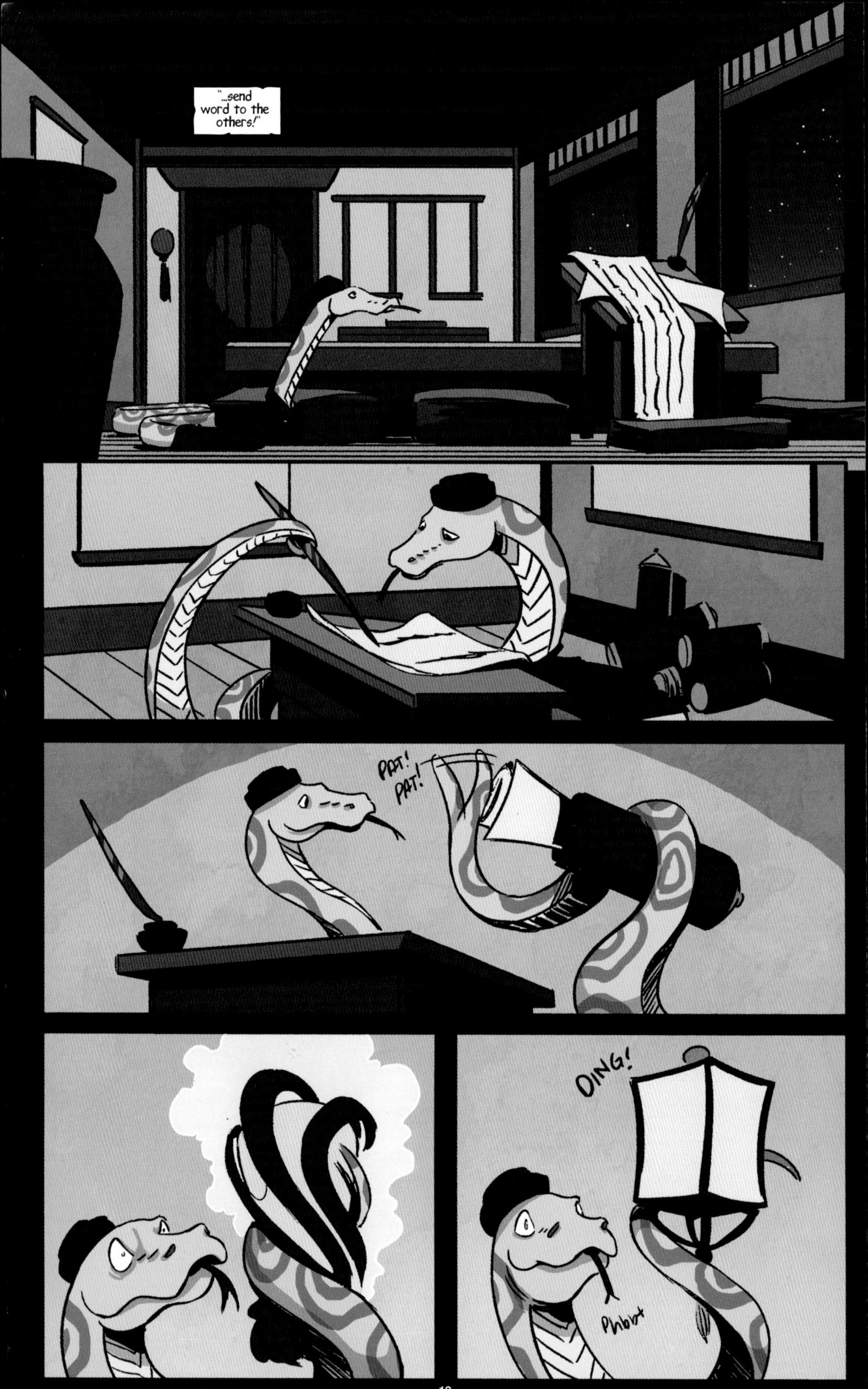
"...send word to the others!"
PAT! PAT!
DING!
Phbbt

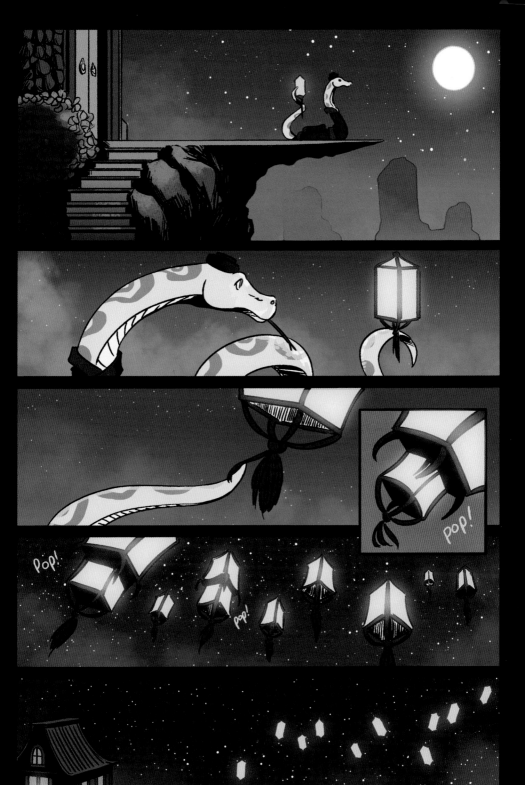

pop!

pop!

pop!

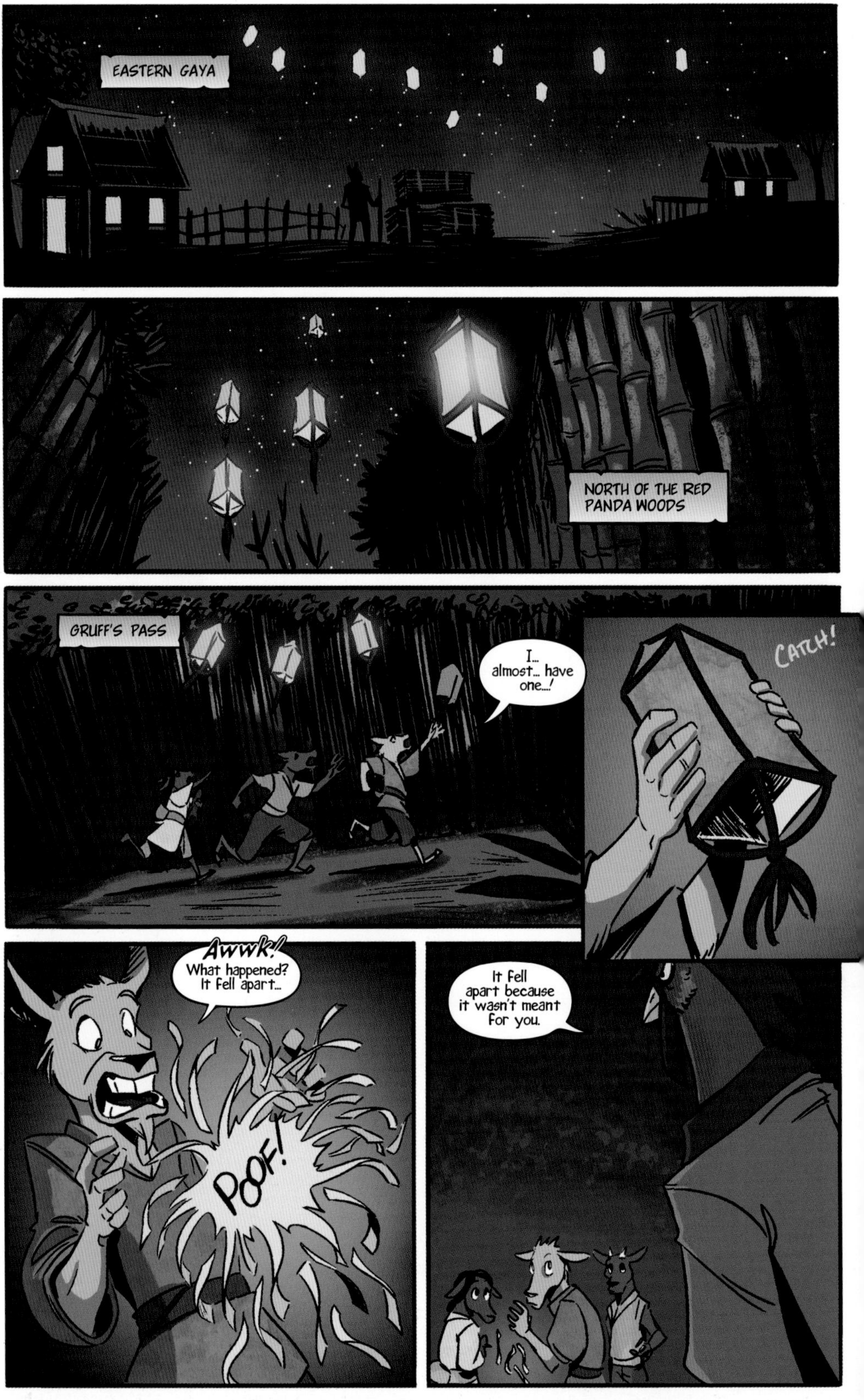
EASTERN GAYA
NORTH OF THE RED PANDA WOODS
GRUFF'S PASS
I... almost... have one...!
CATCH!
Awwk! What happened? It fell apart...
POOF!
It fell apart because it wasn't meant for you.

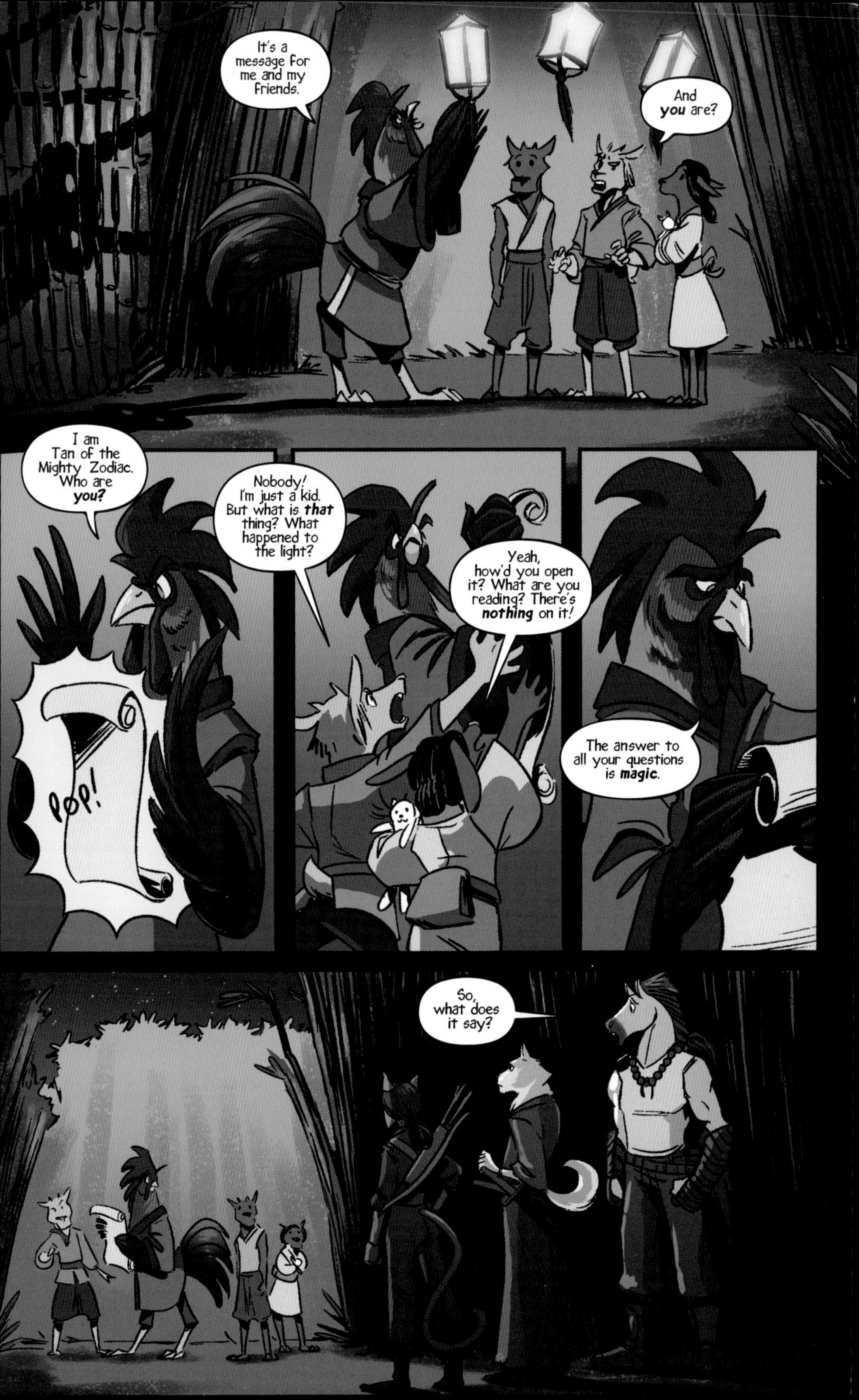
It's a message for me and my friends.
And **you** are?
I am Tan of the Mighty Zodiac. Who are ***you?***
POP!
Nobody! I'm just a kid. But what is ***that*** thing? What happened to the light?
Yeah, how'd you open it? What are you reading? There's ***nothing*** on it!
The answer to all your questions is **magic**.
So, what does it say?

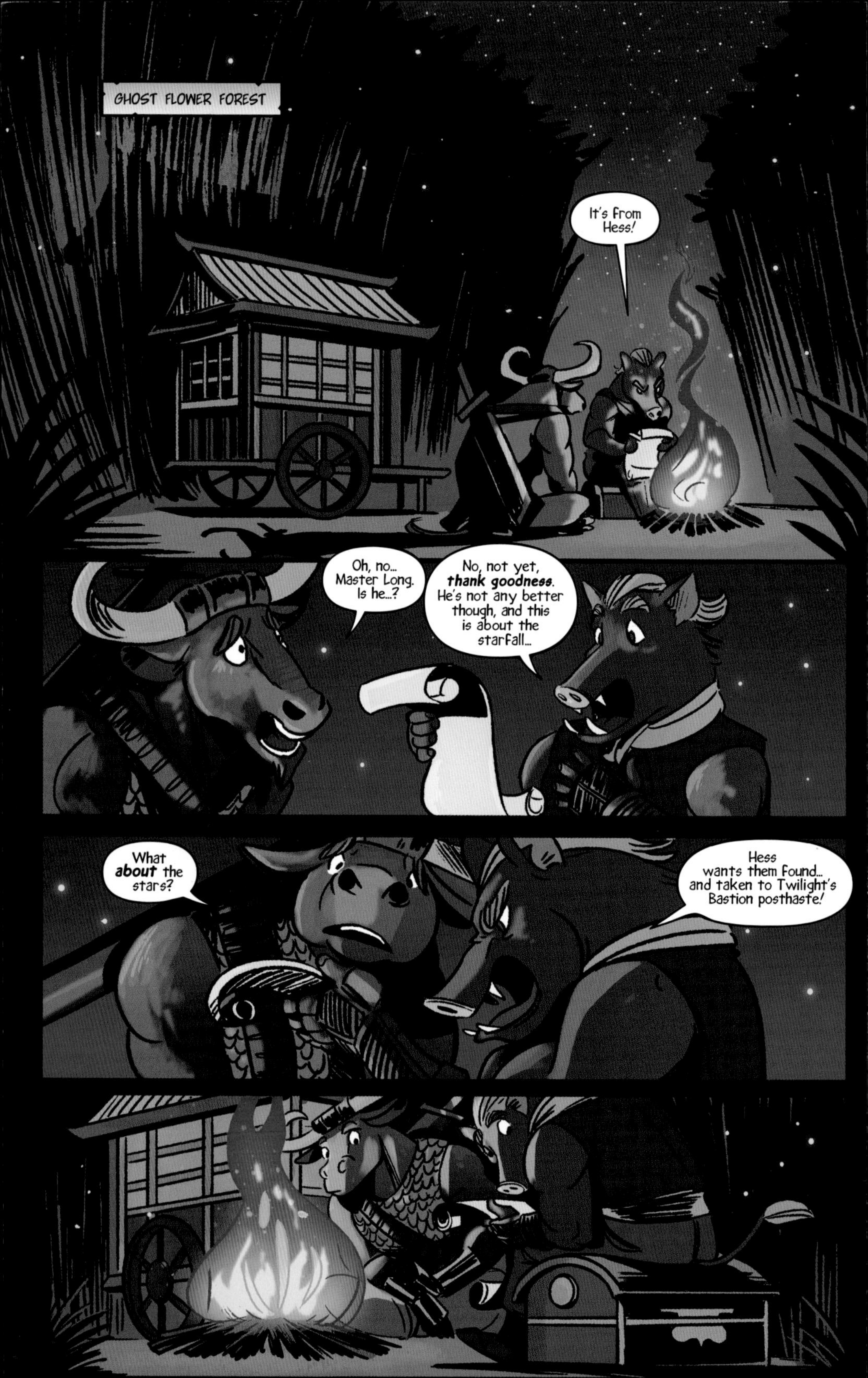
GHOST FLOWER FOREST
It's from Hess!
Oh, no... Master Long. Is he...?
No, not yet, **thank goodness**. He's not any better though, and this is about the starfall...
What **about** the stars?
Hess wants them found... and taken to Twilight's Bastion posthaste!

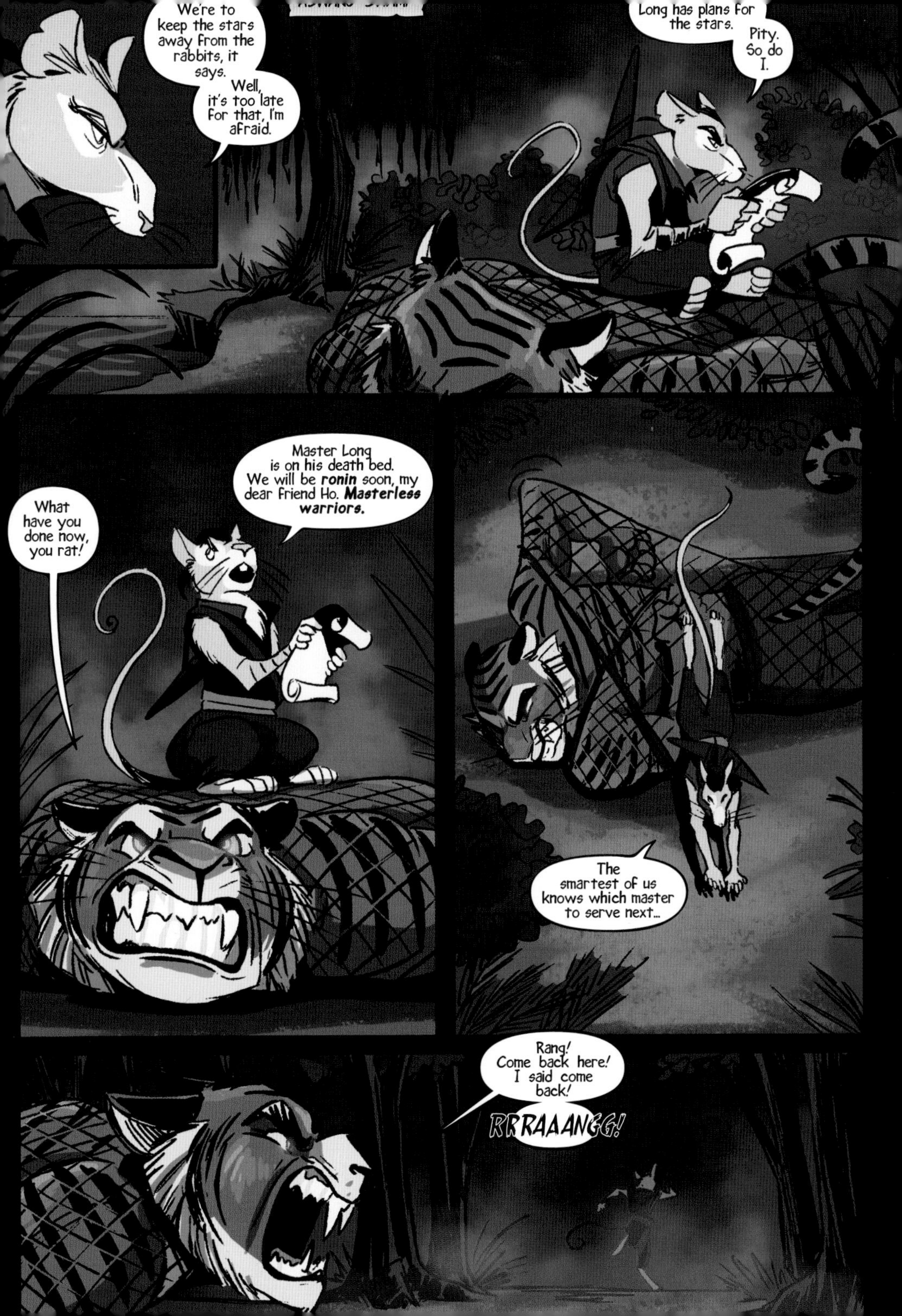
We're to keep the stars away from the rabbits, it says.
Well, it's too late for that, I'm afraid.
Long has plans for the stars.
Pity. So do I.
What have you done now, you rat!
Master Long is on his death bed. We will be **ronin** soon, my dear friend Ho. ***Masterless warriors.***
The smartest of us knows which master to serve next...
Rang! Come back here! I said come back!
RRRAAANGG!

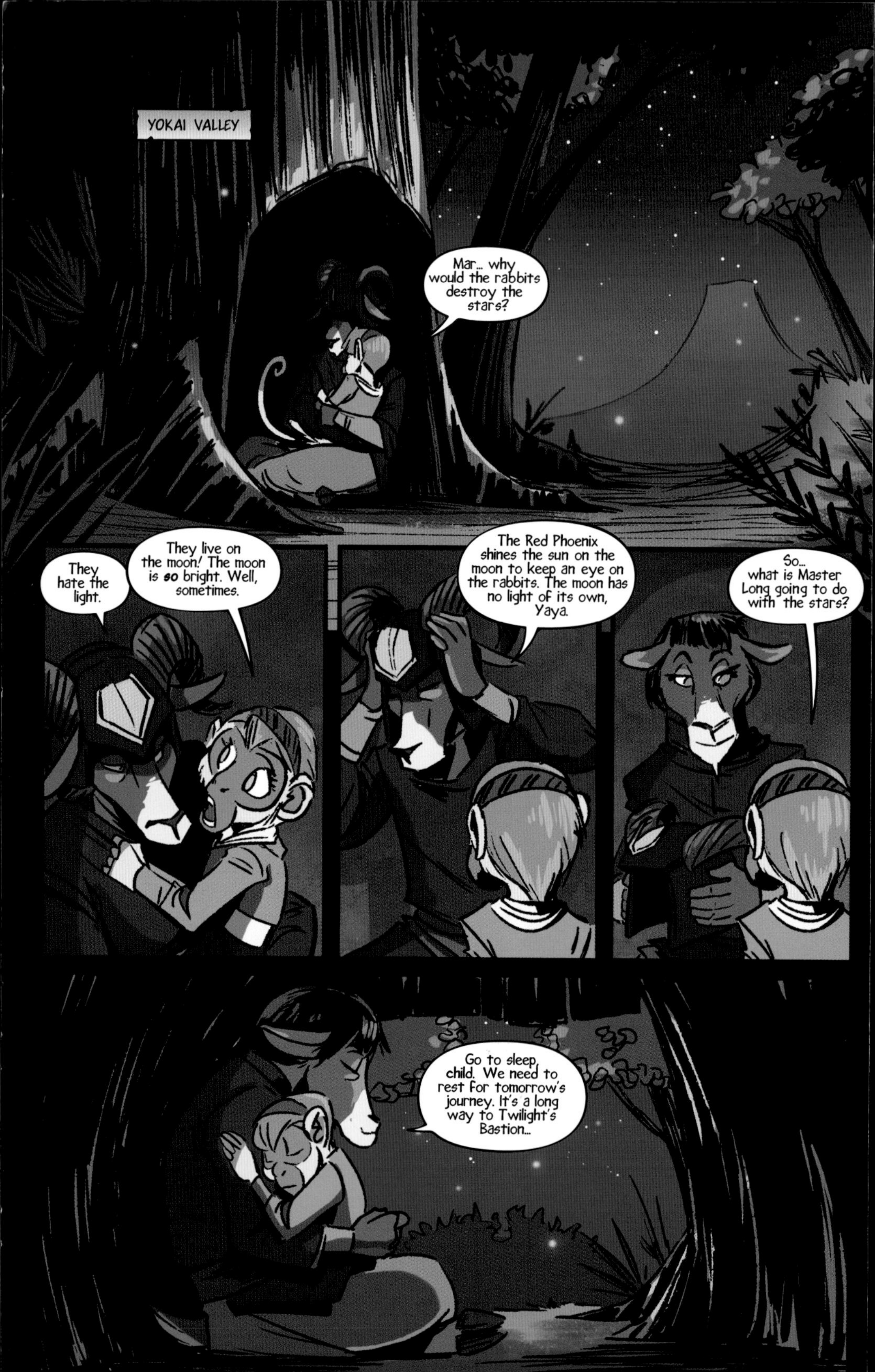

YOKAI VALLEY
Mar... why would the rabbits destroy the stars?
They hate the light.
They live on the moon! The moon is **so** bright. Well, sometimes.
The Red Phoenix shines the sun on the moon to keep an eye on the rabbits. The moon has no light of its own, Yaya.
So... what is Master Long going to do with the stars?
Go to sleep, child. We need to rest for tomorrow's journey. It's a long way to Twilight's Bastion...

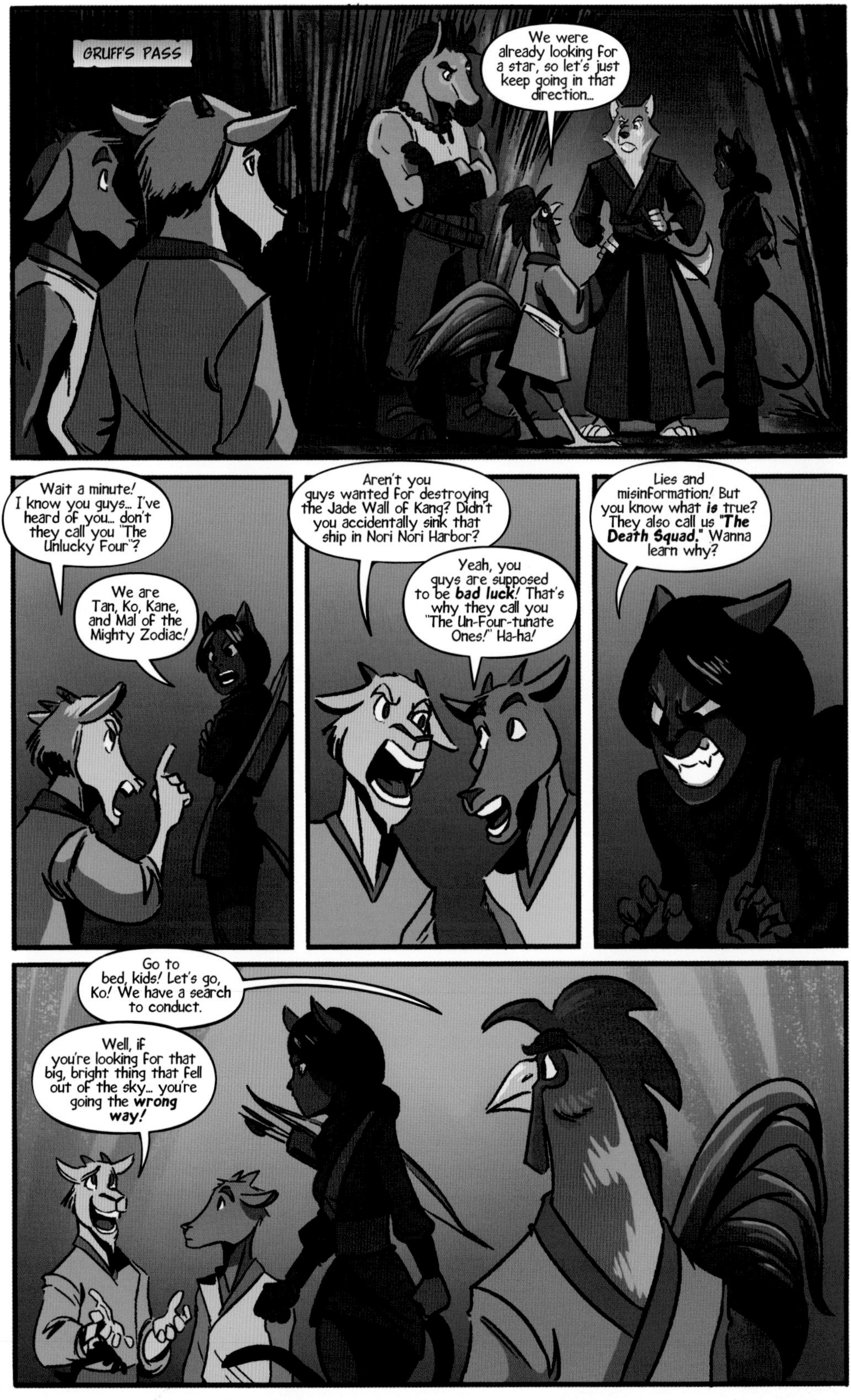
GRUFF'S PASS
We were already looking for a star, so let's just keep going in that direction...
Wait a minute! I know you guys... I've heard of you... don't they call you "The Unlucky Four"?
We are Tan, Ko, Kane, and Mal of the Mighty Zodiac!
Aren't you guys wanted for destroying the Jade Wall of Kang? Didn't you accidentally sink that ship in Nori Nori Harbor?
Yeah, you guys are supposed to be **bad luck**! That's why they call you "The Un-Four-tunate Ones!" Ha-ha!
Lies and misinformation! But you know what *is* true? They also call us **"The Death Squad."** Wanna learn why?
Go to bed, kids! Let's go, Ko! We have a search to conduct.
Well, if you're looking for that big, bright thing that fell out of the sky... you're going the **wrong way!**

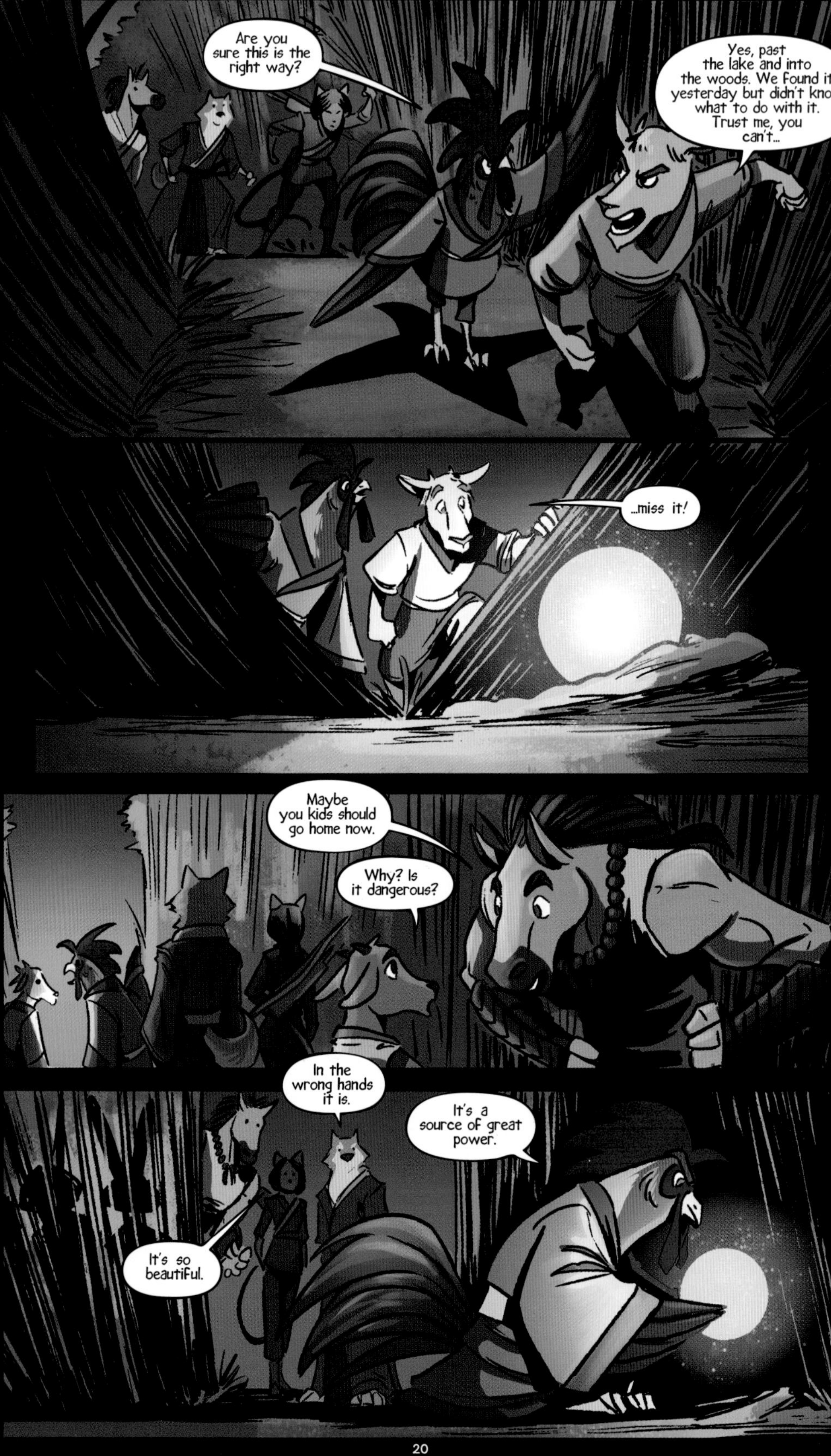
Are you sure this is the right way?
Yes, past the lake and into the woods. We found it yesterday but didn't know what to do with it. Trust me, you can't...
...miss it!
Maybe you kids should go home now.
Why? Is it dangerous?
In the wrong hands it is.
It's a source of great power.
It's so beautiful.

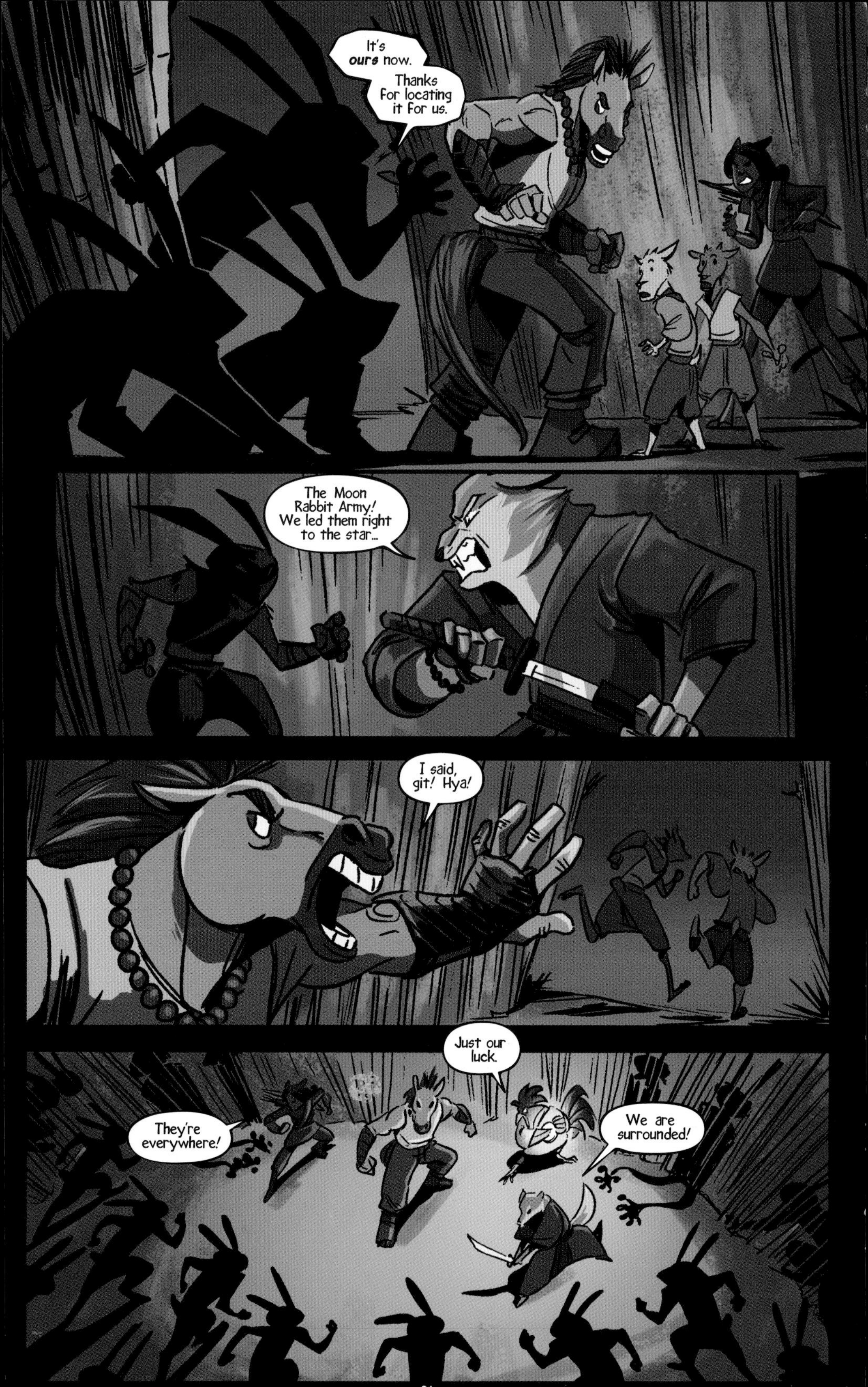
It's **ours** now.
Thanks for locating it for us.
The Moon Rabbit Army! We led them right to the star...
I said, git! Hya!
Just our luck.
They're everywhere!
We are surrounded!

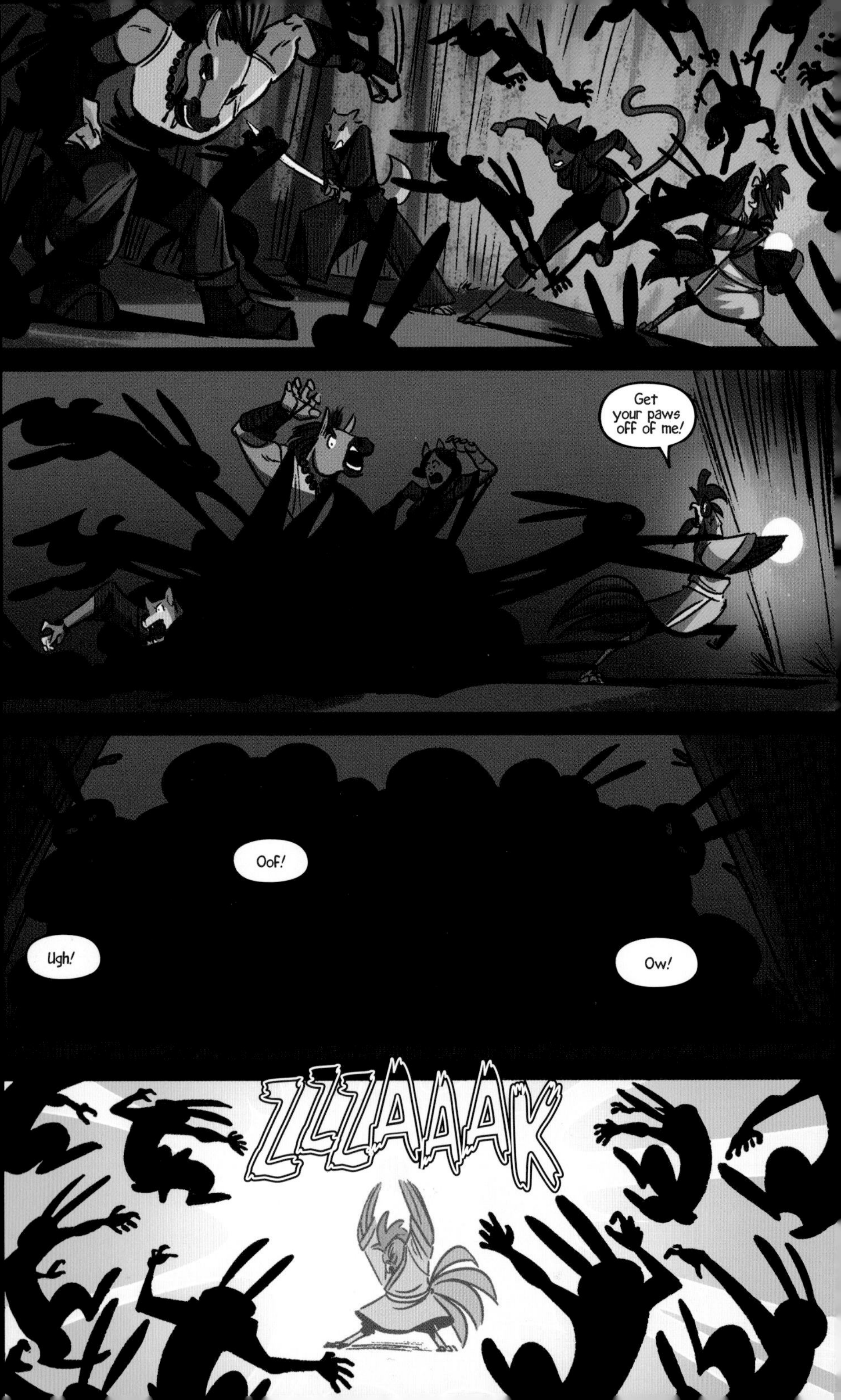
Get your paws off of me!
Oof!
Ugh!
Ow!
ZZZAAAK

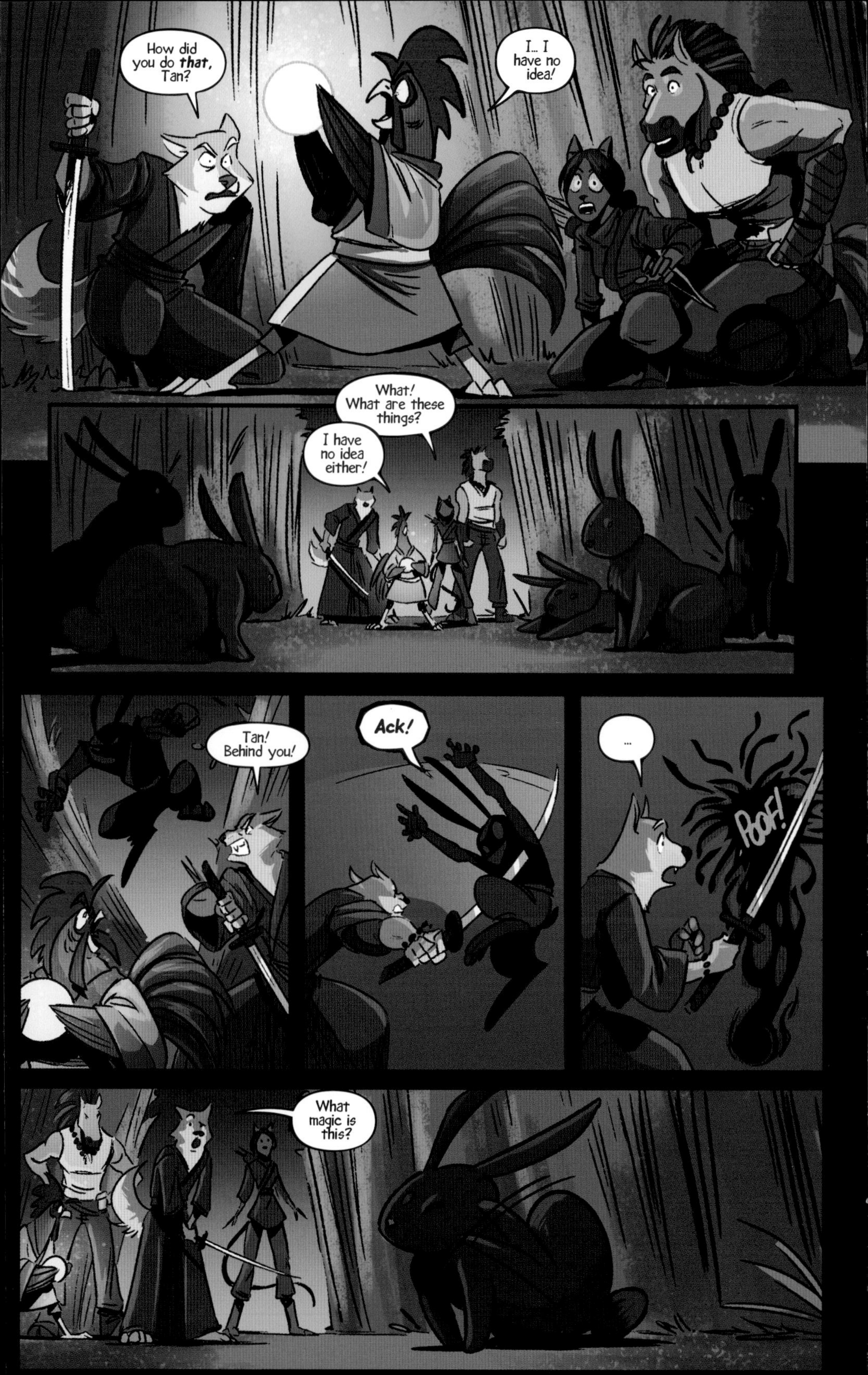
How did you do **that**, Tan?
I... I have no idea!
What! What are these things?
I have no idea either!
Tan! Behind you!
Ack!
...
POOF!
What magic is this?

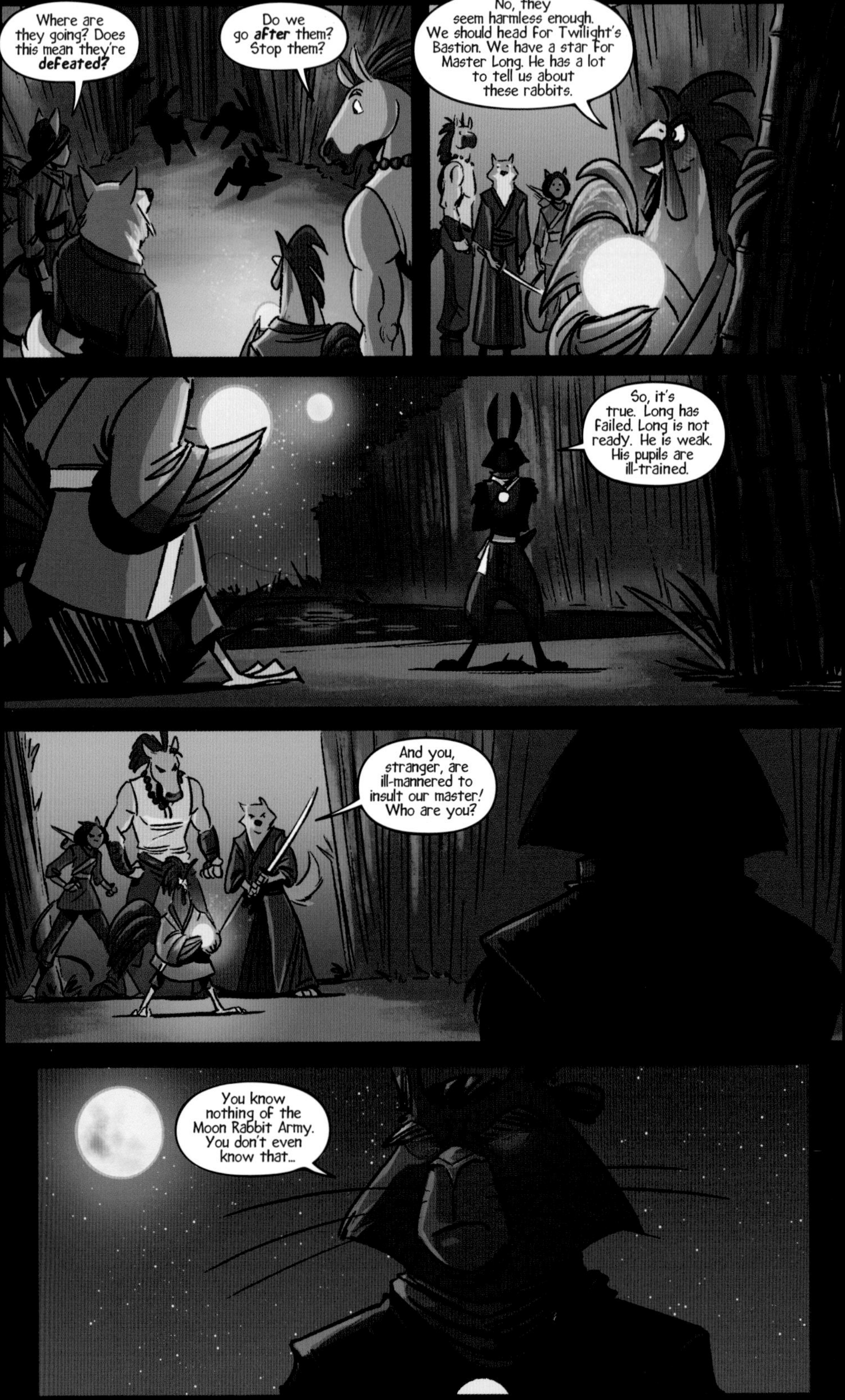
Where are they going? Does this mean they're **defeated?**
Do we go **after** them? Stop them?
No, they seem harmless enough. We should head for Twilight's Bastion. We have a star for Master Long. He has a lot to tell us about these rabbits.
So, it's true. Long has failed. Long is not ready. He is weak. His pupils are ill-trained.
And you, stranger, are ill-mannered to insult our master! Who are you?
You know nothing of the Moon Rabbit Army. You don't even know that...

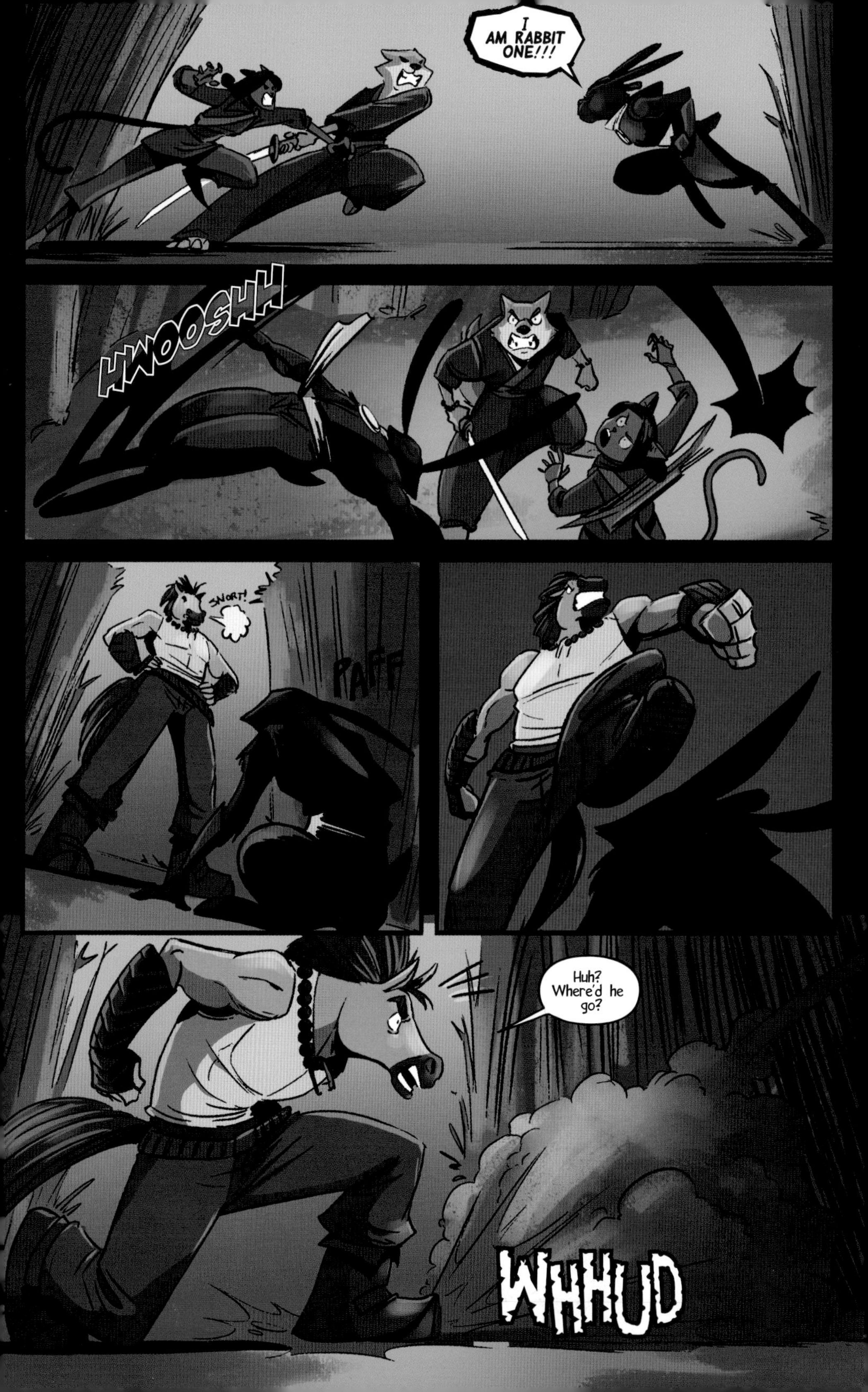
I AM RABBIT ONE!!!
HWOOSHH
SNORT!
PAFF
Huh? Where'd he go?
WHHUD

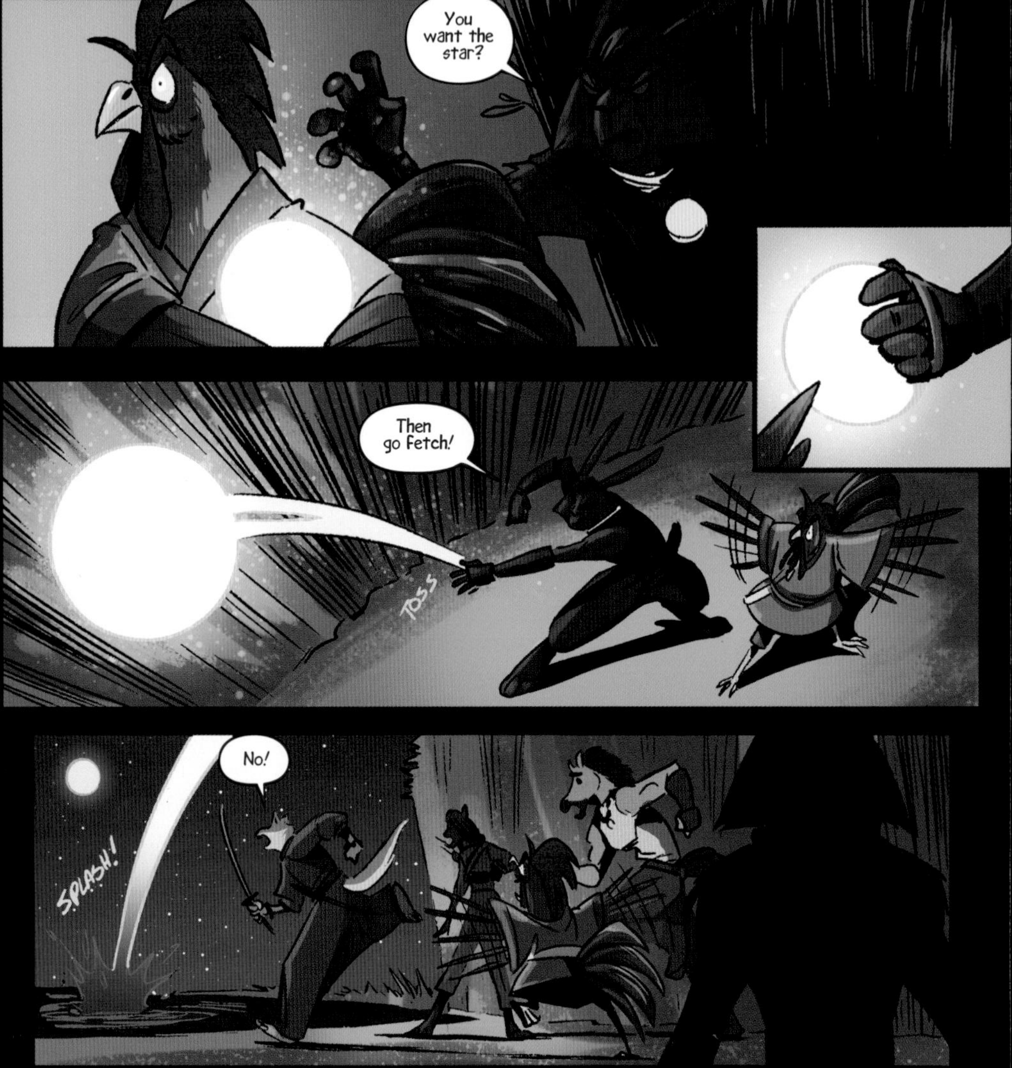
You want the star?
Then go fetch!
TOSS
No!
SPLASH!

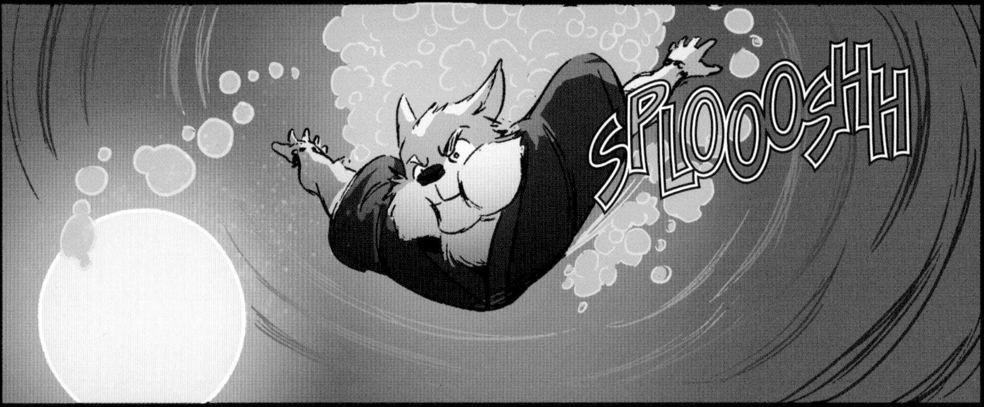
SPLOOOSHH
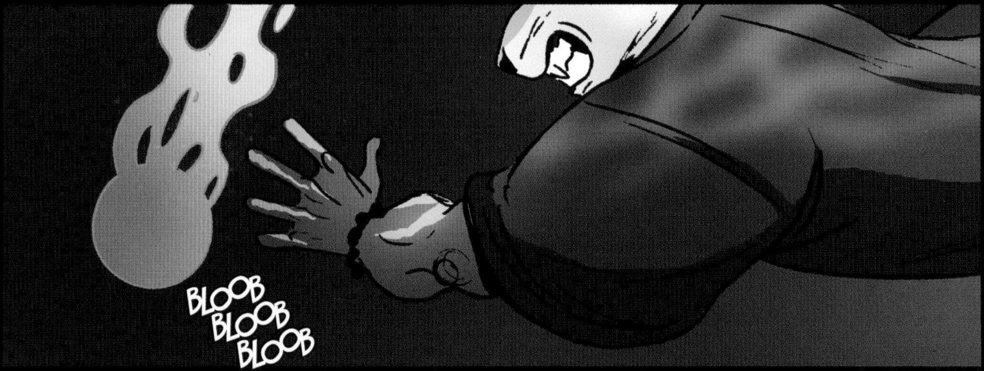
BLOOB
BLOOB
BLOOB
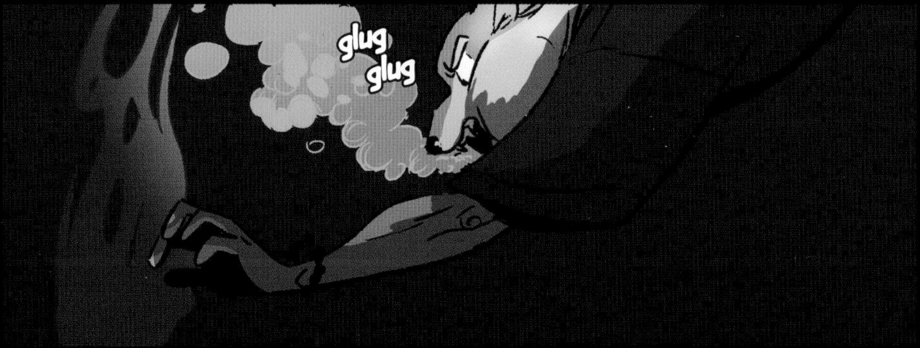
glug
glug
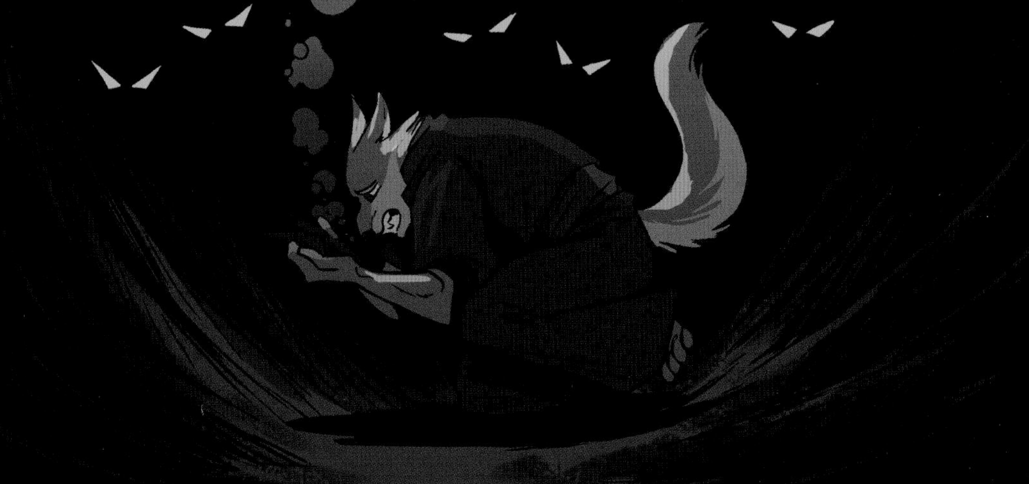

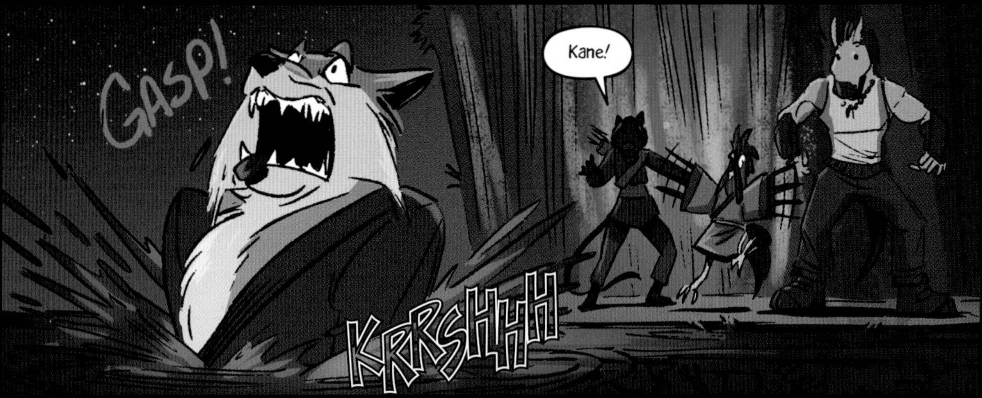
GASP!
Kane!
KRRSHHH
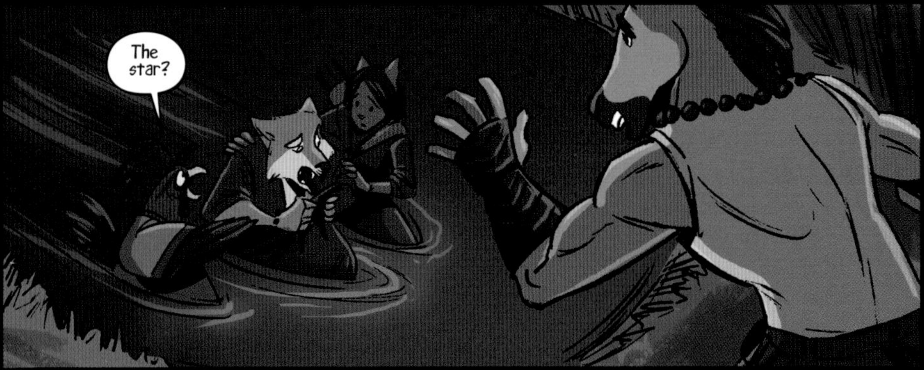
The star?
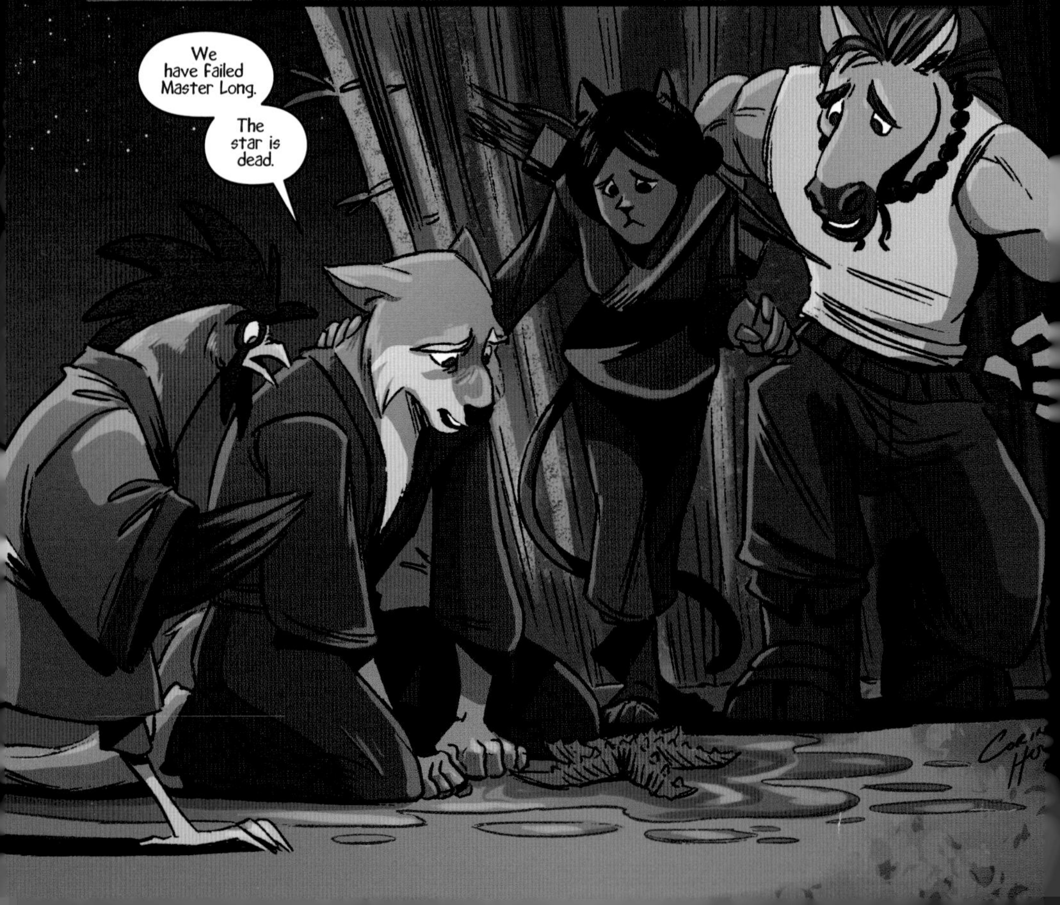
We have failed Master Long.
The star is dead.

CHAPTER TWO

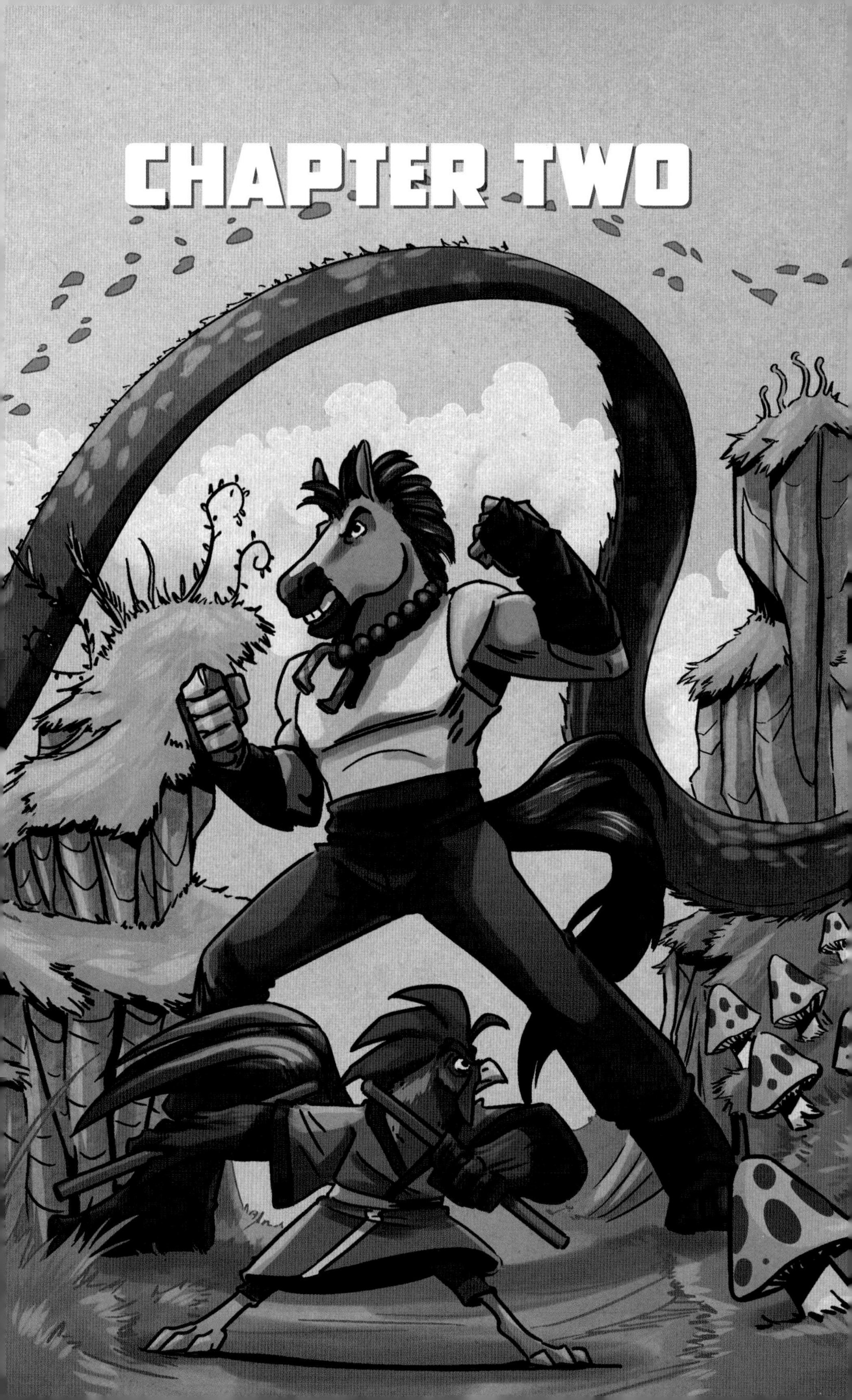

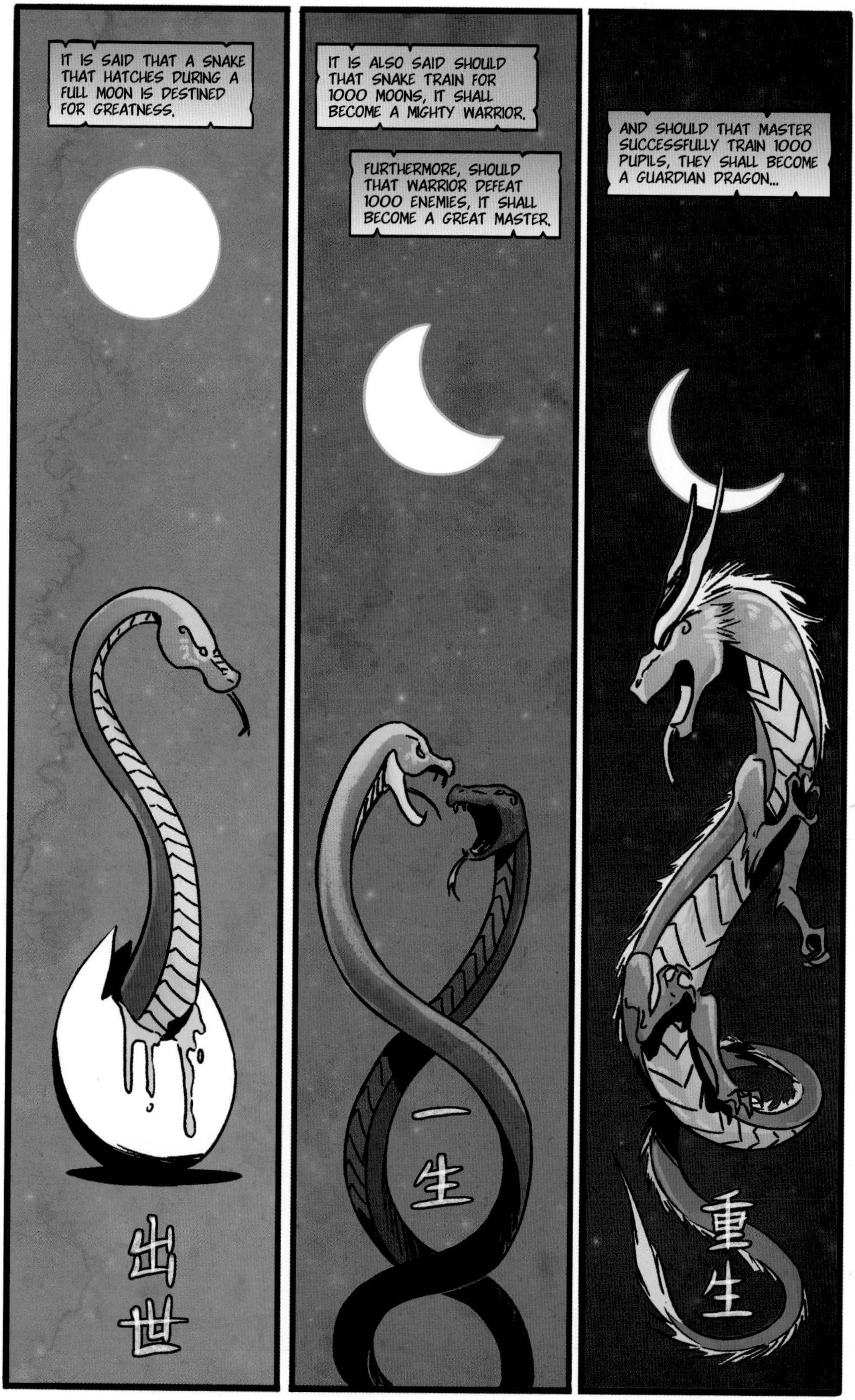
IT IS SAID THAT A SNAKE THAT HATCHES DURING A FULL MOON IS DESTINED FOR GREATNESS.
出世
IT IS ALSO SAID SHOULD THAT SNAKE TRAIN FOR 1000 MOONS, IT SHALL BECOME A MIGHTY WARRIOR.
FURTHERMORE, SHOULD THAT WARRIOR DEFEAT 1000 ENEMIES, IT SHALL BECOME A GREAT MASTER.
一生
AND SHOULD THAT MASTER SUCCESSFULLY TRAIN 1000 PUPILS, THEY SHALL BECOME A GUARDIAN DRAGON...
重生

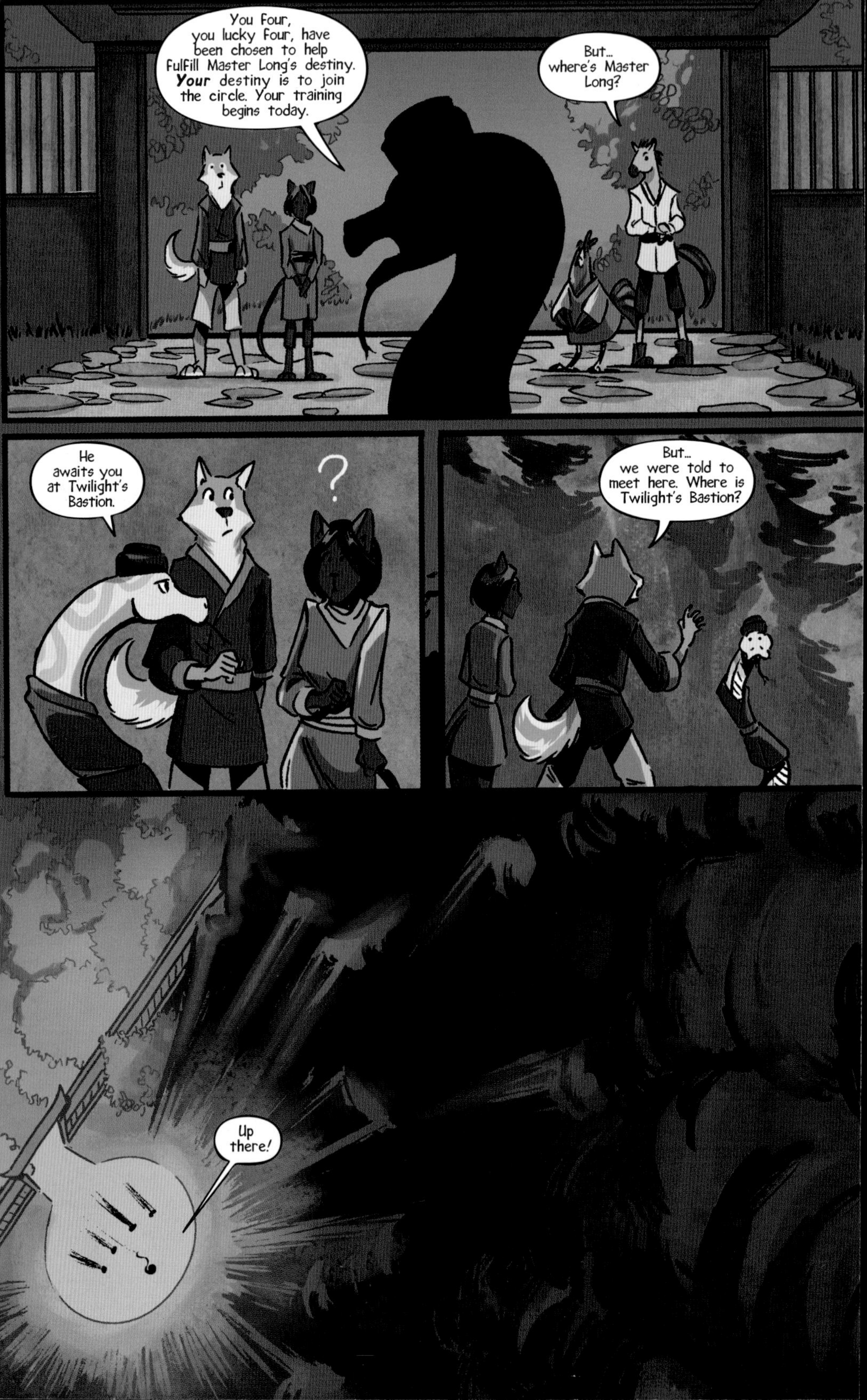
You Four, you lucky Four, have been chosen to help fulfill Master Long's destiny. **Your** destiny is to join the circle. Your training begins today.
But... where's Master Long?
He awaits you at Twilight's Bastion.
?
But... we were told to meet here. Where is Twilight's Bastion?
Up there!

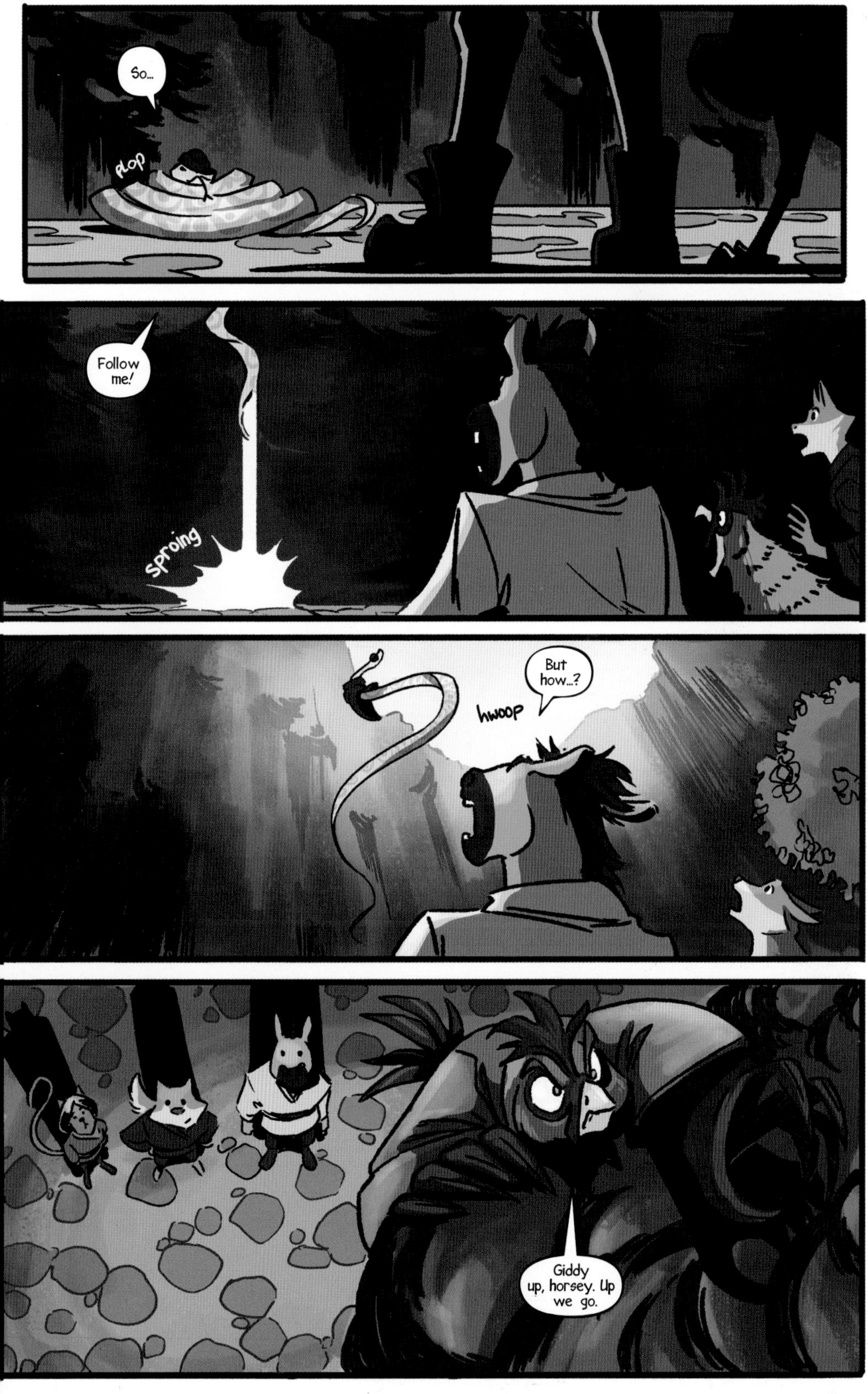
So...
plop
Follow me!
sproing
But how...?
hwoop
Giddy up, horsey. Up we go.

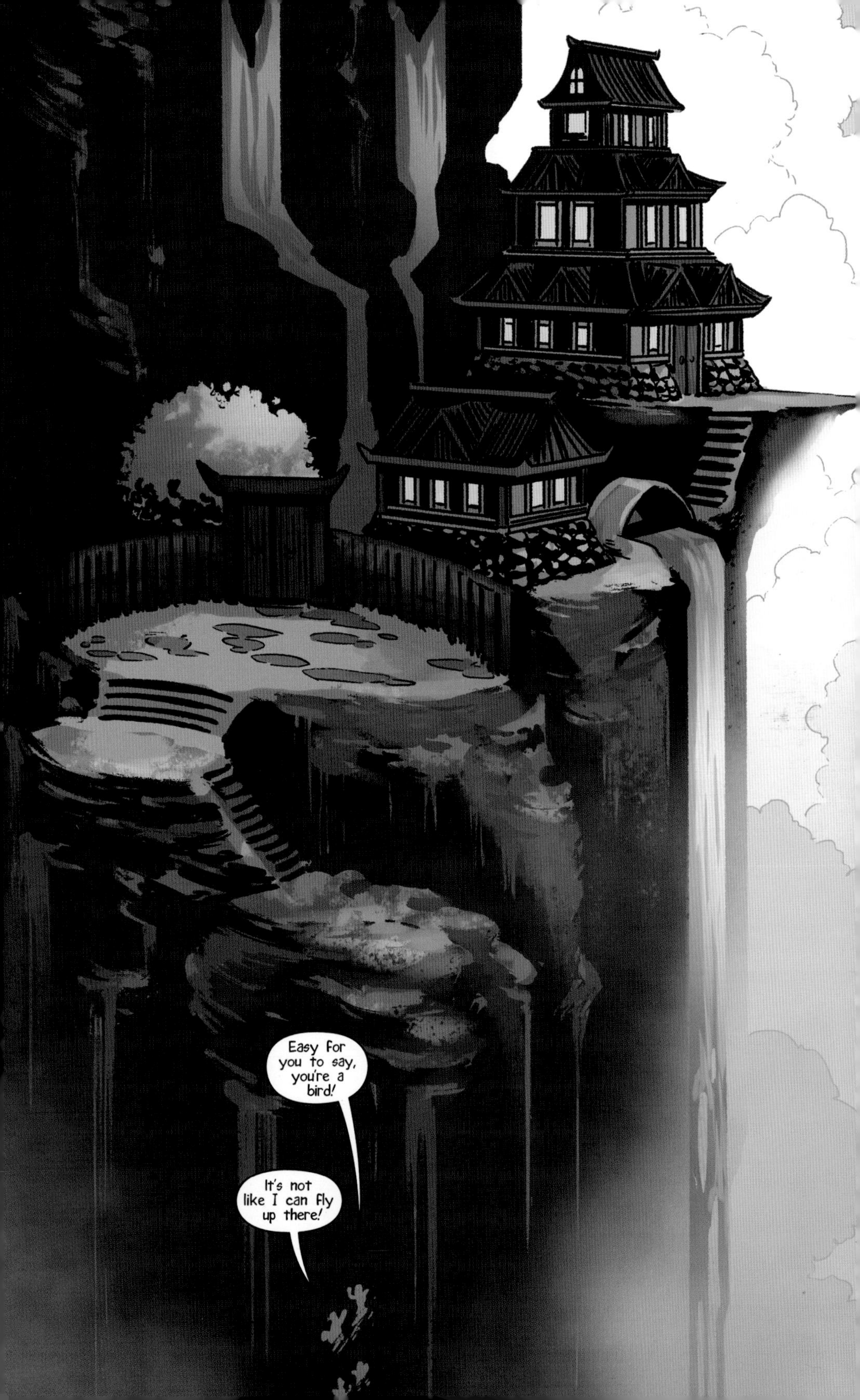
Easy for you to say, you're a bird!
It's not like I can fly up there!

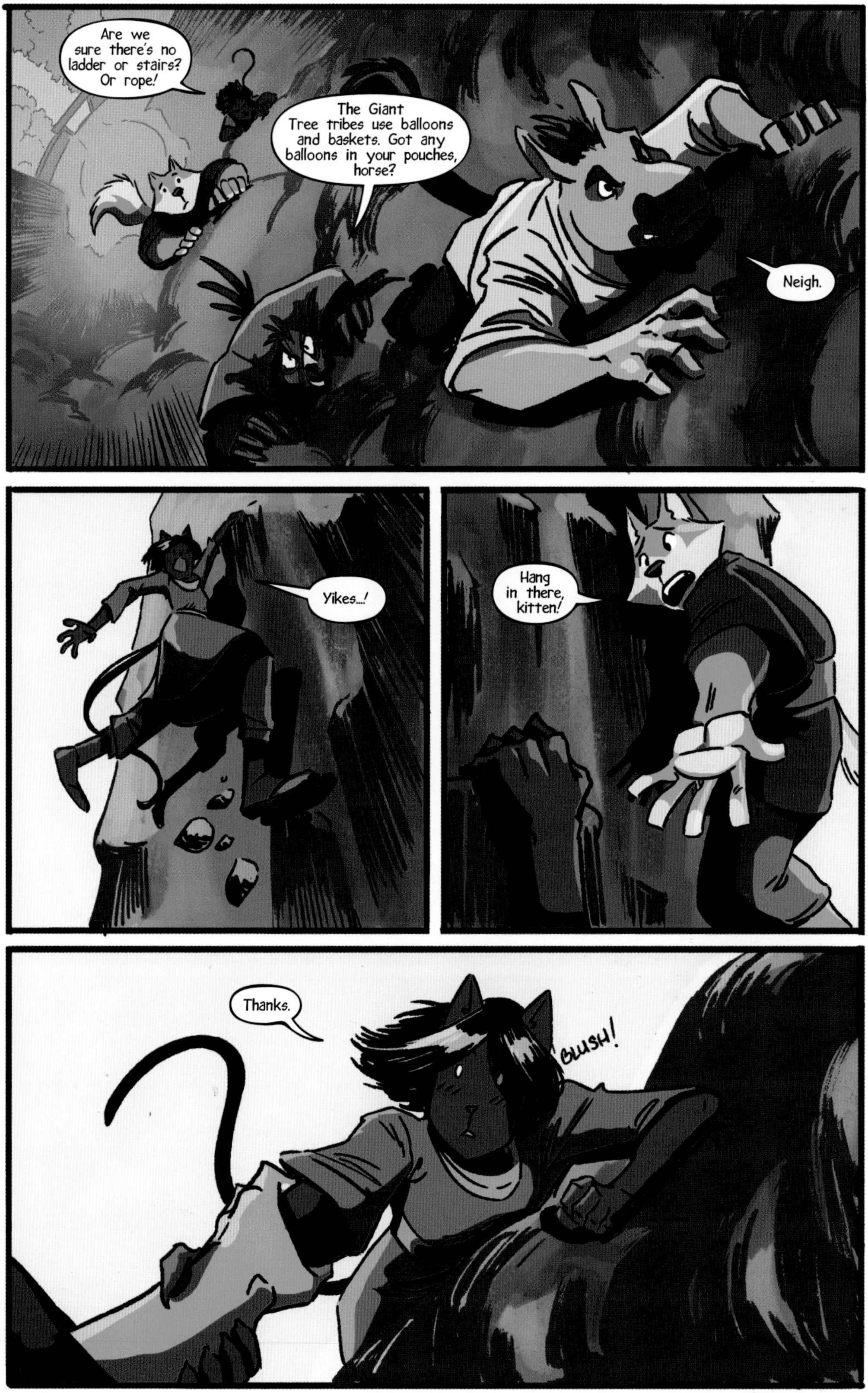
Are we sure there's no ladder or stairs? Or rope!
The Giant Tree tribes use balloons and baskets. Got any balloons in your pouches, horse?
Neigh.
Yikes...!
Hang in there, kitten!
Thanks.
BLUSH!

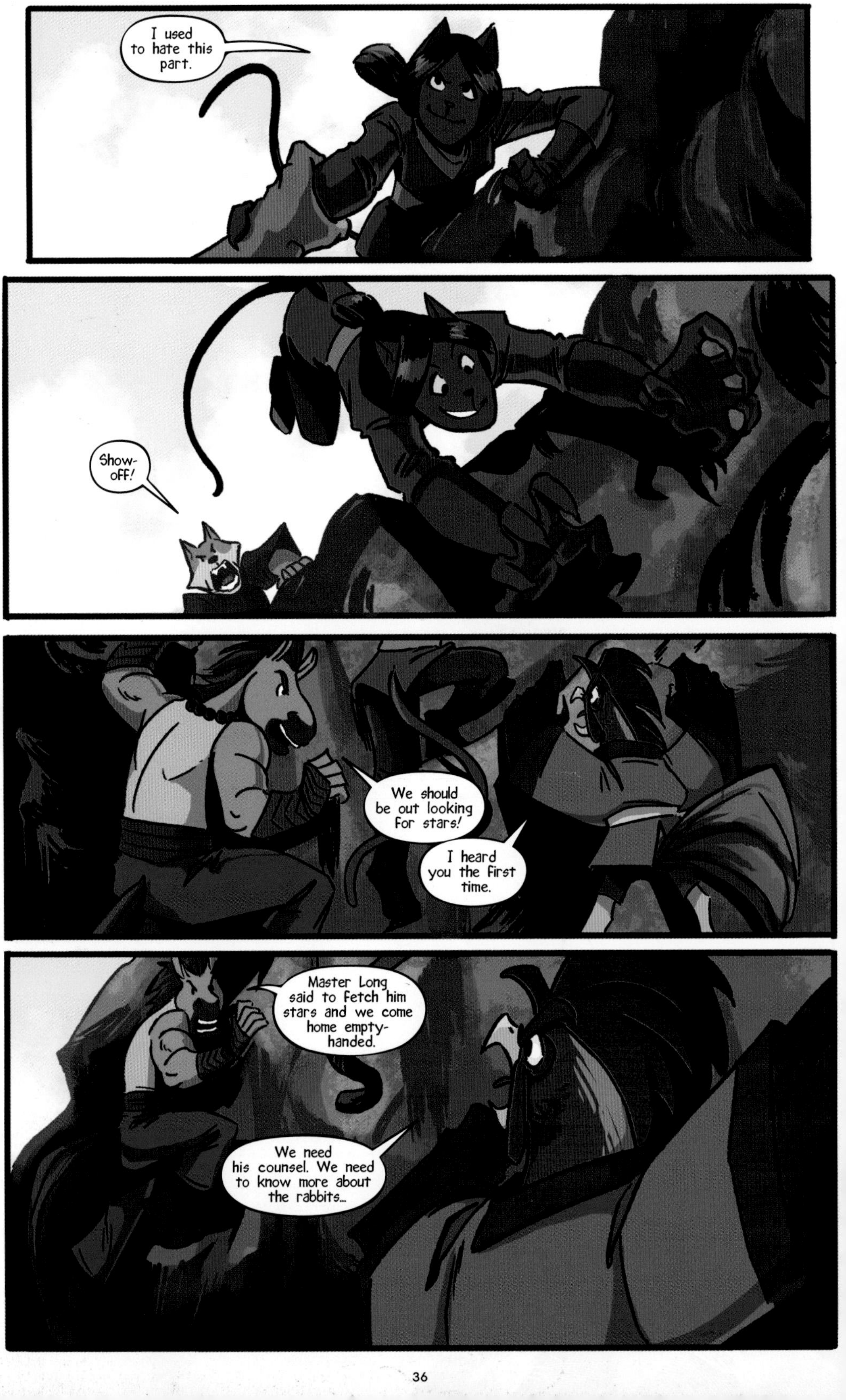

I used to hate this part.
Show-off!
We should be out looking for stars!
I heard you the first time.
Master Long said to fetch him stars and we come home empty-handed.
We need his counsel. We need to know more about the rabbits...

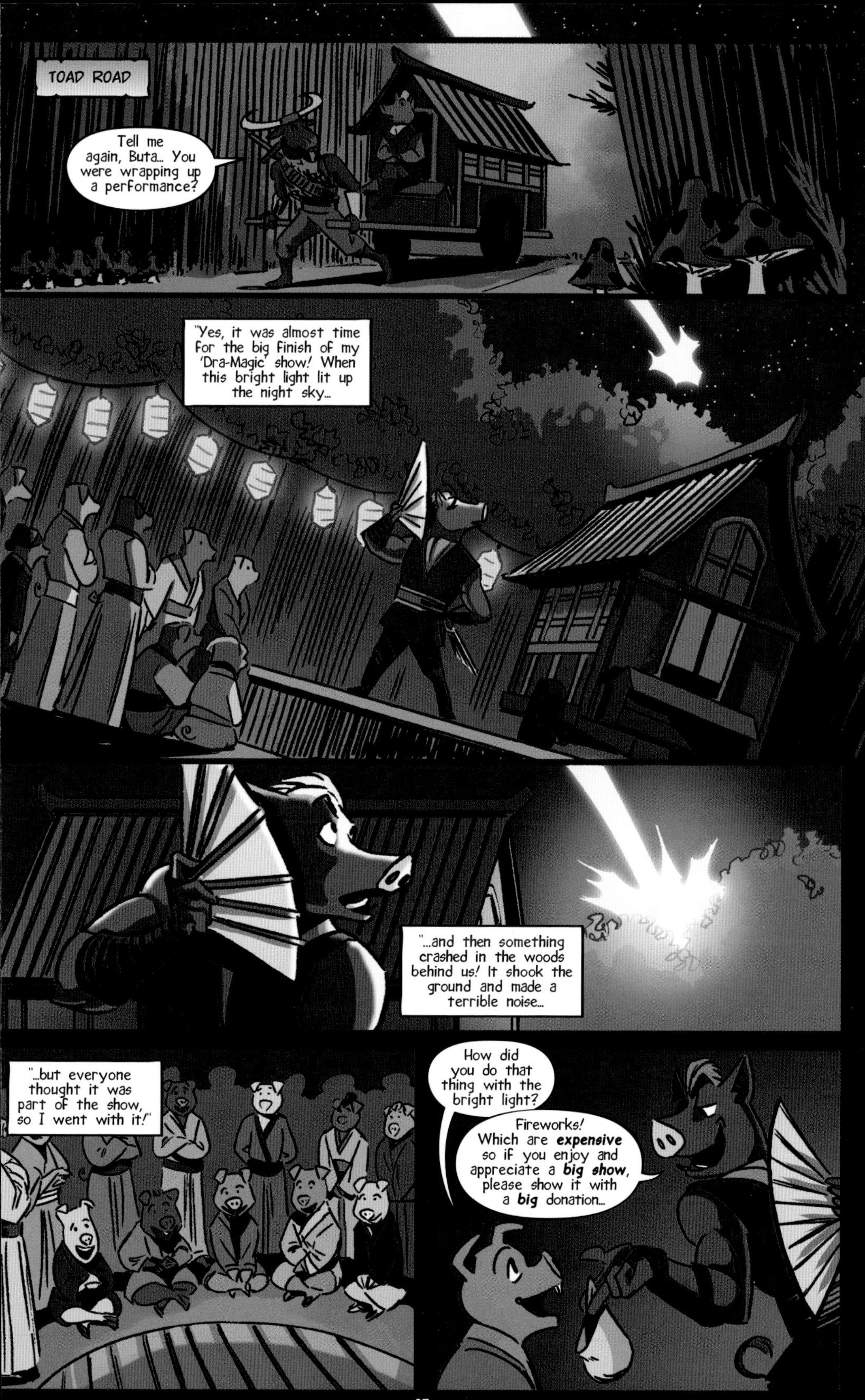
TOAD ROAD
Tell me again, Buta... You were wrapping up a performance?
"Yes, it was almost time for the big finish of my 'Dra-Magic' show! When this bright light lit up the night sky...
"...and then something crashed in the woods behind us! It shook the ground and made a terrible noise...
"...but everyone thought it was part of the show, so I went with it!"
How did you do that thing with the bright light?
Fireworks! Which are **expensive** so if you enjoy and appreciate a **big show**, please show it with a **big** donation...

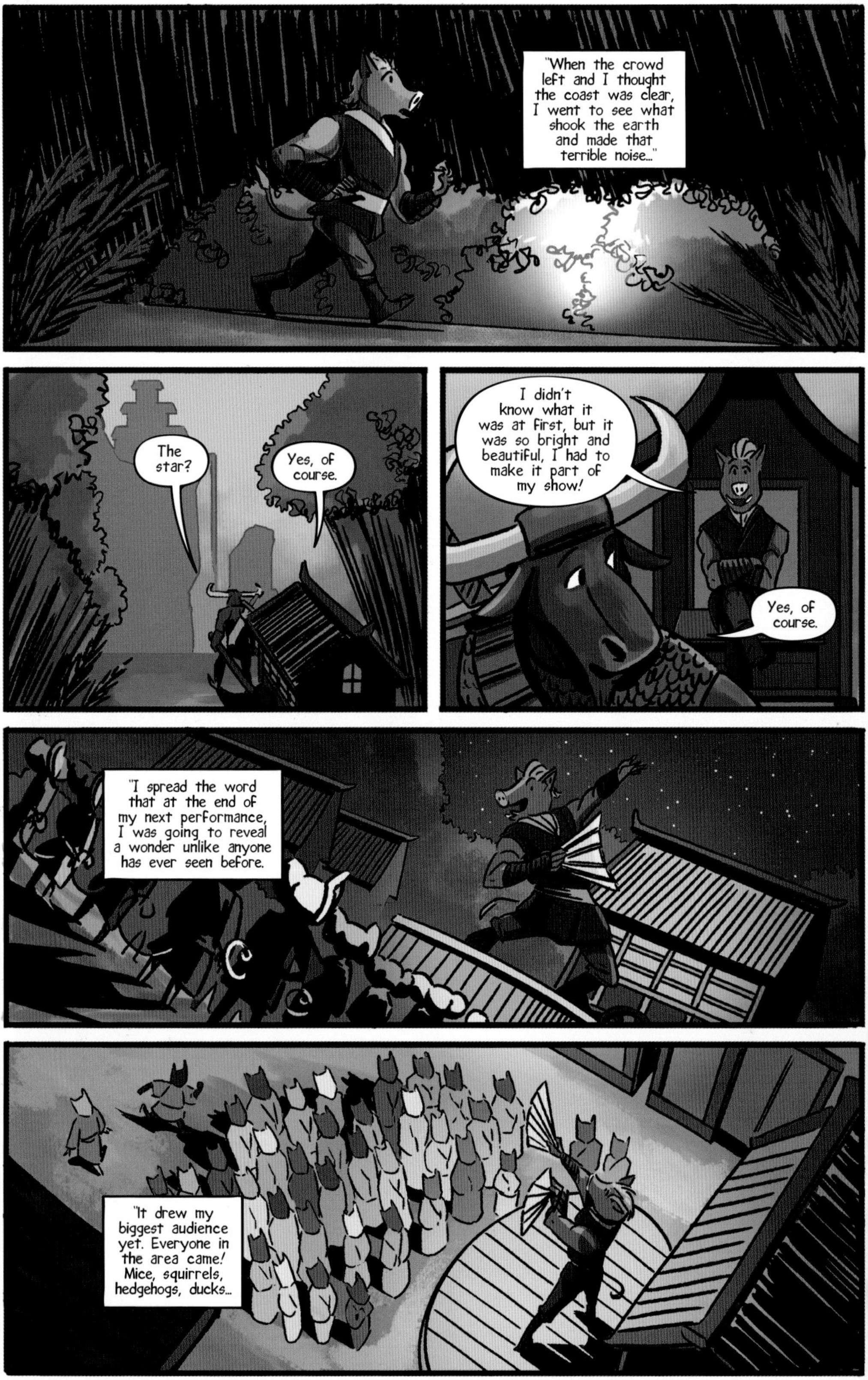
"When the crowd left and I thought the coast was clear, I went to see what shook the earth and made that terrible noise..."
The star?
Yes, of course.
I didn't know what it was at first, but it was so bright and beautiful, I had to make it part of my show!
Yes, of course.
"I spread the word that at the end of my next performance, I was going to reveal a wonder unlike anyone has ever seen before.
"It drew my biggest audience yet. Everyone in the area came! Mice, squirrels, hedgehogs, ducks...

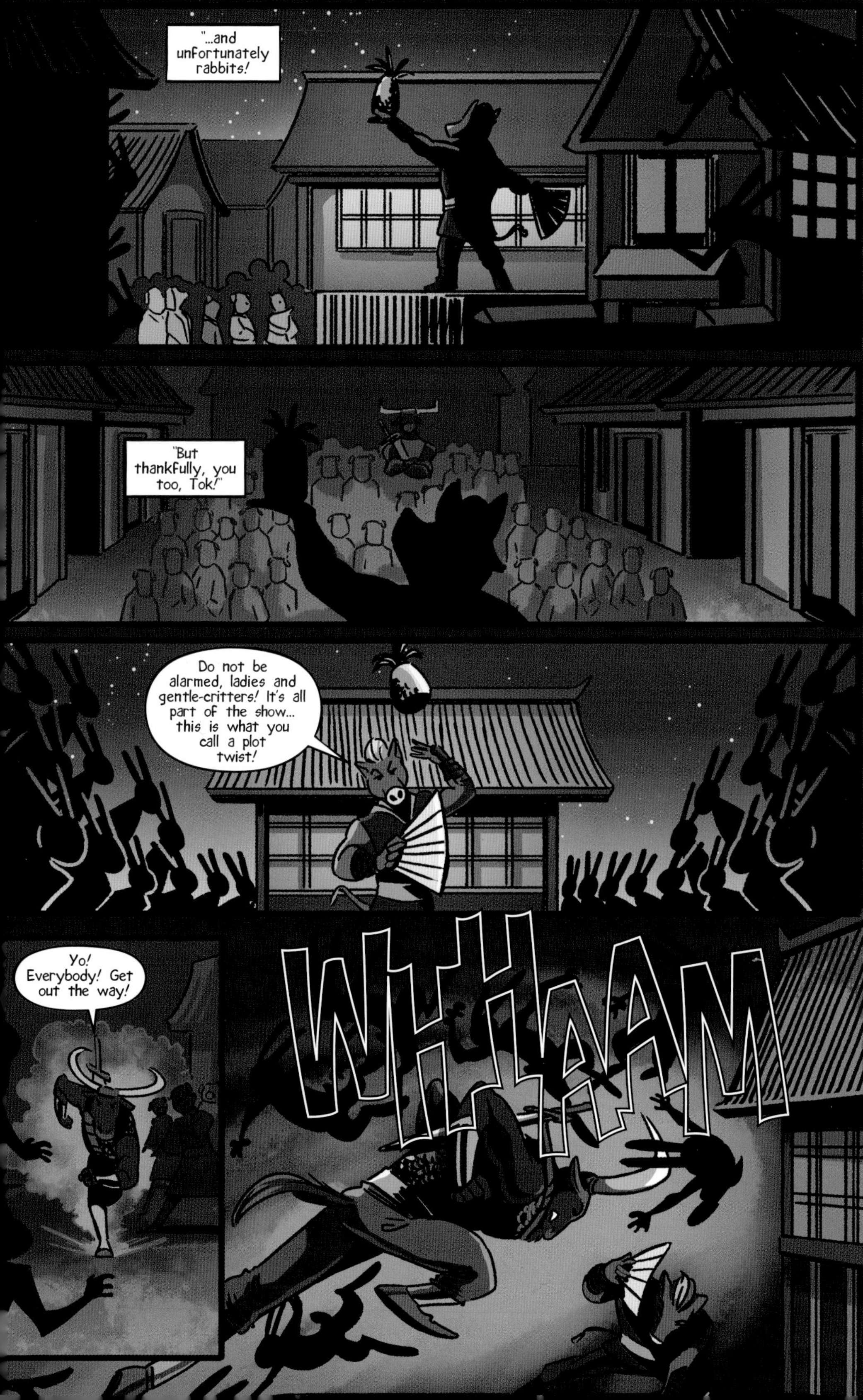
"...and unfortunately rabbits!"
"But thankfully, you too, Tok!"
Do not be alarmed, ladies and gentle-critters! It's all part of the show... this is what you call a plot twist!
Yo! Everybody! Get out the way!
WHHAAM

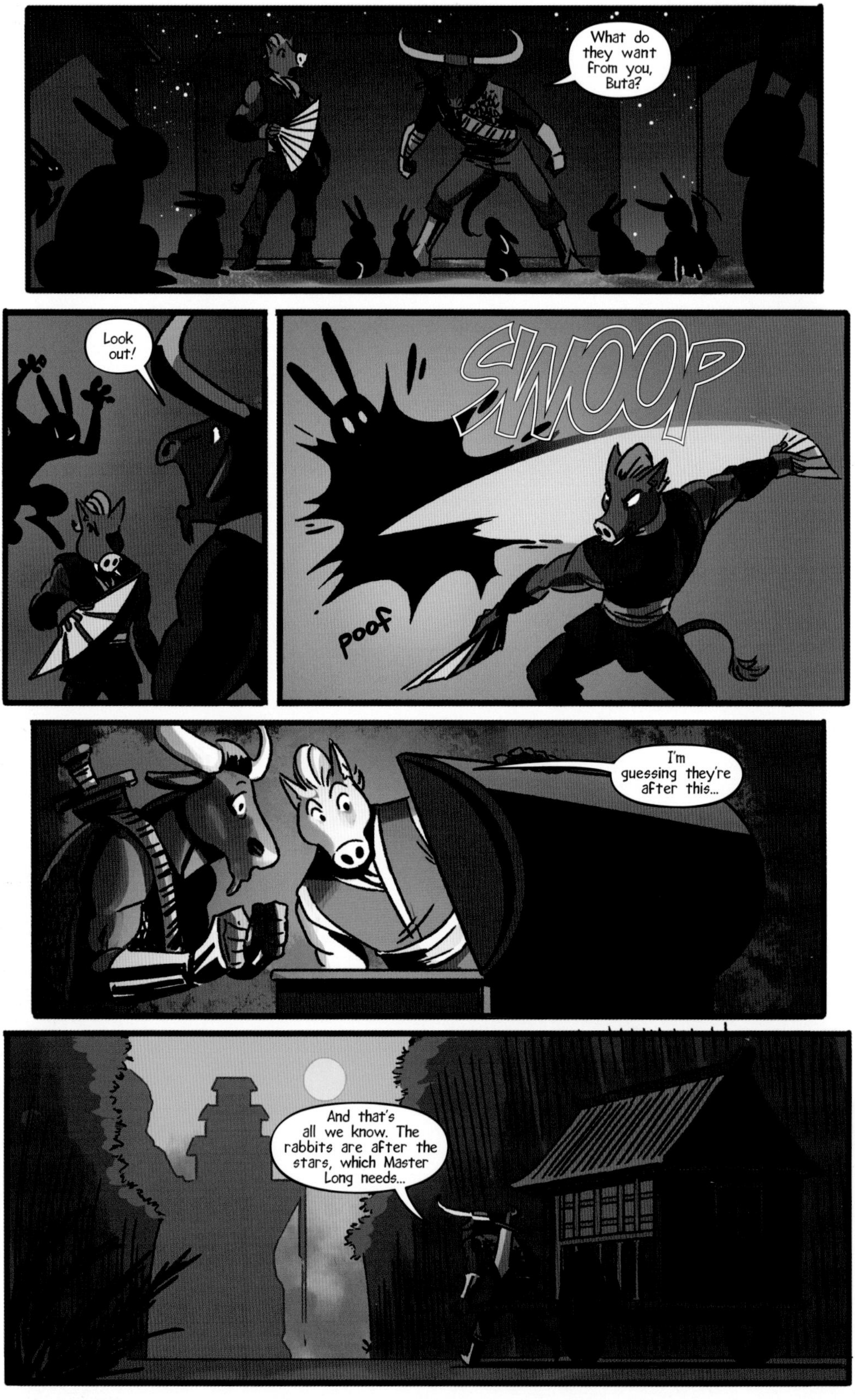
What do they want from you, Buta?
Look out!
SWOOP
poof
I'm guessing they're after this...
And that's all we know. The rabbits are after the stars, which Master Long needs...

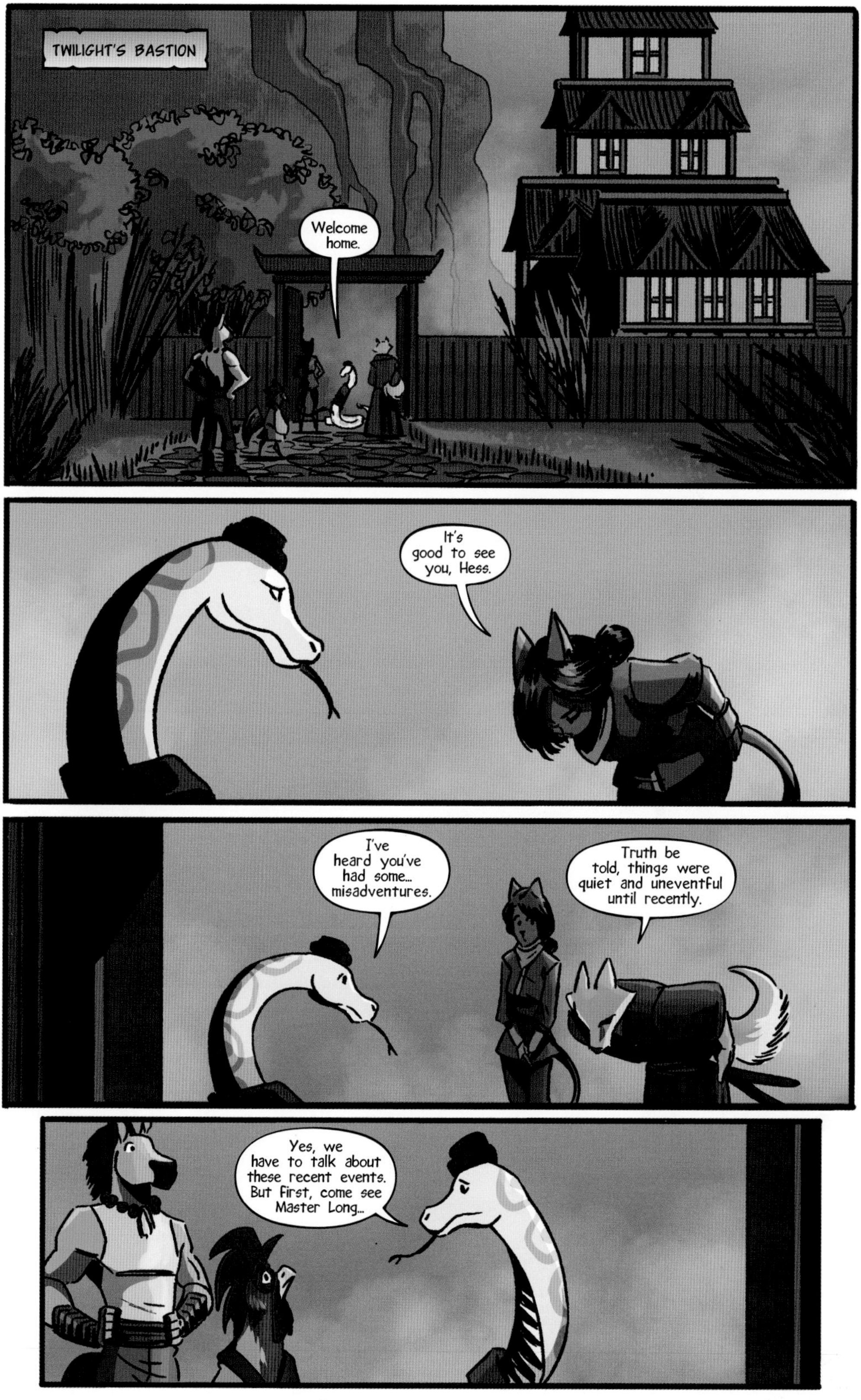
TWILIGHT'S BASTION
Welcome home.
It's good to see you, Hess.
I've heard you've had some... misadventures.
Truth be told, things were quiet and uneventful until recently.
Yes, we have to talk about these recent events. But first, come see Master Long...

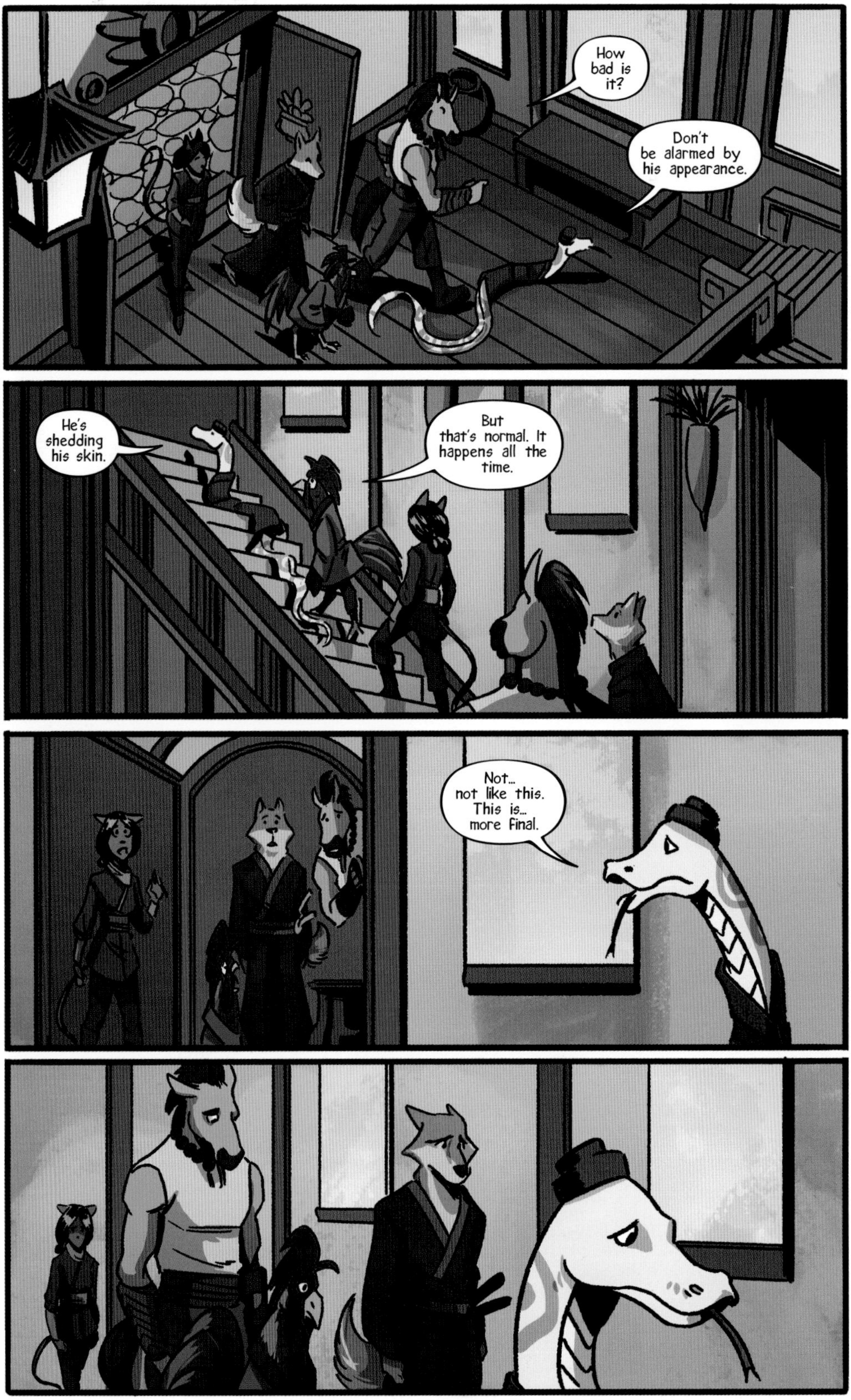
How bad is it?
Don't be alarmed by his appearance.
He's shedding his skin.
But that's normal. It happens all the time.
Not... not like this. This is... more final.

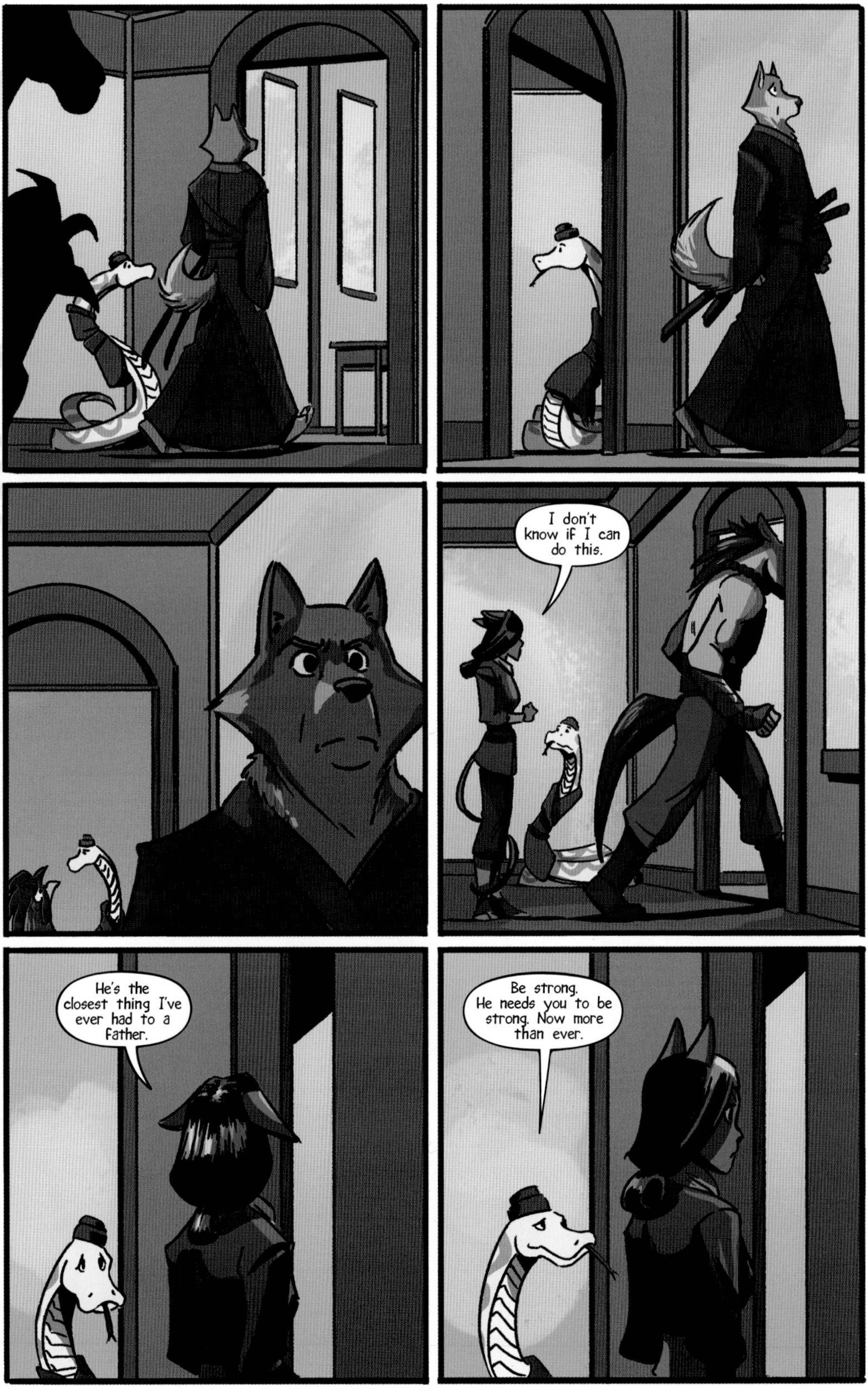
I don't know if I can do this.
He's the closest thing I've ever had to a father.
Be strong. He needs you to be strong. Now more than ever.

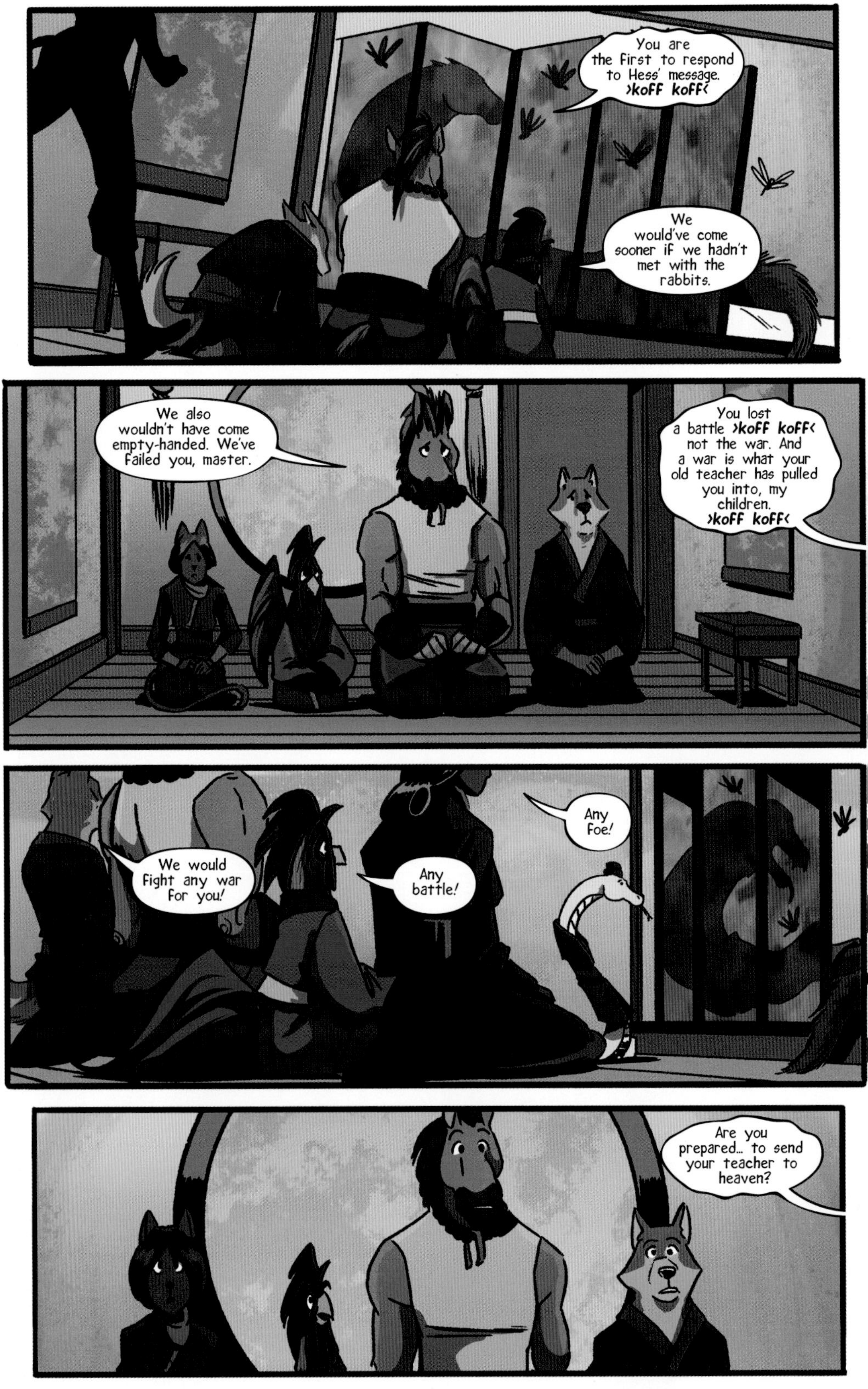
You are the first to respond to Hess' message. >koff koff<
We would've come sooner if we hadn't met with the rabbits.
We also wouldn't have come empty-handed. We've failed you, master.
You lost a battle >koff koff< not the war. And a war is what your old teacher has pulled you into, my children. >koff koff<
We would fight any war for you!
Any battle!
Any Foe!
Are you prepared... to send your teacher to heaven?

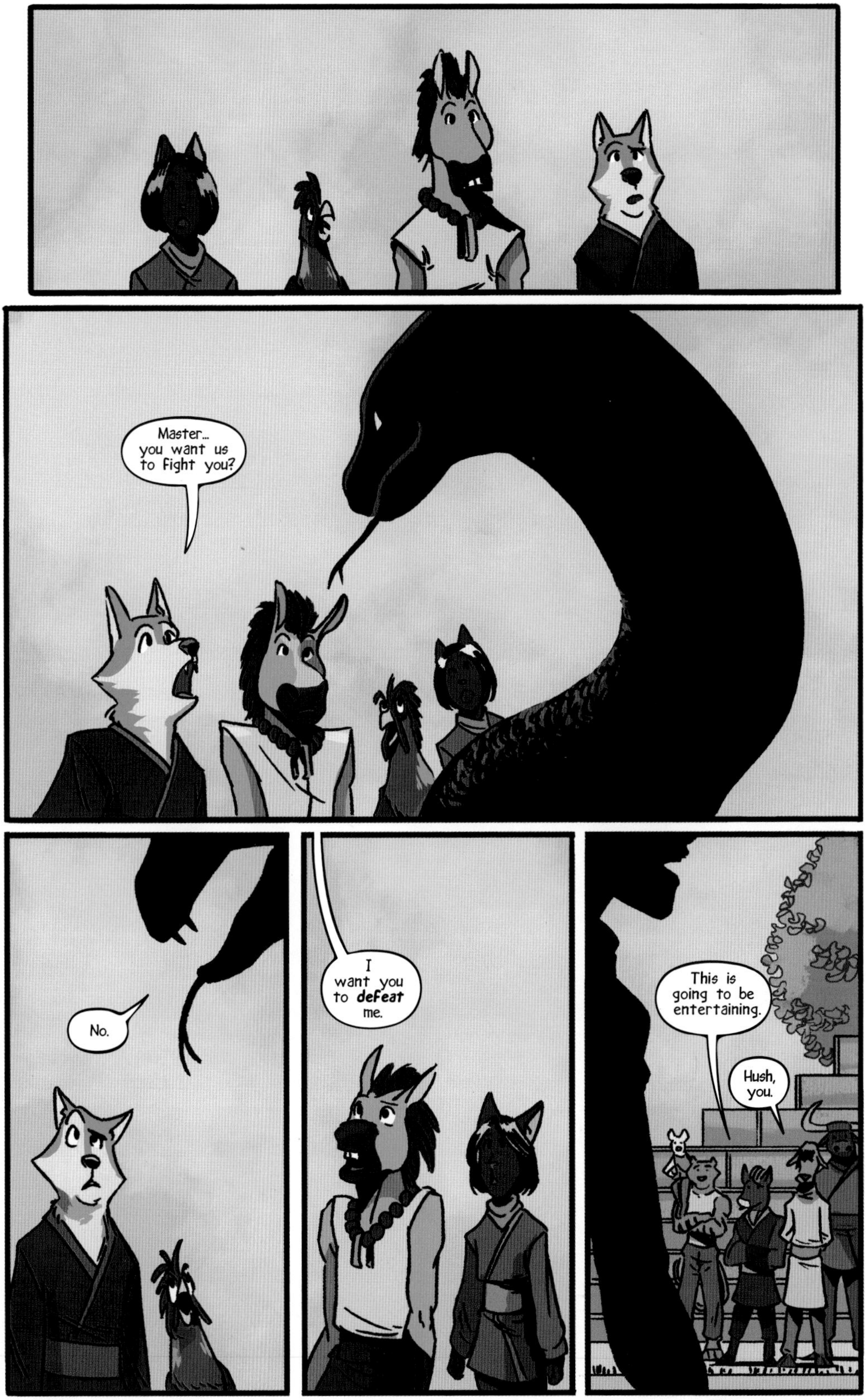
Master... you want us to fight you?
No.
I want you to **defeat** me.
This is going to be entertaining.
Hush, you.

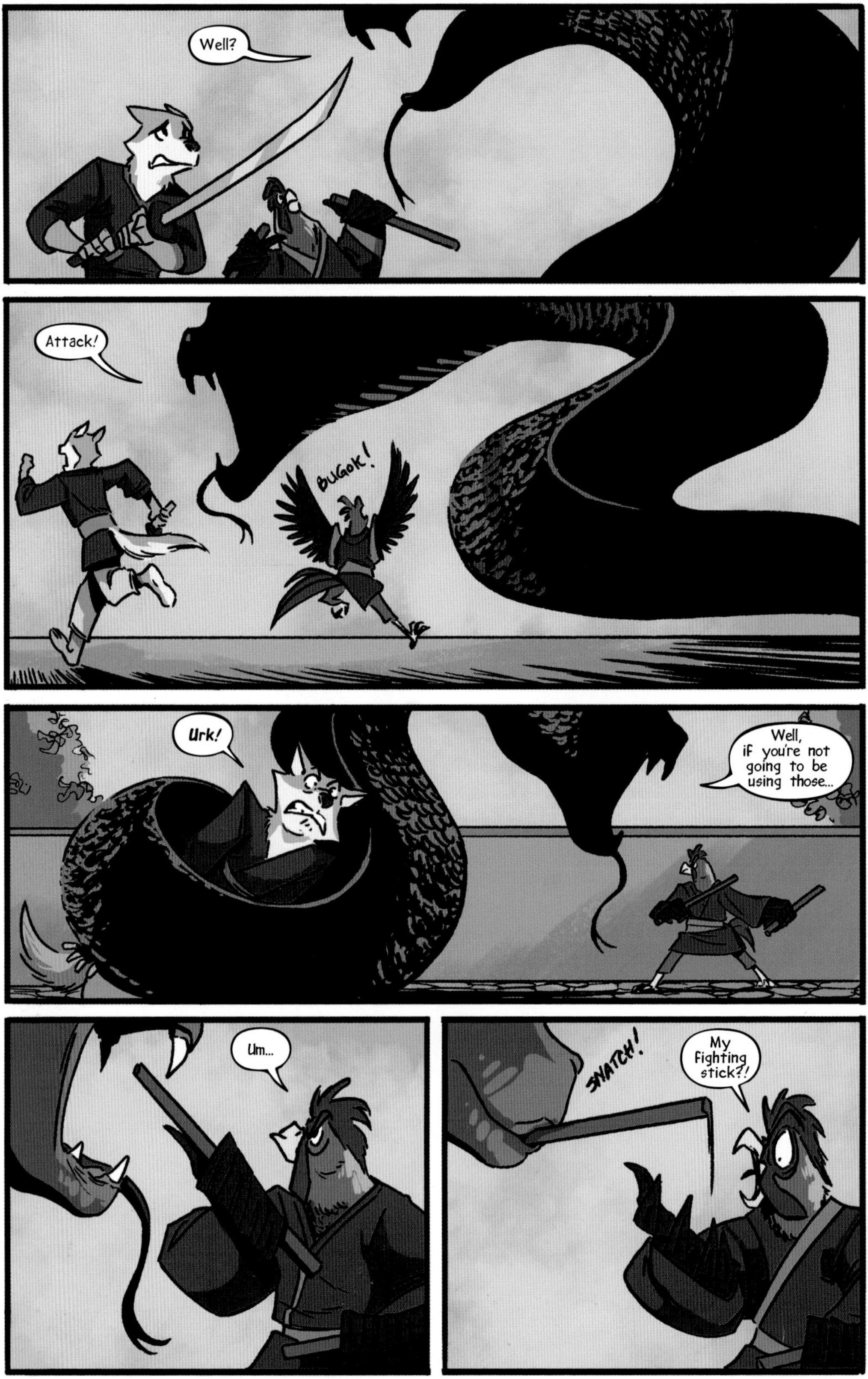
Well?
Attack!
BUGOK!
Urk!
Well, if you're not going to be using those...
Um...
SNATCH!
My Fighting stick?!

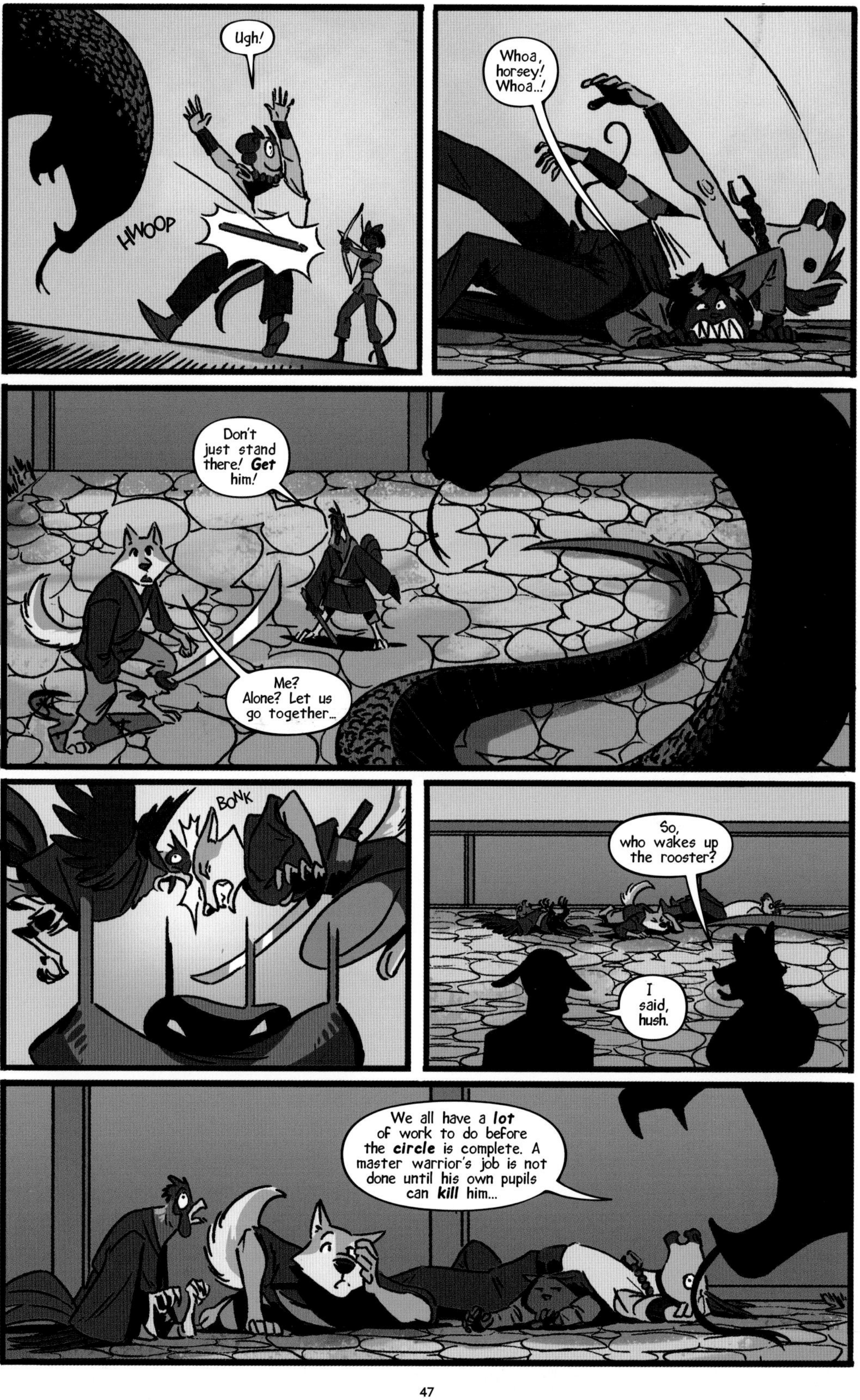
Ugh!
HWOOP
Whoa, horsey! Whoa...!
Don't just stand there! Get him!
Me? Alone? Let us go together...
BONK
So, who wakes up the rooster?
I said, hush.
We all have a lot of work to do before the circle is complete. A master warrior's job is not done until his own pupils can kill him...

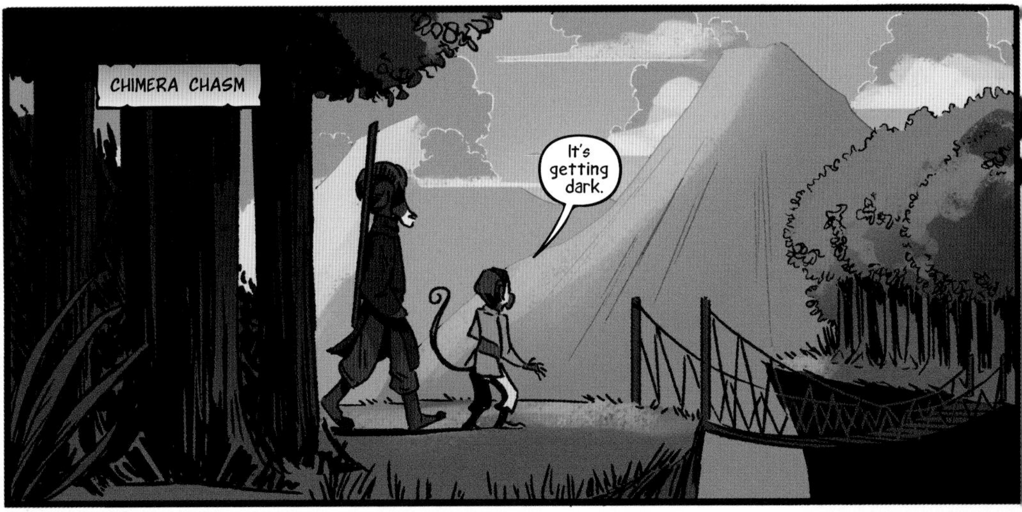
CHIMERA CHASM
It's getting dark.
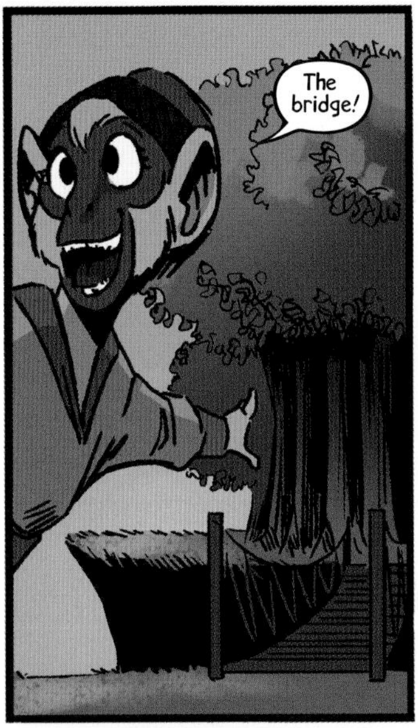
The bridge!
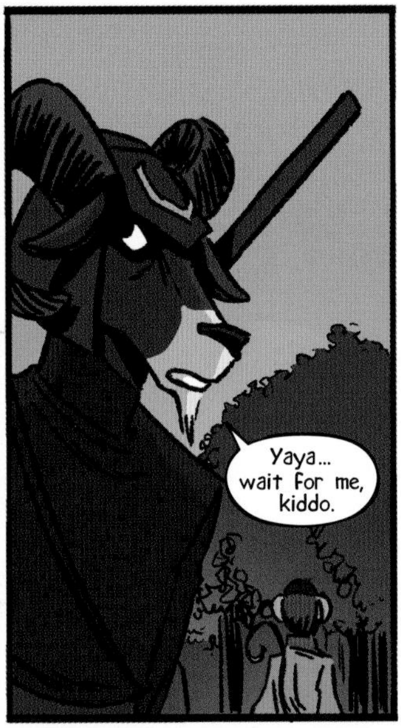
Yaya... wait for me, kiddo.
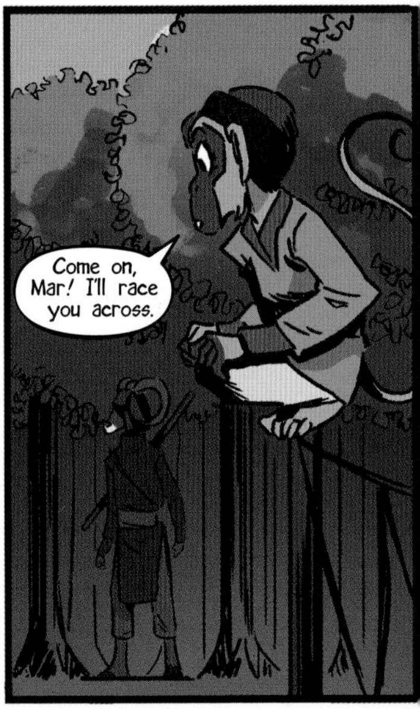
Come on, Mar! I'll race you across.
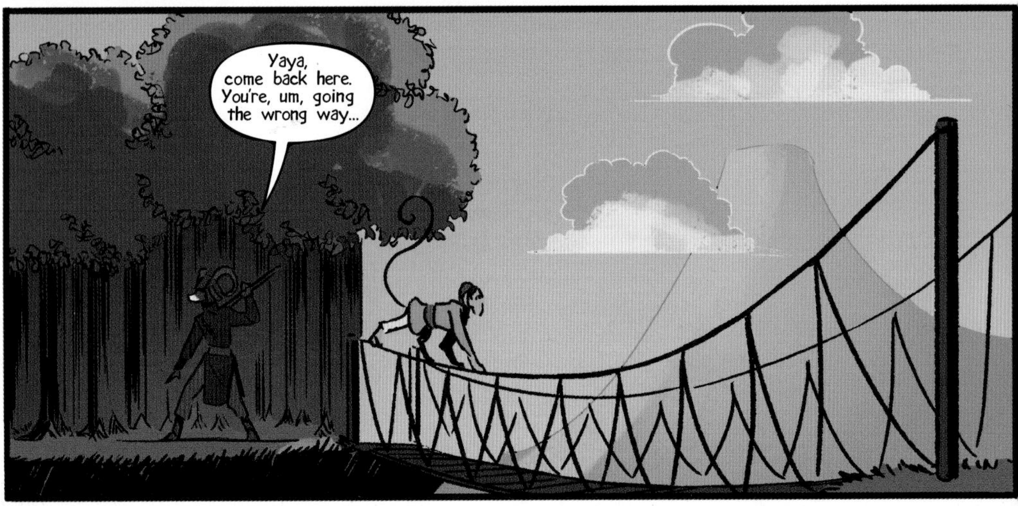
Yaya, come back here. You're, um, going the wrong way...

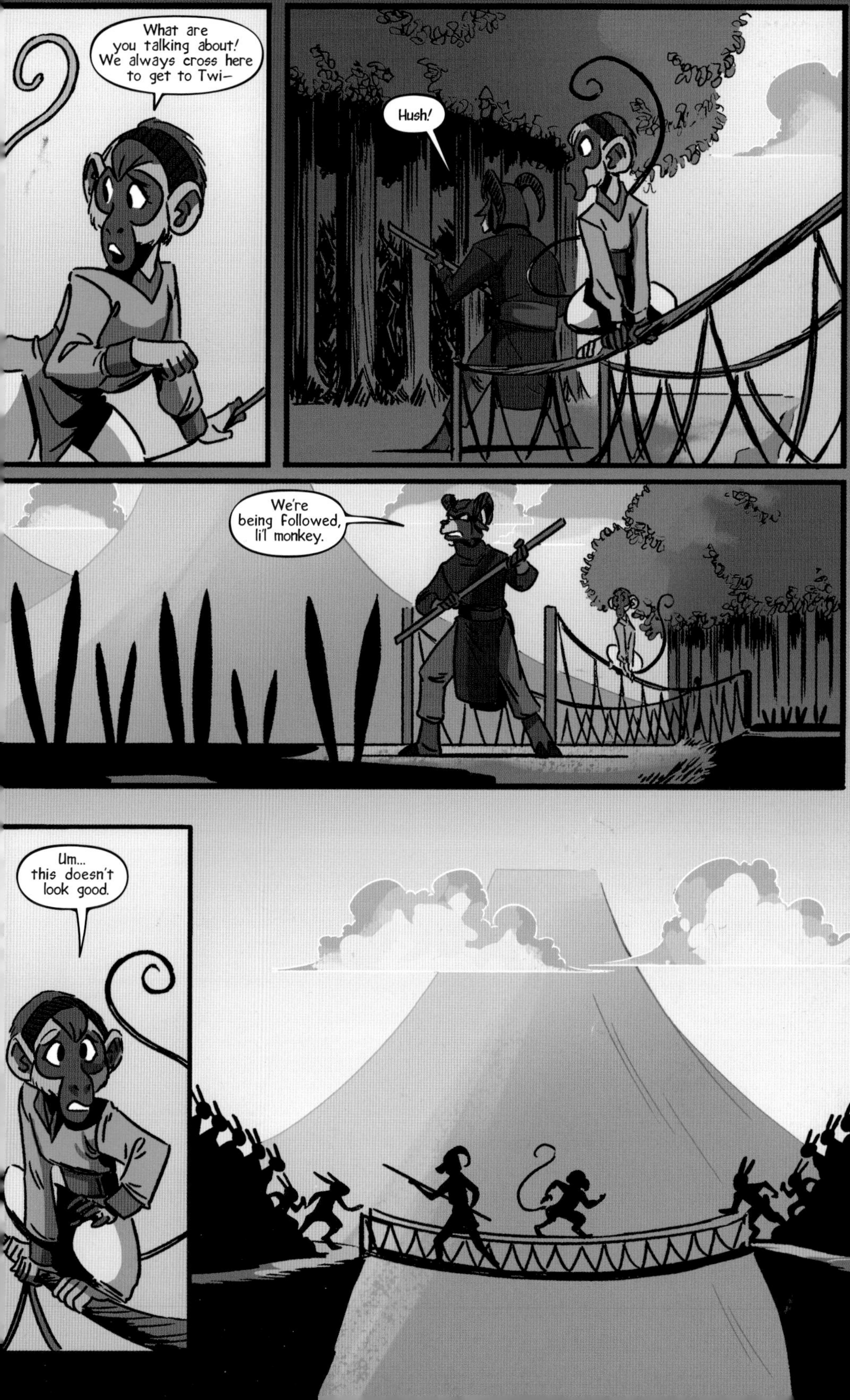
What are you talking about! We always cross here to get to Twi—
Hush!
We're being followed, li'l monkey.
Um... this doesn't look good.

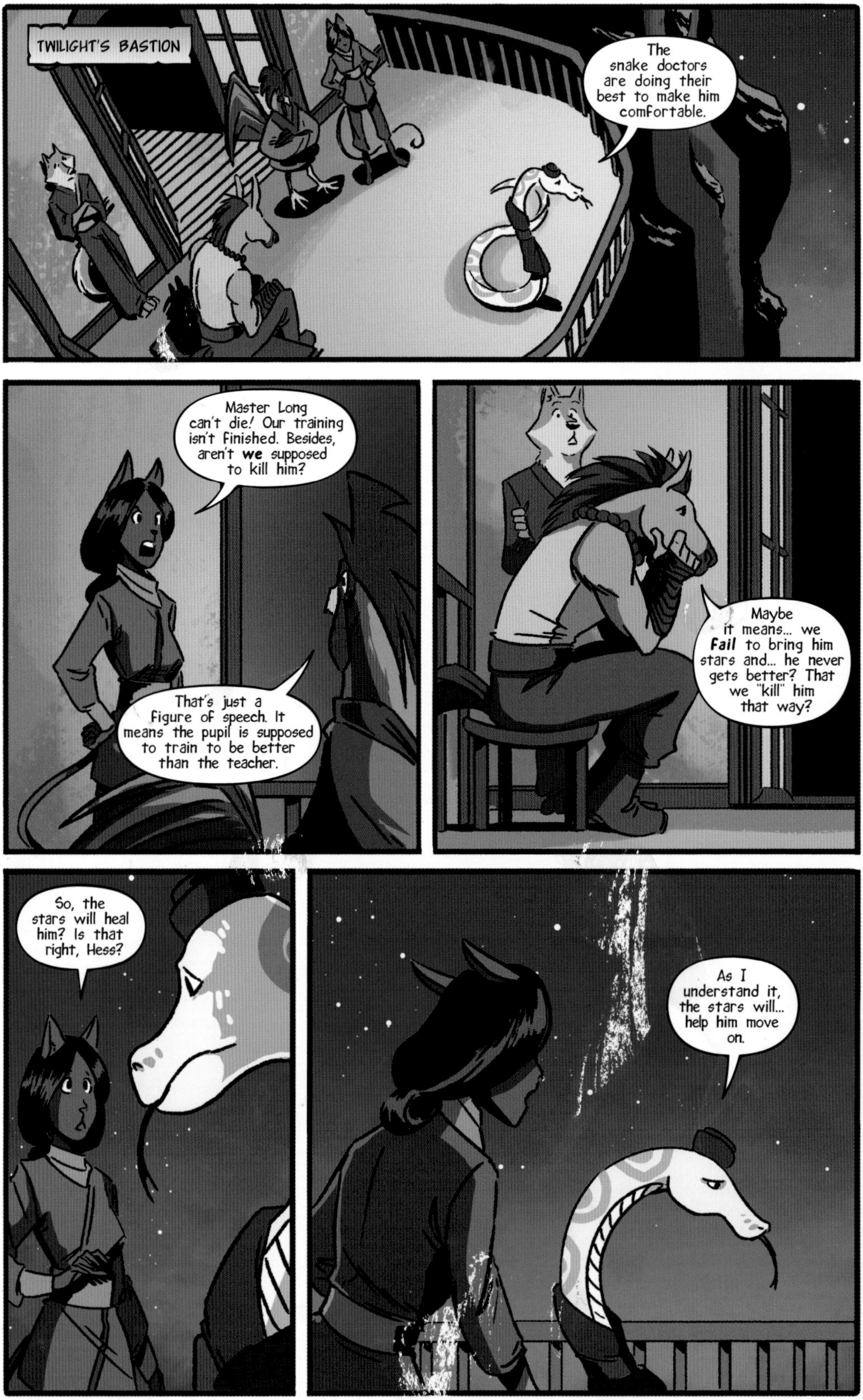
TWILIGHT'S BASTION
The snake doctors are doing their best to make him comfortable.
Master Long can't die! Our training isn't finished. Besides, aren't **we** supposed to kill him?
That's just a figure of speech. It means the pupil is supposed to train to be better than the teacher.
Maybe it means... we **Fail** to bring him stars and... he never gets better? That we "kill" him that way?
So, the stars will heal him? Is that right, Hess?
As I understand it, the stars will... help him move on.

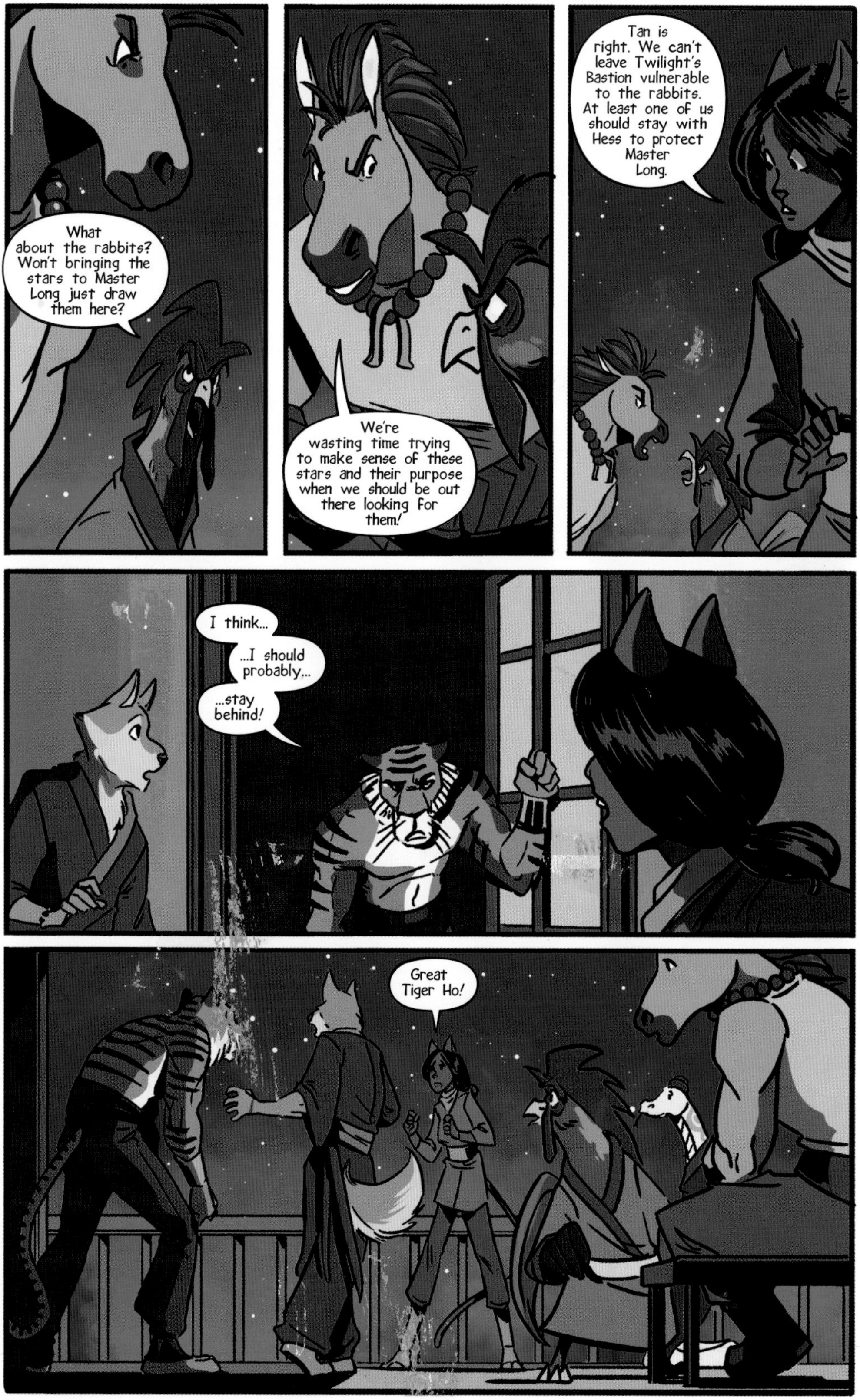
What about the rabbits? Won't bringing the stars to Master Long just draw them here?
We're wasting time trying to make sense of these stars and their purpose when we should be out there looking for them!
Tan is right. We can't leave Twilight's Bastion vulnerable to the rabbits. At least one of us should stay with Hess to protect Master Long.
I think...
...I should probably...
...stay behind!
Great Tiger Ho!

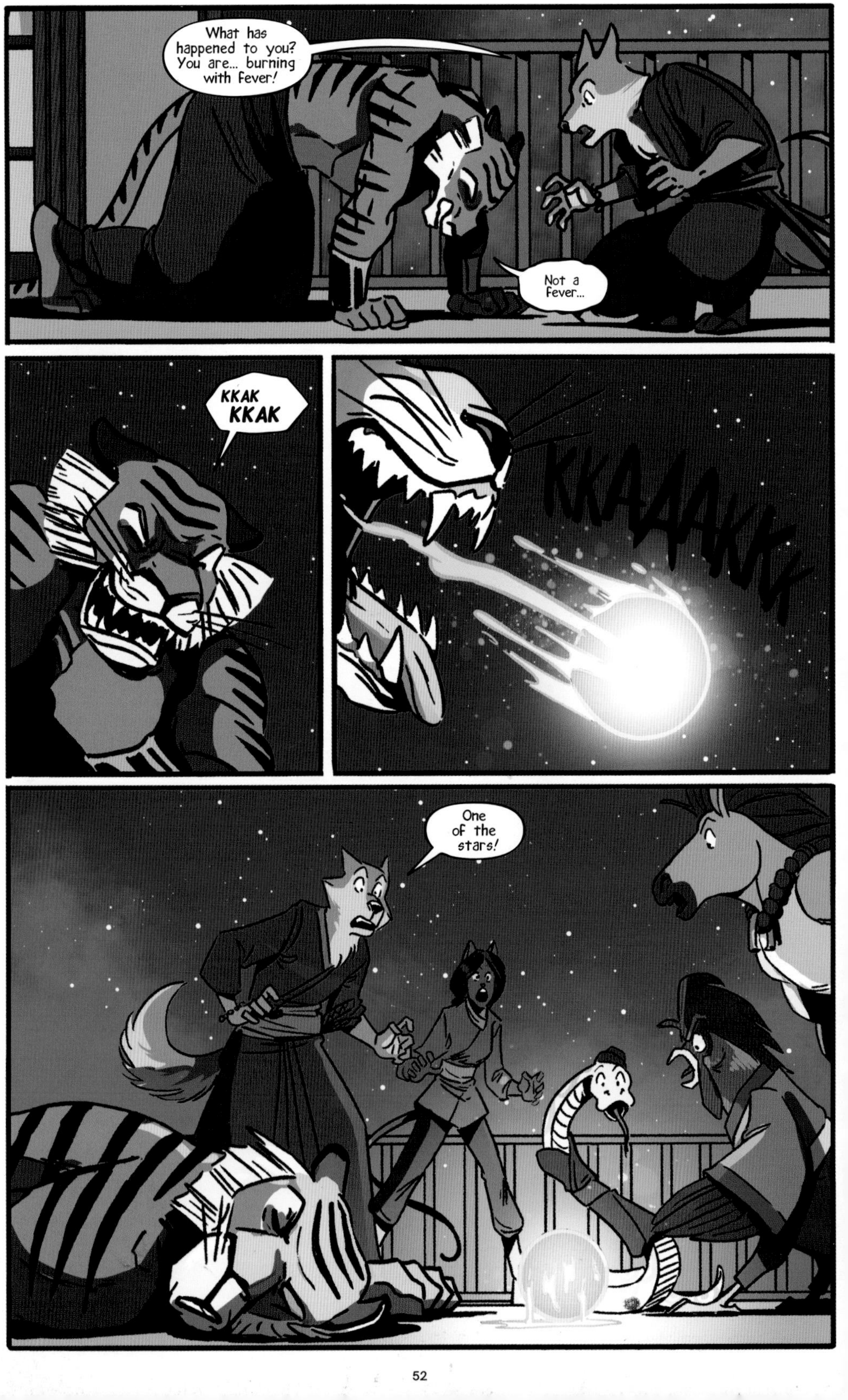
What has happened to you? You are... burning with fever!
Not a fever...
KKAK KKAK
KKAAAKK
One of the stars!

CHAPTER THREE

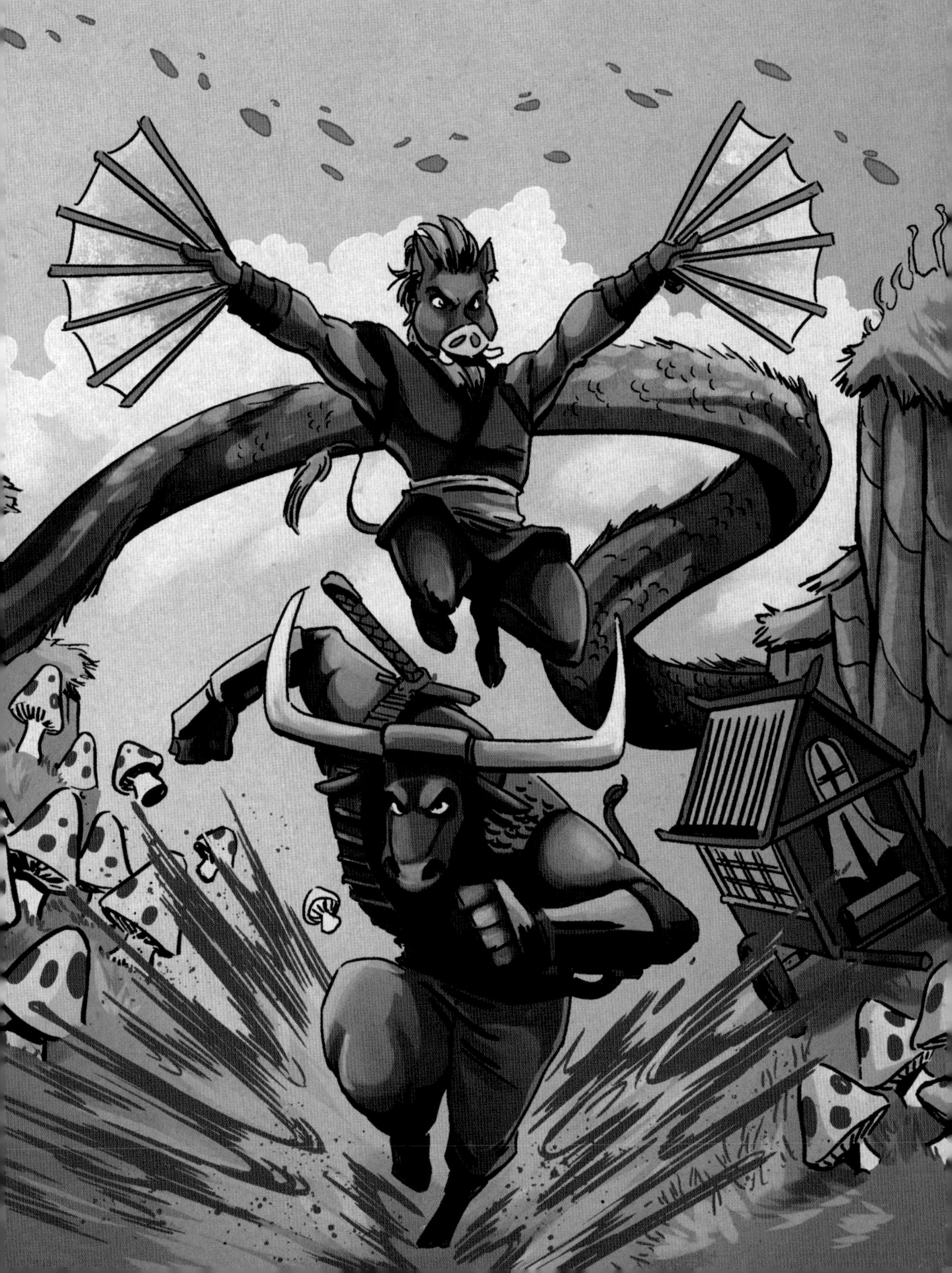

A LONG TIME AGO, THE WORLD WAS ONE. THERE WAS ONLY PEACE AND HARMONY IN THE GARDEN.

THE GUARDIANS OF THE SKY GAVE THE TRIBES DRAGON FRUIT TO EAT. IT WAS THE ONLY FOOD THEY NEEDED.

THERE WAS ONLY ONE RULE IN THE GARDEN: SHARE.

BUT THE RABBITS STOLE THE DRAGON FRUIT, HID IT FROM THE OTHERS, AND KEPT IT FOR THEMSELVES.

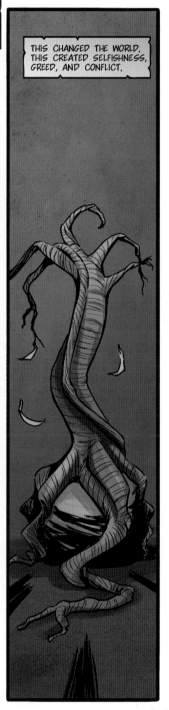

THIS CHANGED THE WORLD. THIS CREATED SELFISHNESS, GREED, AND CONFLICT.

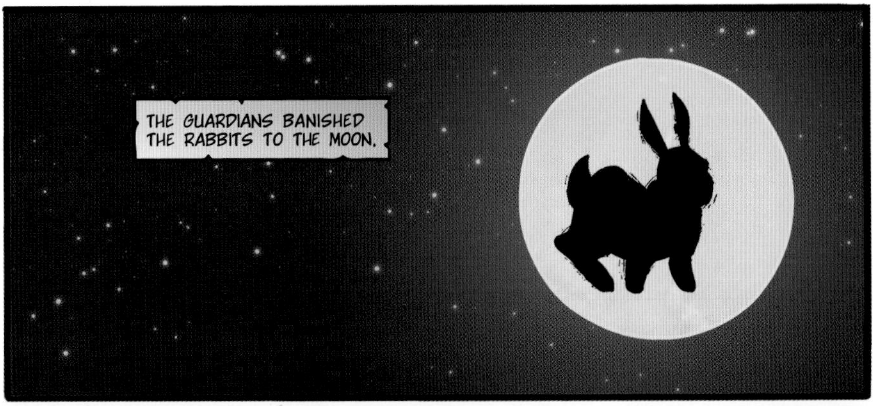
THE GUARDIANS BANISHED THE RABBITS TO THE MOON.

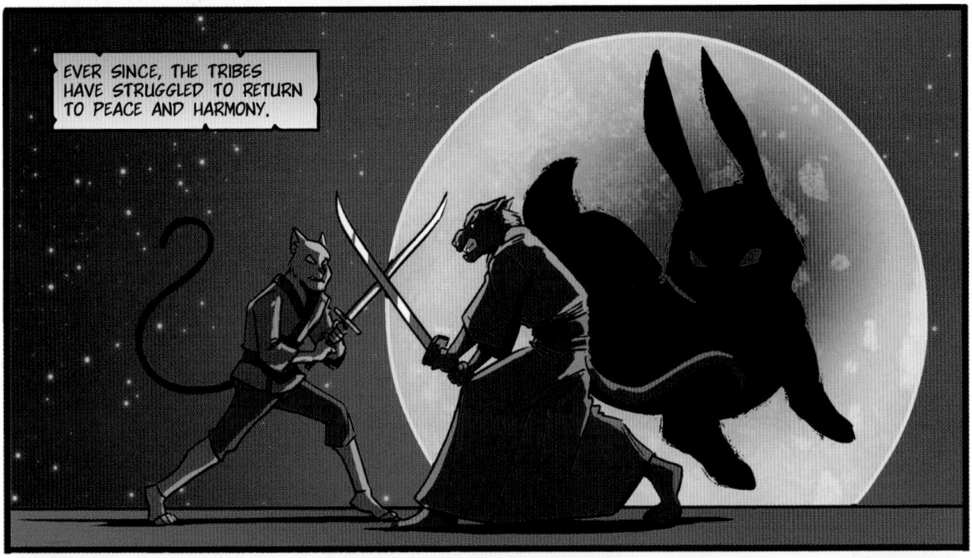
EVER SINCE, THE TRIBES HAVE STRUGGLED TO RETURN TO PEACE AND HARMONY.

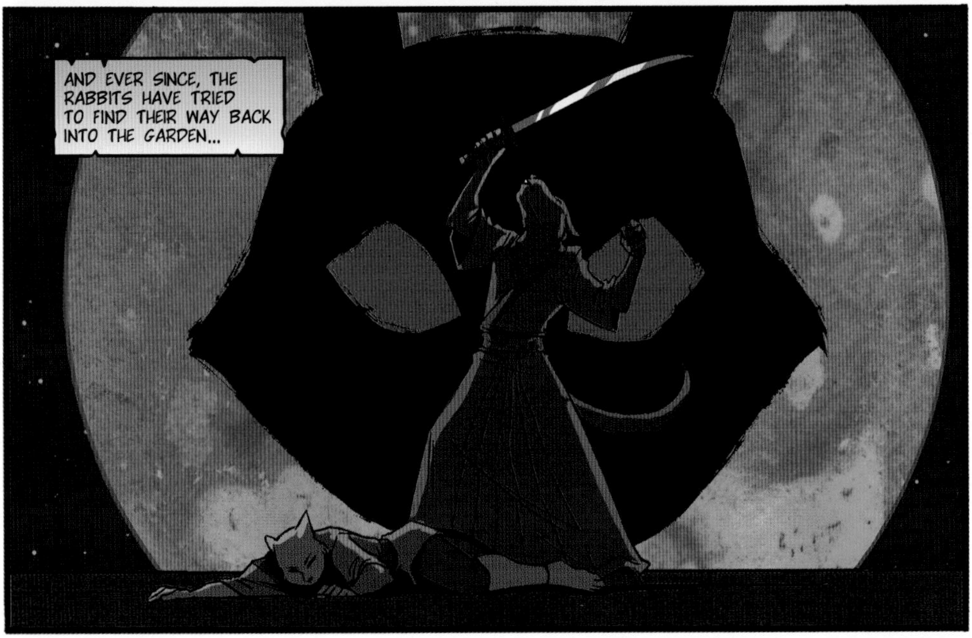
AND EVER SINCE, THE RABBITS HAVE TRIED TO FIND THEIR WAY BACK INTO THE GARDEN...

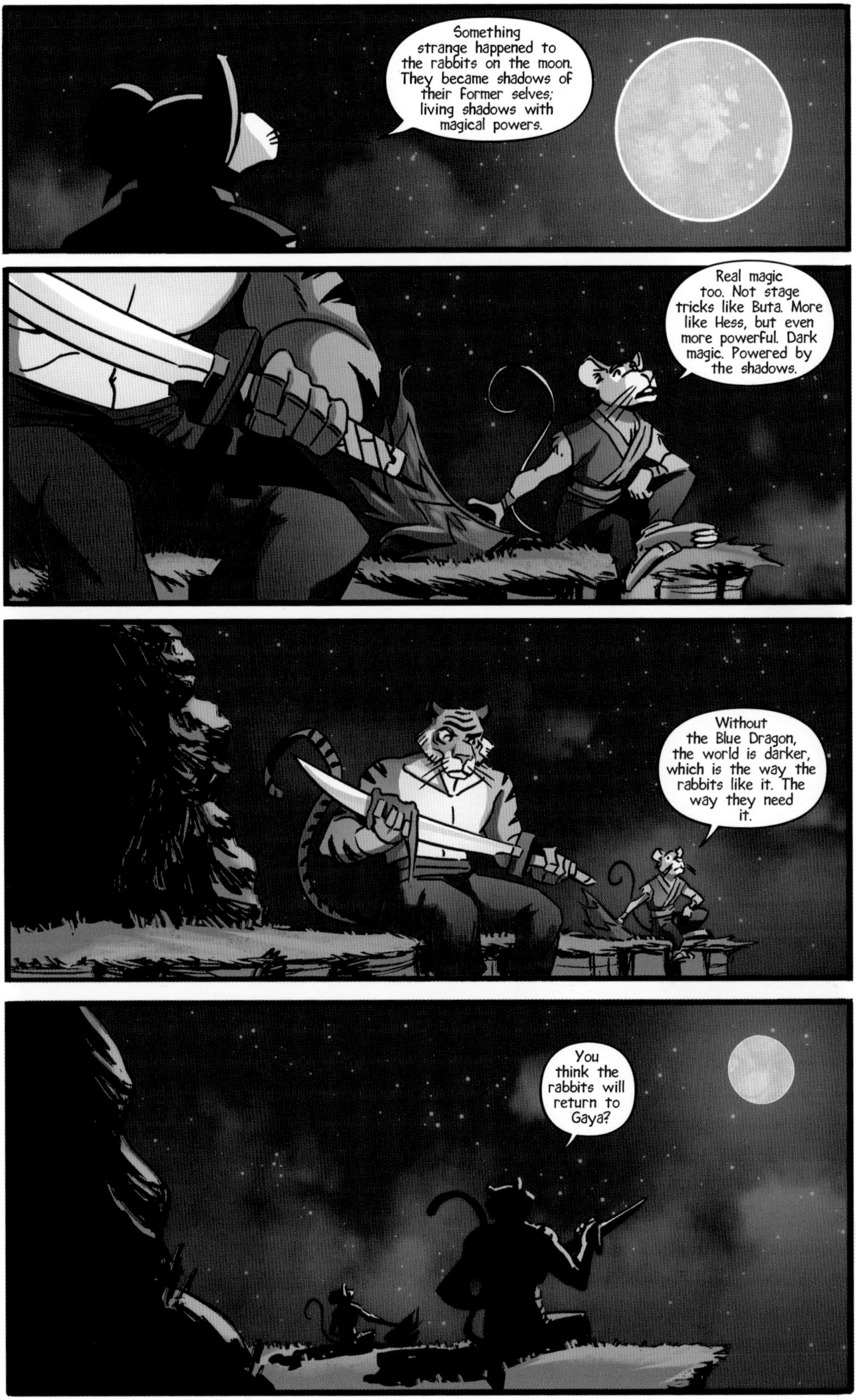
Something strange happened to the rabbits on the moon. They became shadows of their former selves; living shadows with magical powers.
Real magic too. Not stage tricks like Buta. More like Hess, but even more powerful. Dark magic. Powered by the shadows.
Without the Blue Dragon, the world is darker, which is the way the rabbits like it. The way they need it.
You think the rabbits will return to Gaya?

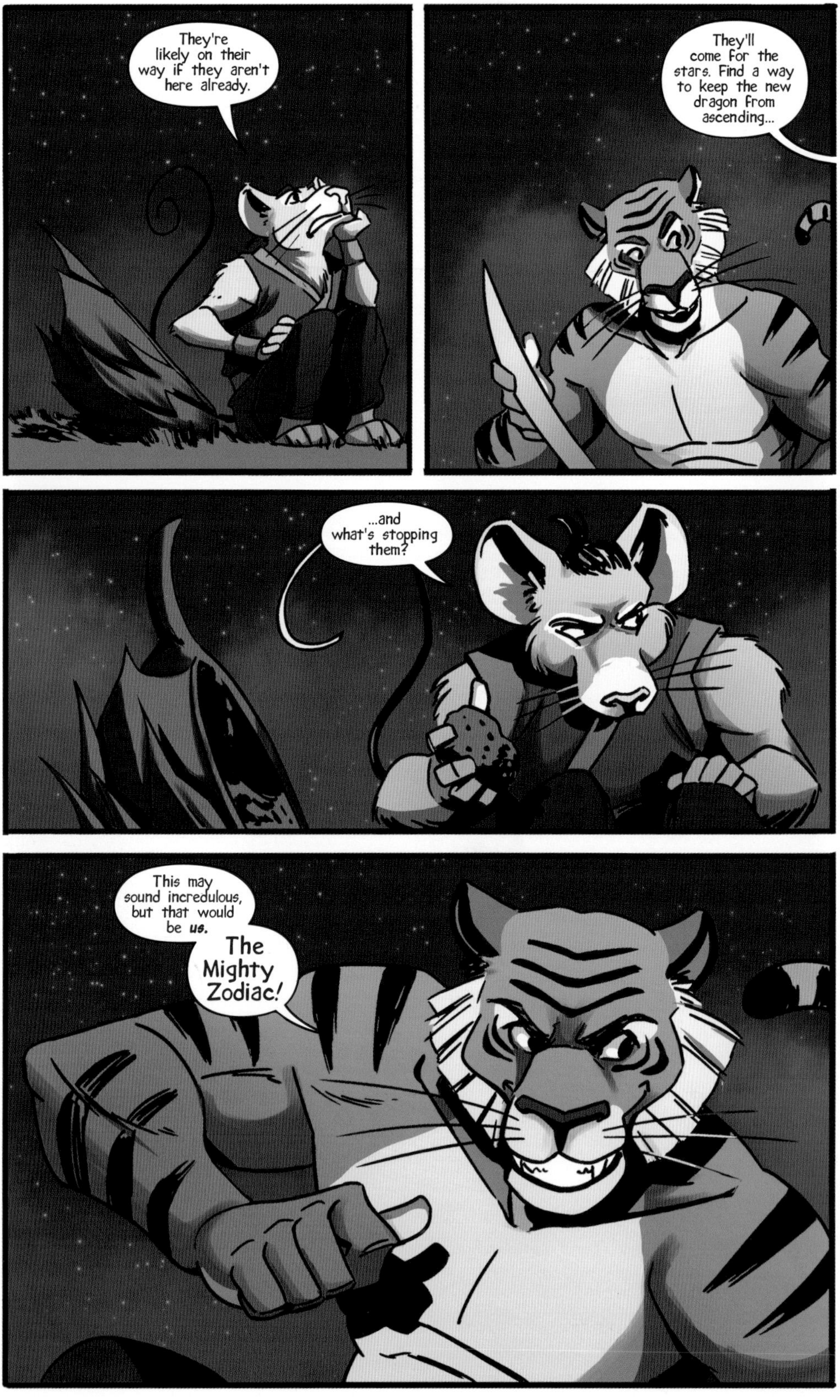
They're likely on their way if they aren't here already.
They'll come for the stars. Find a way to keep the new dragon from ascending...
...and what's stopping them?
This may sound incredulous, but that would be *us.*
The Mighty Zodiac!

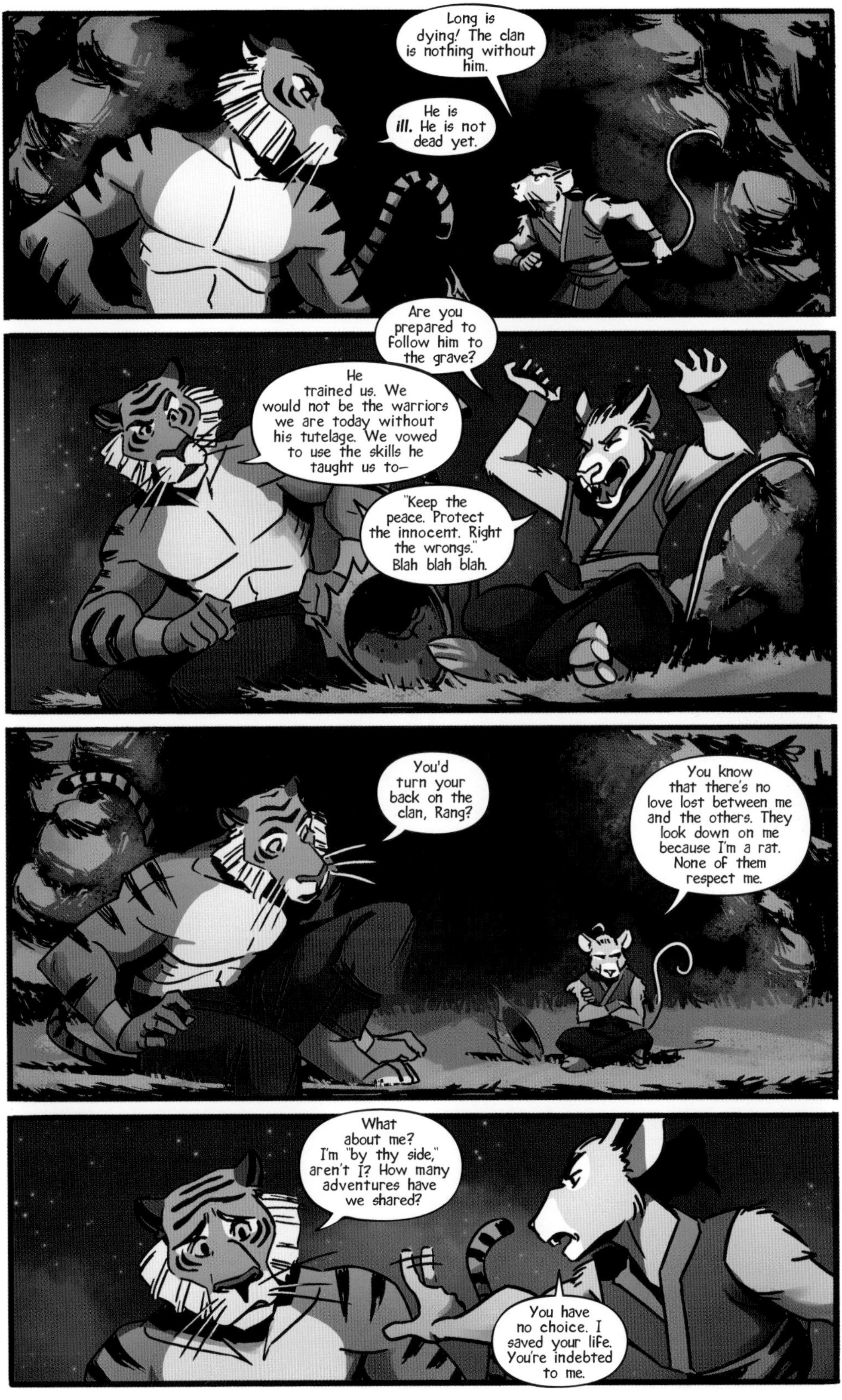
Long is dying! The clan is nothing without him.
He is **ill.** He is not dead yet.
Are you prepared to follow him to the grave?
He trained us. We would not be the warriors we are today without his tutelage. We vowed to use the skills he taught us to—
"Keep the peace. Protect the innocent. Right the wrongs." Blah blah blah.
You'd turn your back on the clan, Rang?
You know that there's no love lost between me and the others. They look down on me because I'm a rat. None of them respect me.
What about me? I'm "by thy side," aren't I? How many adventures have we shared?
You have no choice. I saved your life. You're indebted to me.

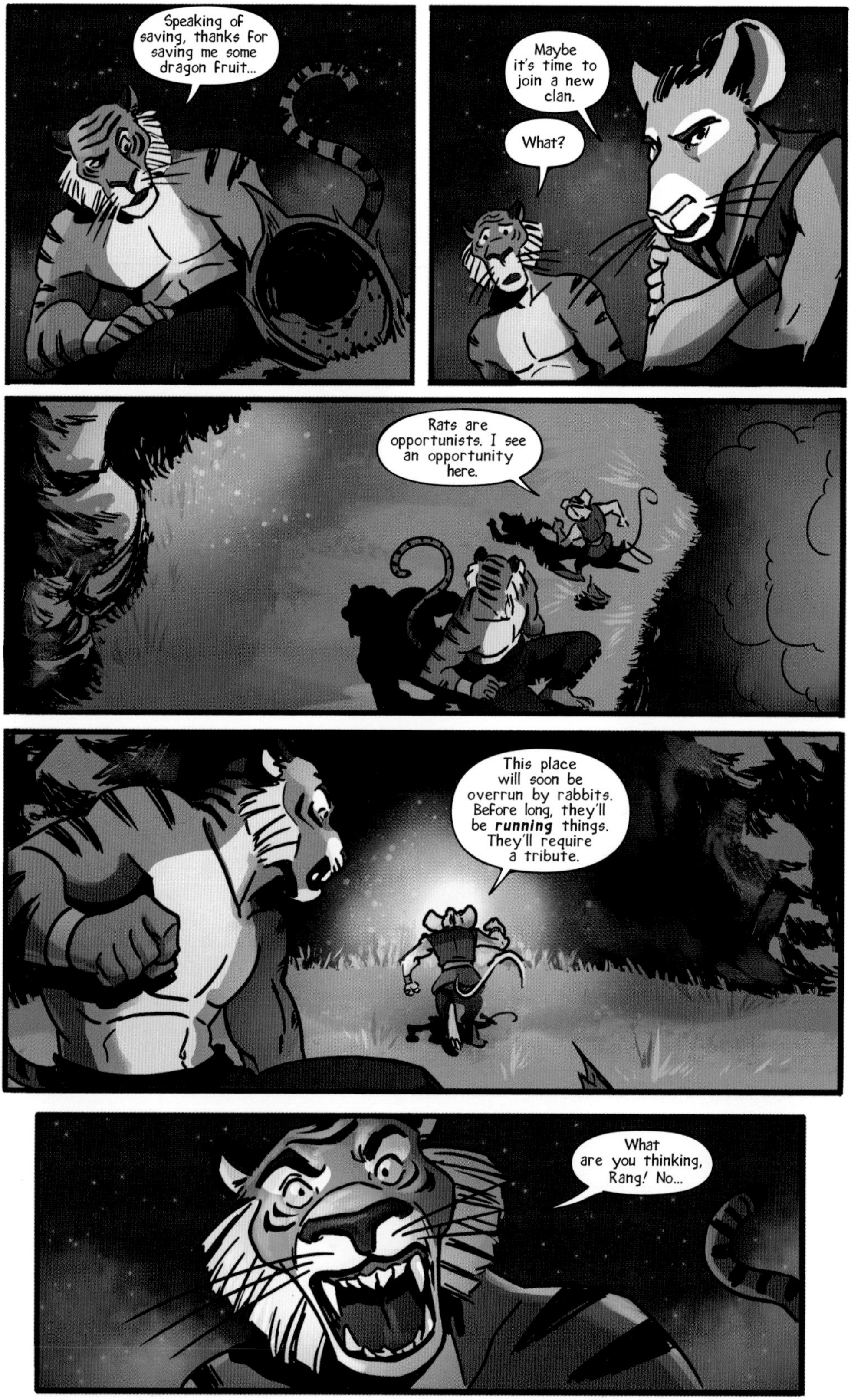
Speaking of saving, thanks for saving me some dragon fruit...
Maybe it's time to join a new clan.
What?
Rats are opportunists. I see an opportunity here.
This place will soon be overrun by rabbits. Before long, they'll be ***running*** things. They'll require a tribute.
What are you thinking, Rang! No...

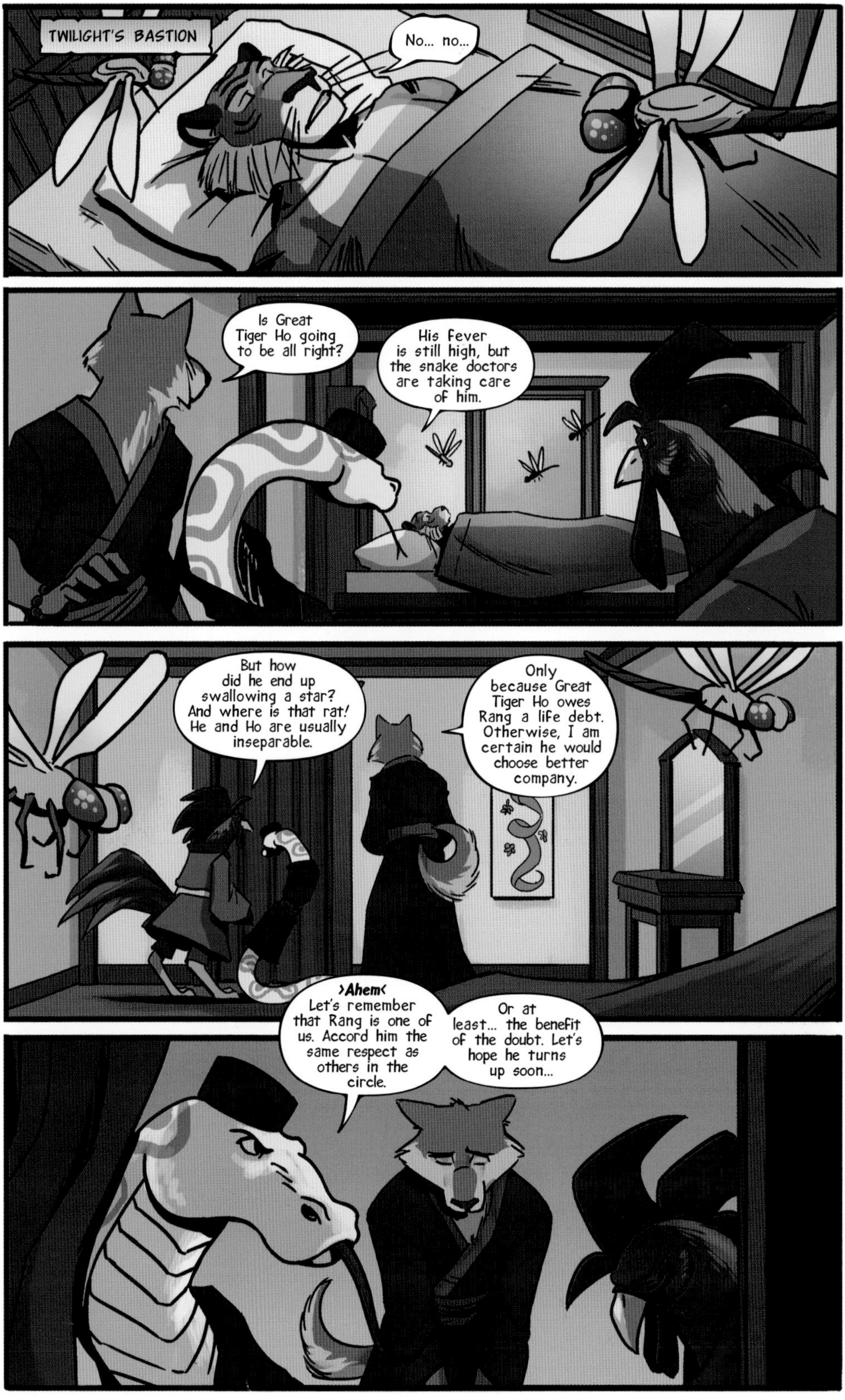
TWILIGHT'S BASTION
No... no...
Is Great Tiger Ho going to be all right?
His fever is still high, but the snake doctors are taking care of him.
But how did he end up swallowing a star? And where is that rat! He and Ho are usually inseparable.
Only because Great Tiger Ho owes Rang a life debt. Otherwise, I am certain he would choose better company.
›Ahem‹ Let's remember that Rang is one of us. Accord him the same respect as others in the circle.
Or at least... the benefit of the doubt. Let's hope he turns up soon...

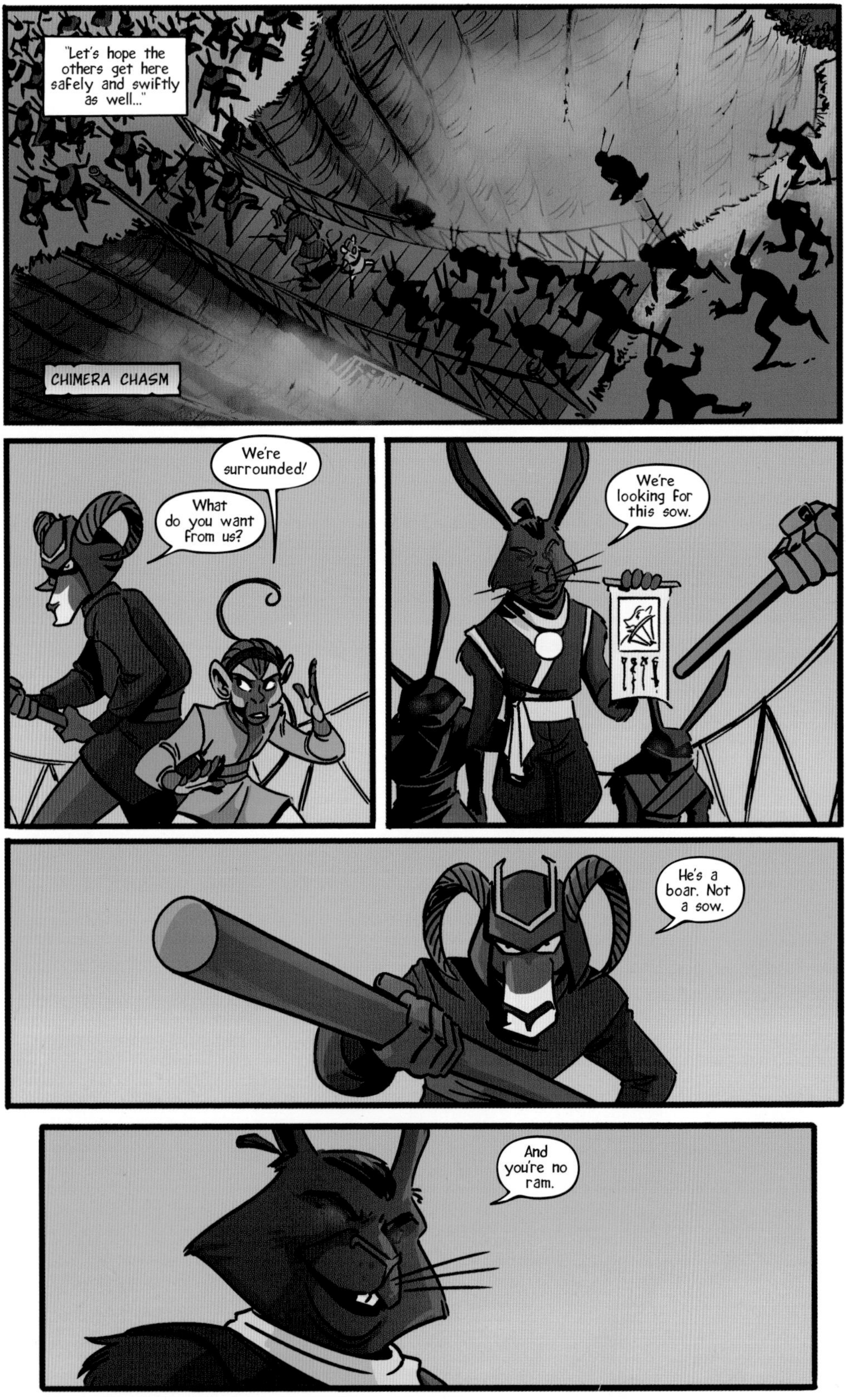
"Let's hope the others get here safely and swiftly as well..."
CHIMERA CHASM
We're surrounded!
What do you want from us?
We're looking for this sow.
He's a boar. Not a sow.
And you're no ram.

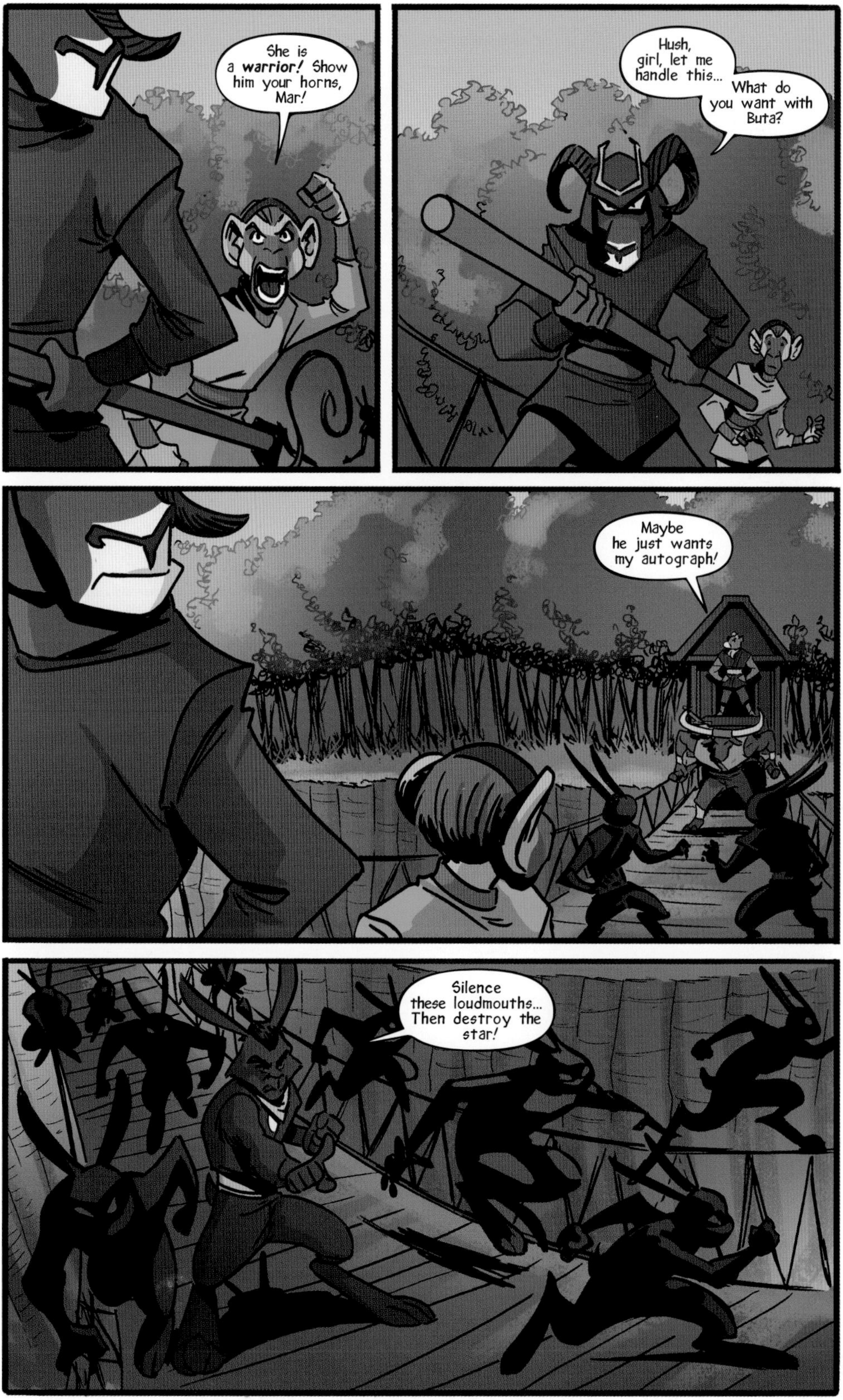
She is a **warrior!** Show him your horns, Mar!
Hush, girl, let me handle this...
What do you want with Buta?
Maybe he just wants my autograph!
Silence these loudmouths... Then destroy the star!

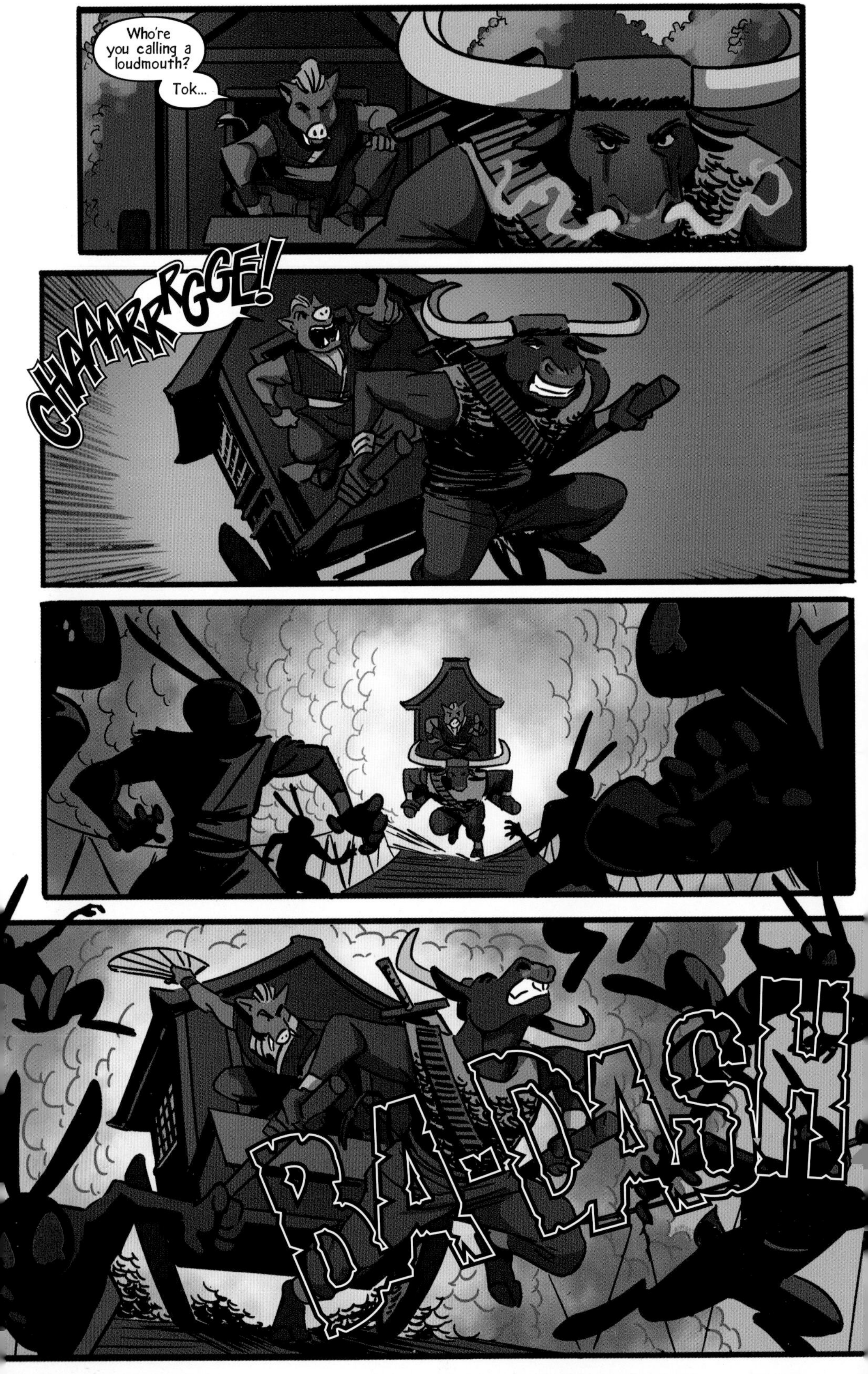
Who're you calling a loudmouth?
Tok...
CHAAARRRGGE!
BADASH

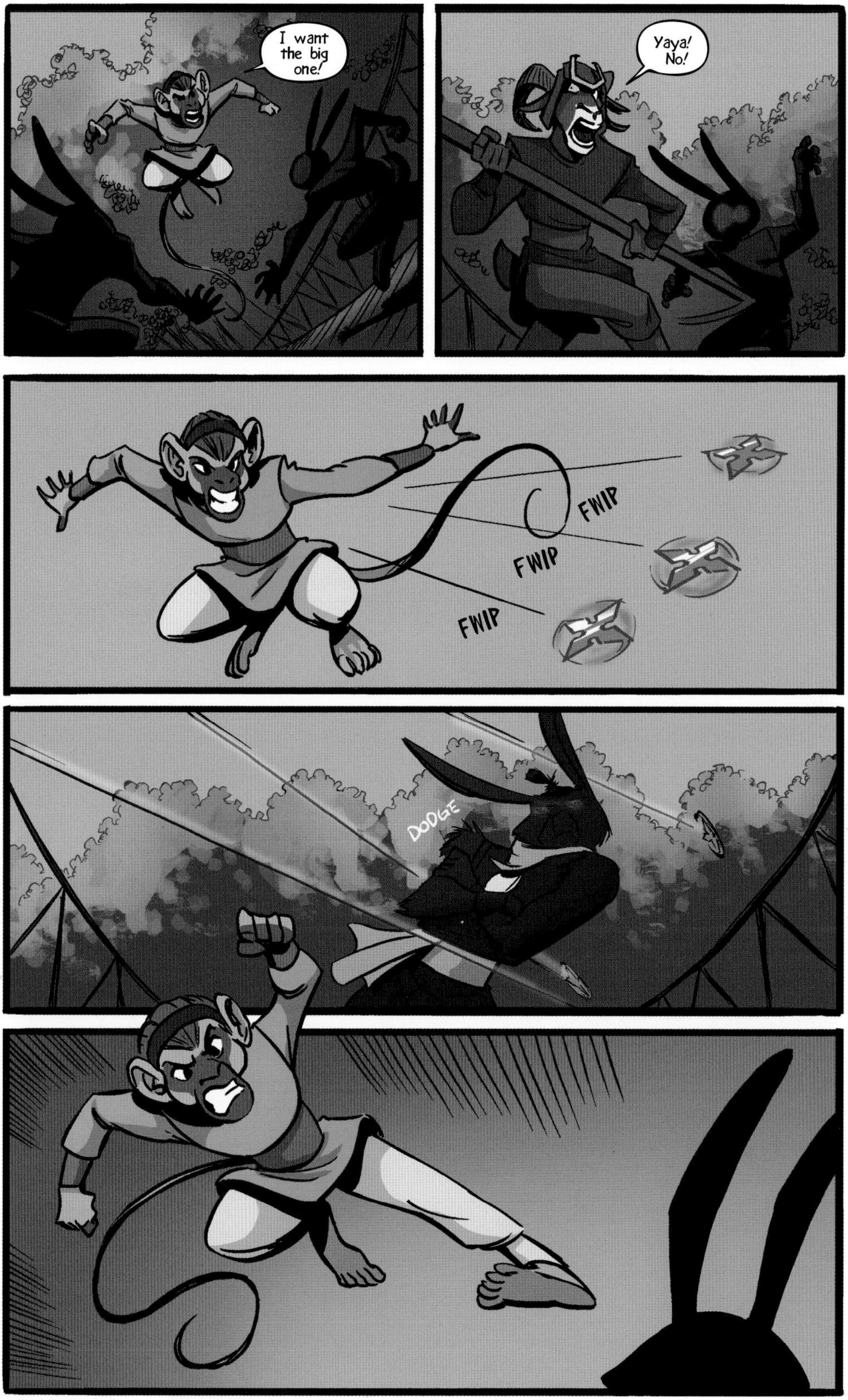
I want the big one!
Yaya! No!
FWIP
FWIP
FWIP
DODGE

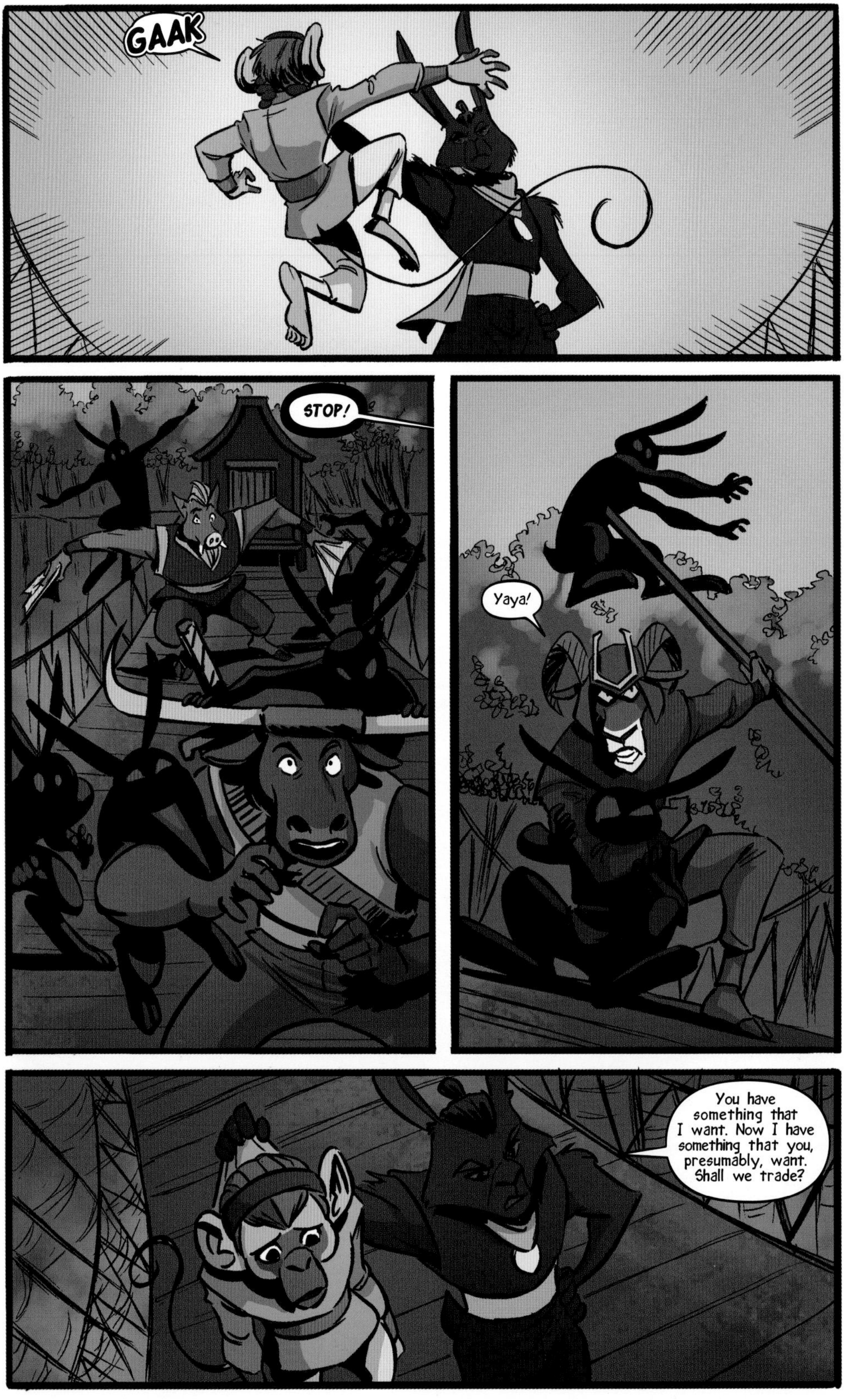
GAAK
STOP!
Yaya!
You have something that I want. Now I have something that you, presumably, want. Shall we trade?

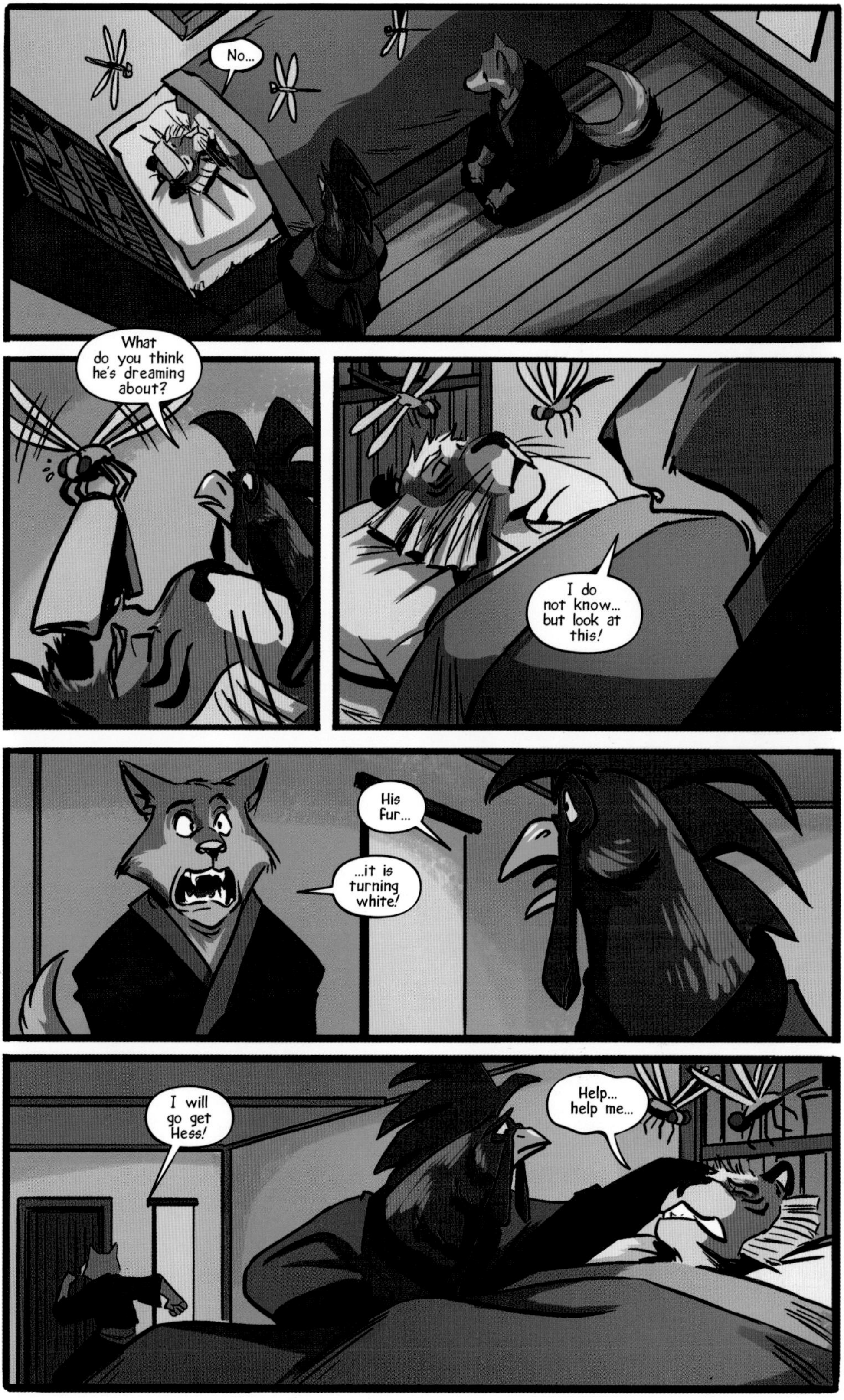
No...
What do you think he's dreaming about?
I do not know... but look at this!
His fur...
...it is turning white!
I will go get Hess!
Help... help me...

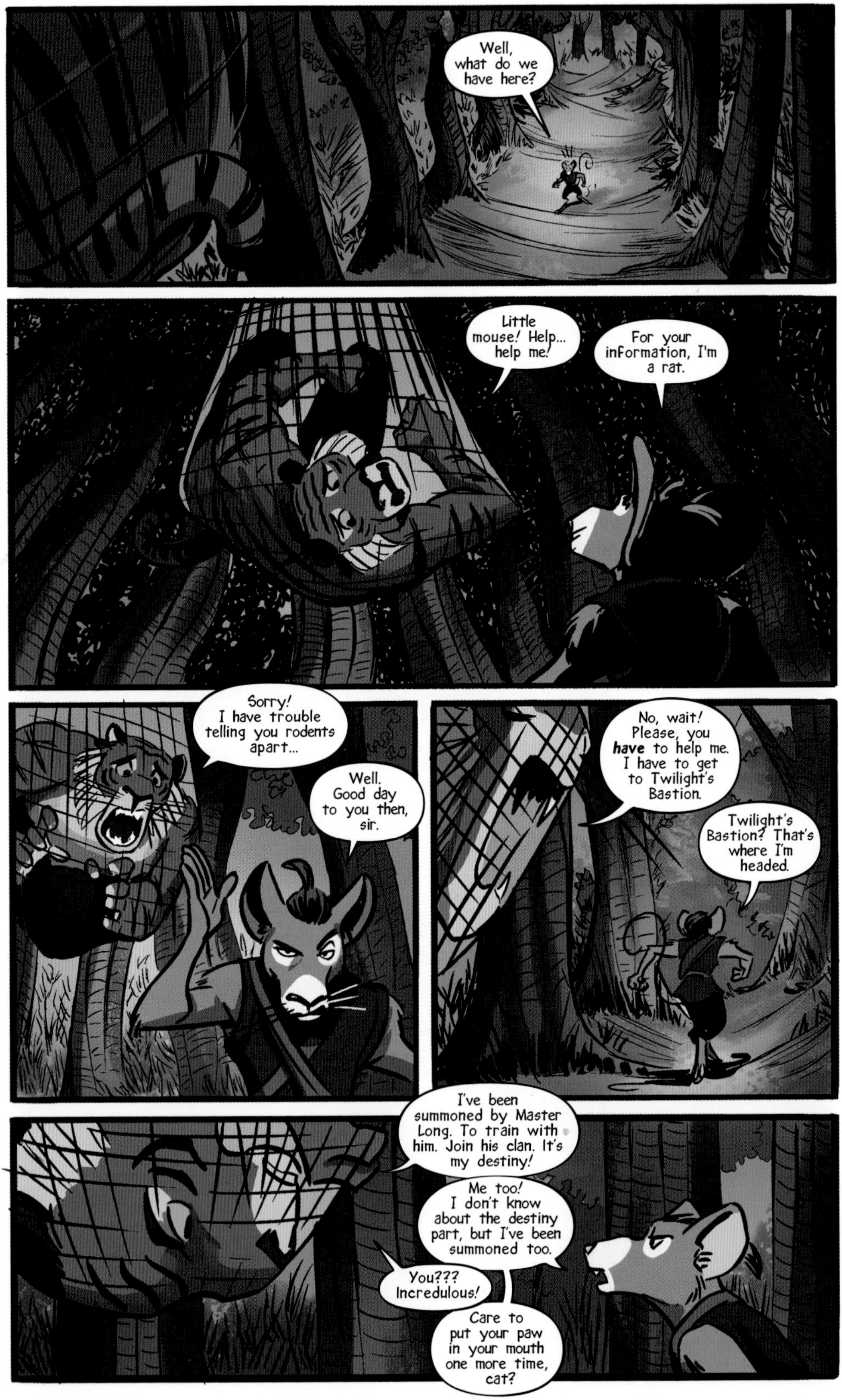
Well, what do we have here?
Little mouse! Help... help me!
For your information, I'm a rat.
Sorry! I have trouble telling you rodents apart...
Well. Good day to you then, sir.
No, wait! Please, you **have** to help me. I have to get to Twilight's Bastion.
Twilight's Bastion? That's where I'm headed.
I've been summoned by Master Long. To train with him. Join his clan. It's my destiny!
Me too! I don't know about the destiny part, but I've been summoned too.
You??? Incredulous!
Care to put your paw in your mouth one more time, cat?

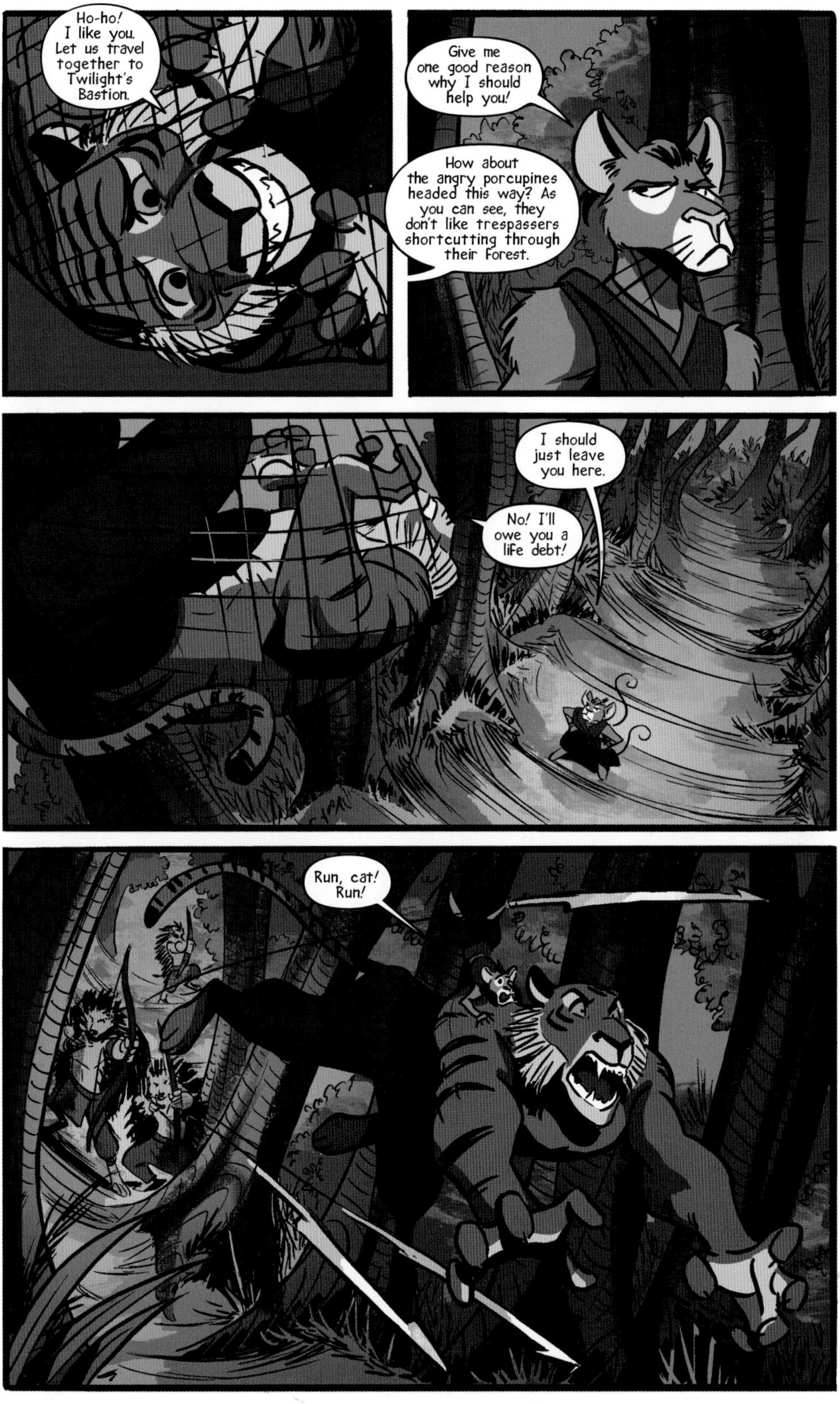
Ho-ho! I like you. Let us travel together to Twilight's Bastion.
Give me one good reason why I should help you!
How about the angry porcupines headed this way? As you can see, they don't like trespassers shortcutting through their forest.
I should just leave you here.
No! I'll owe you a life debt!
Run, cat! Run!

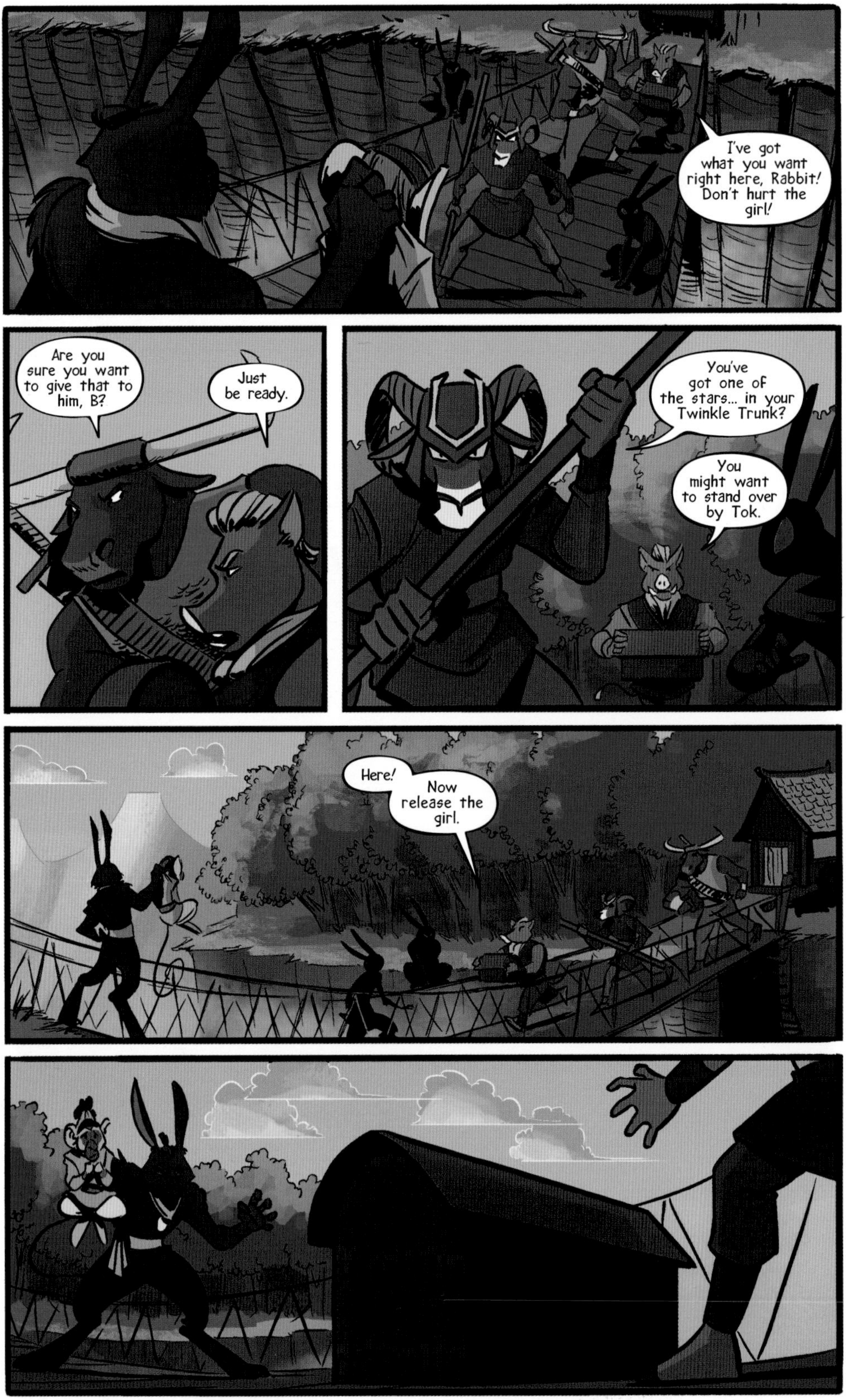
I've got what you want right here, Rabbit! Don't hurt the girl!
Are you sure you want to give that to him, B?
Just be ready.
You've got one of the stars... in your Twinkle Trunk?
You might want to stand over by Tok.
Here!
Now release the girl.

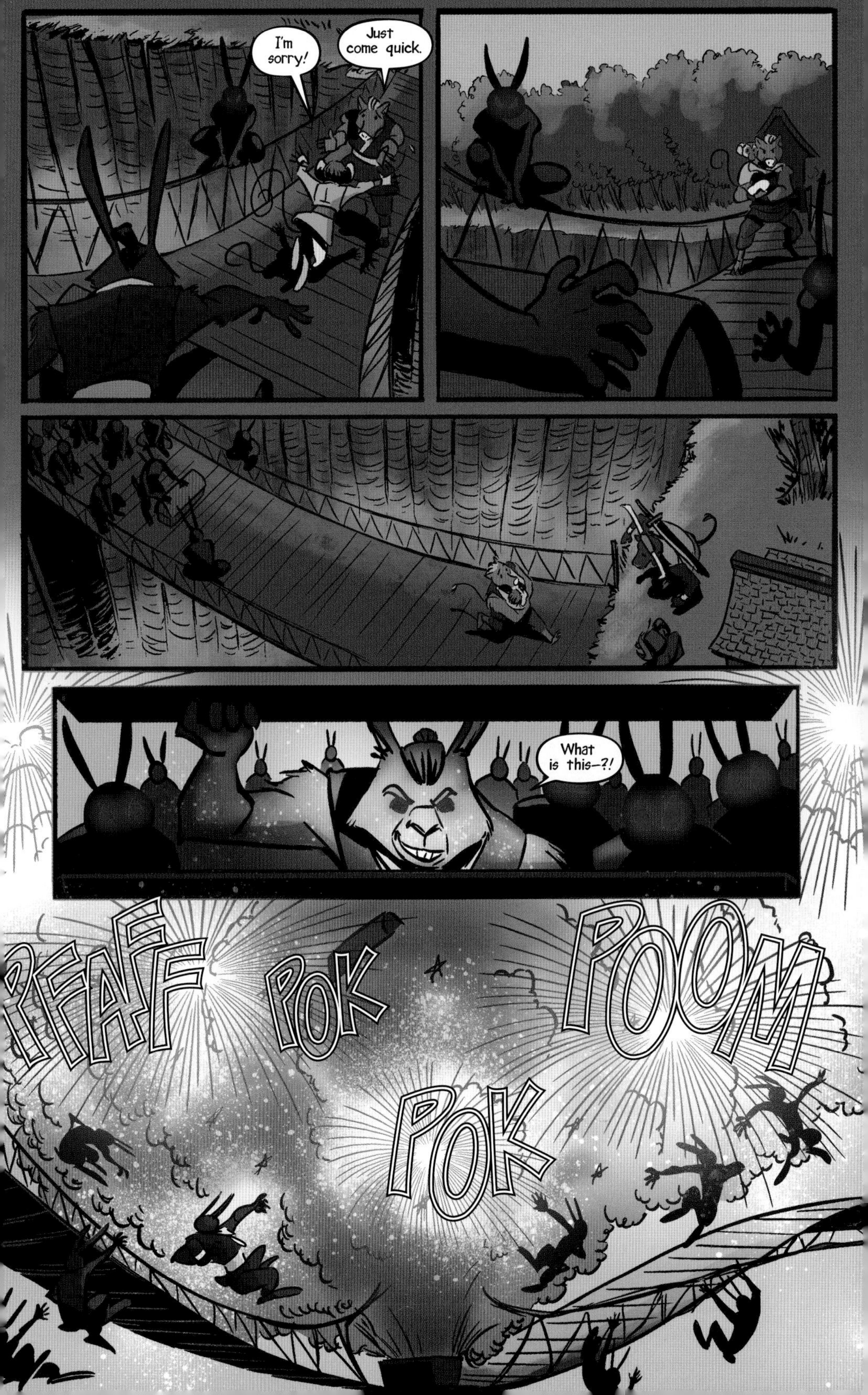
I'm sorry!
Just come quick.
What is this—?!
PFAFF
POK
POOM
POK

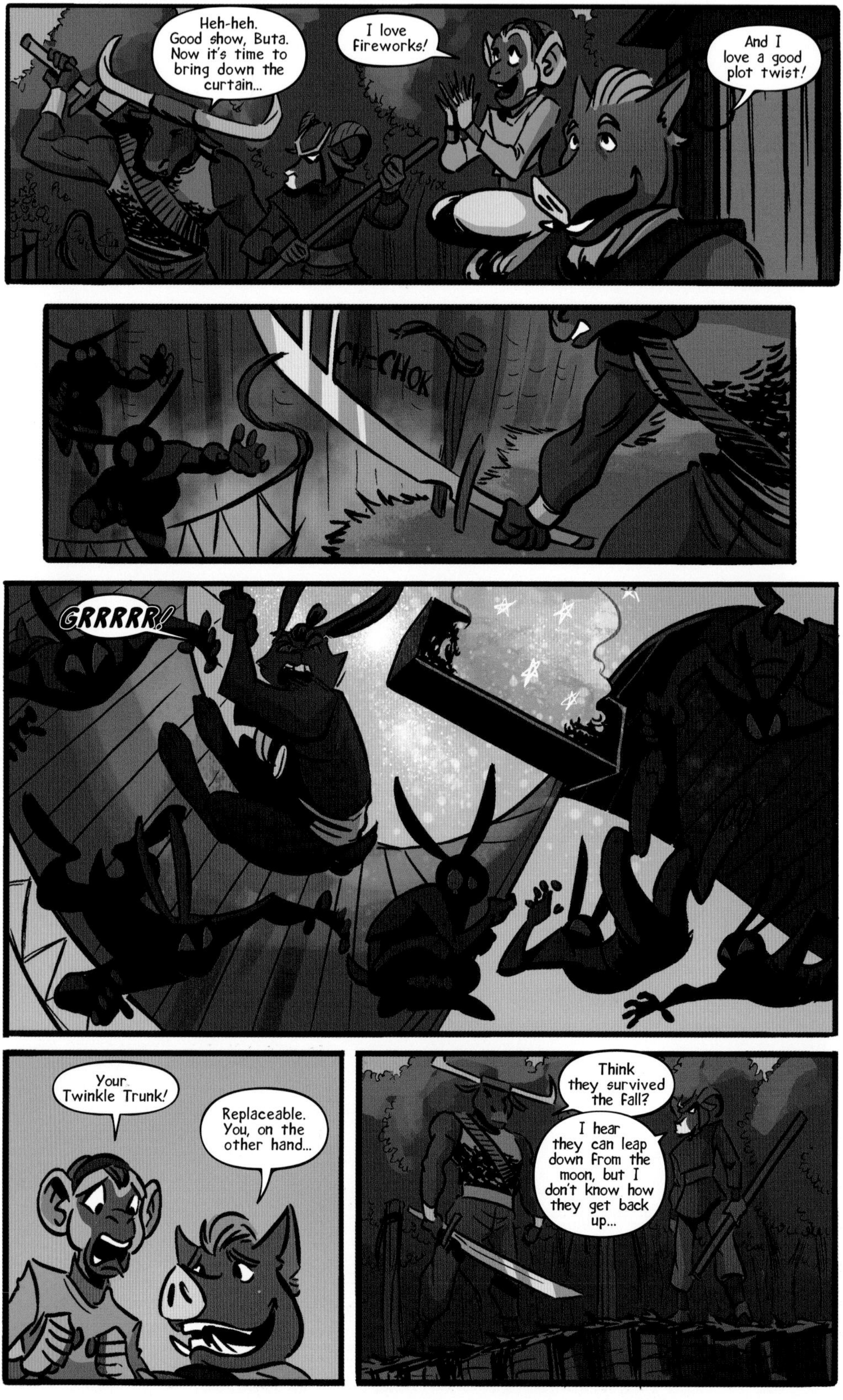
Heh-heh. Good show, Buta. Now it's time to bring down the curtain...
I love fireworks!
And I love a good plot twist!
CH-CHOK
GRRRRR!
Your Twinkle Trunk!
Replaceable. You, on the other hand...
Think they survived the fall?
I hear they can leap down from the moon, but I don't know how they get back up...

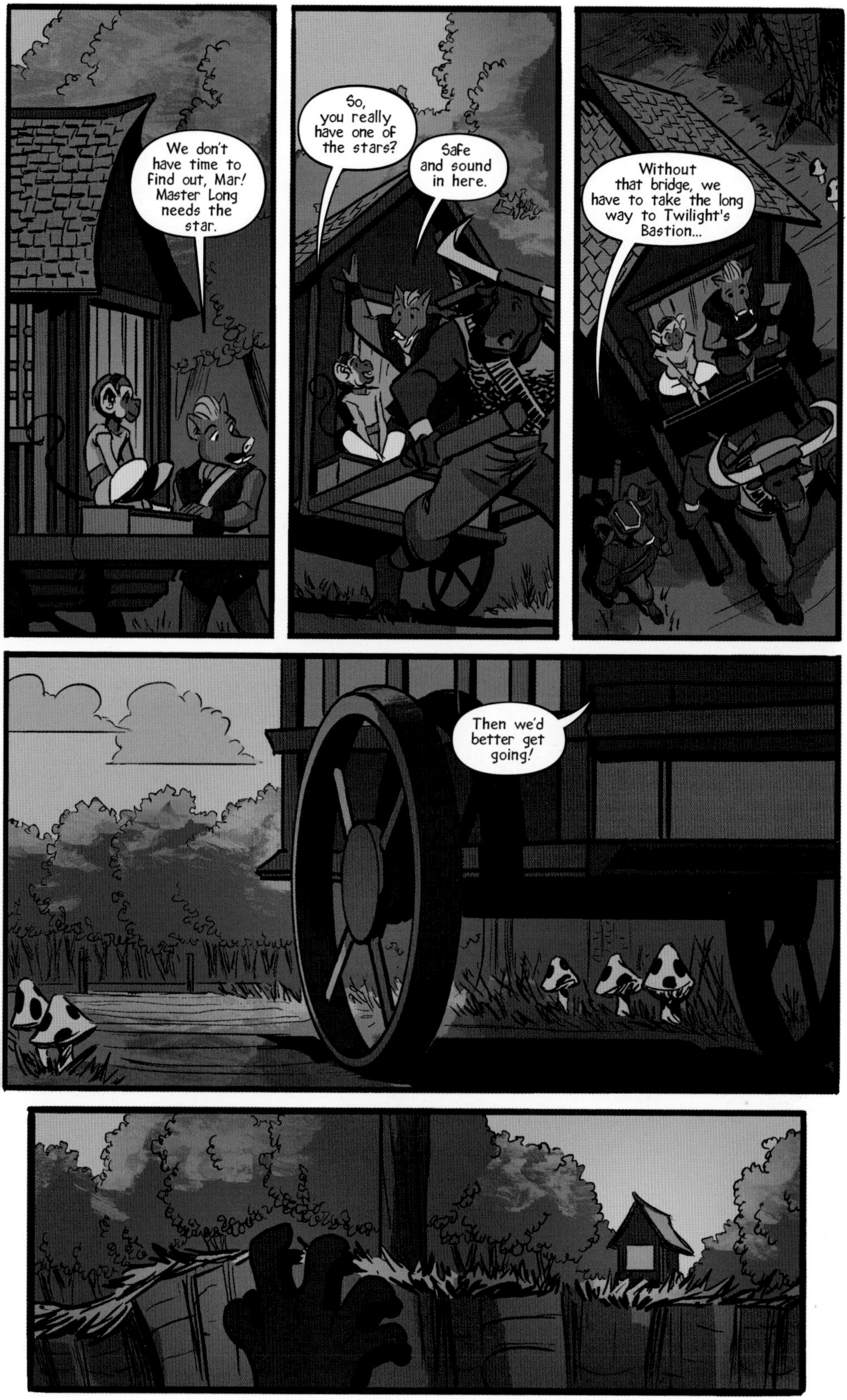
We don't have time to find out, Mar! Master Long needs the star.
So, you really have one of the stars?
Safe and sound in here.
Without that bridge, we have to take the long way to Twilight's Bastion...
Then we'd better get going!

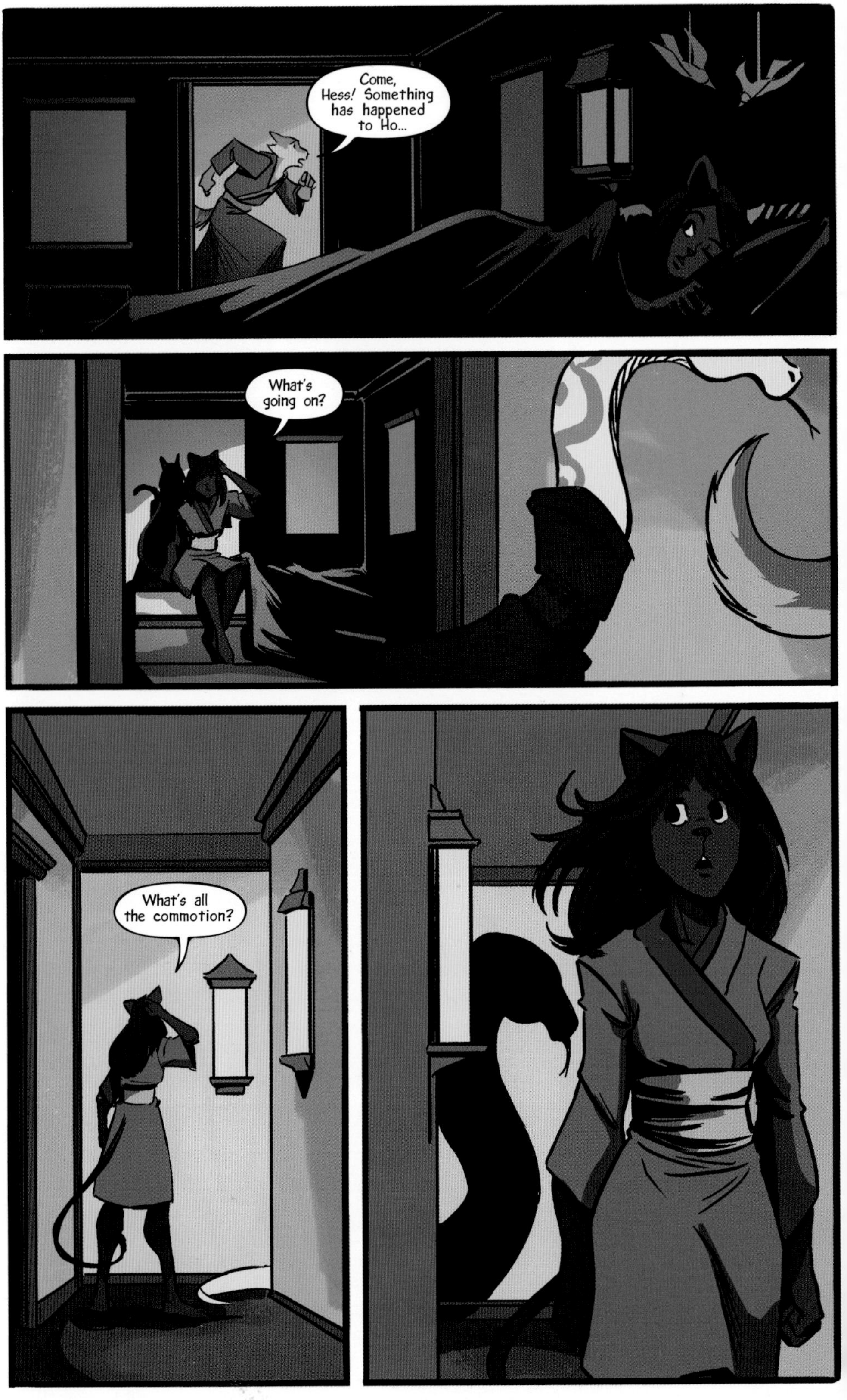
Come, Hess! Something has happened to Ho...
What's going on?
What's all the commotion?

This is the star's doing.

But what is happening to him? What does this mean?

It means he's being transformed...

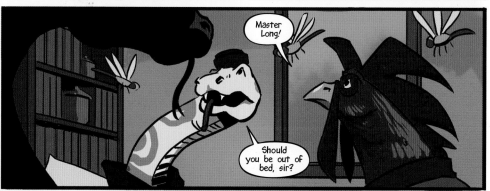

Master Long!

Should you be out of bed, sir?

The true power of the star is in transformation. But it is not Ho's time to be transformed. It is mine. So now, I must do as he did...

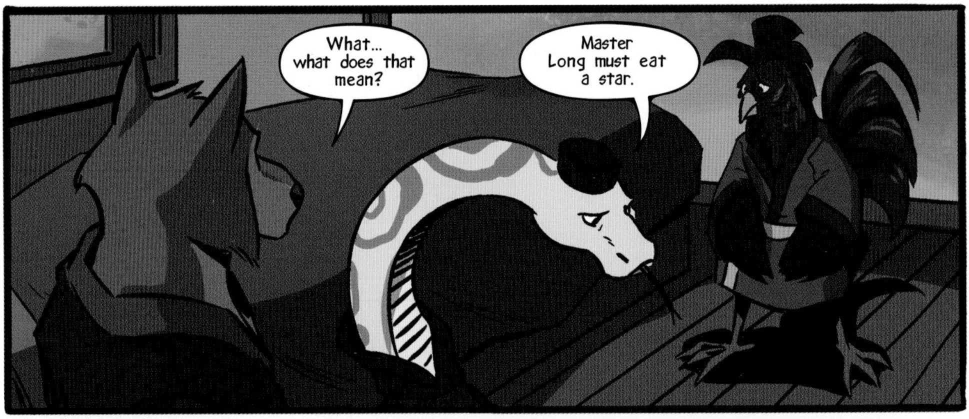
What... what does that mean?
Master Long must eat a star.

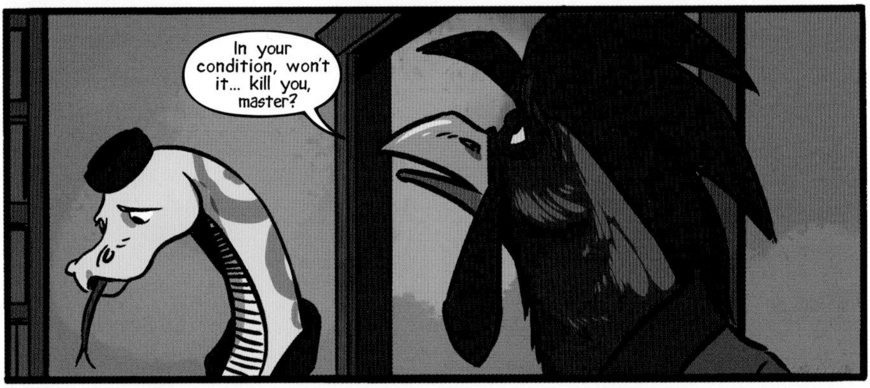
In your condition, won't it... kill you, master?

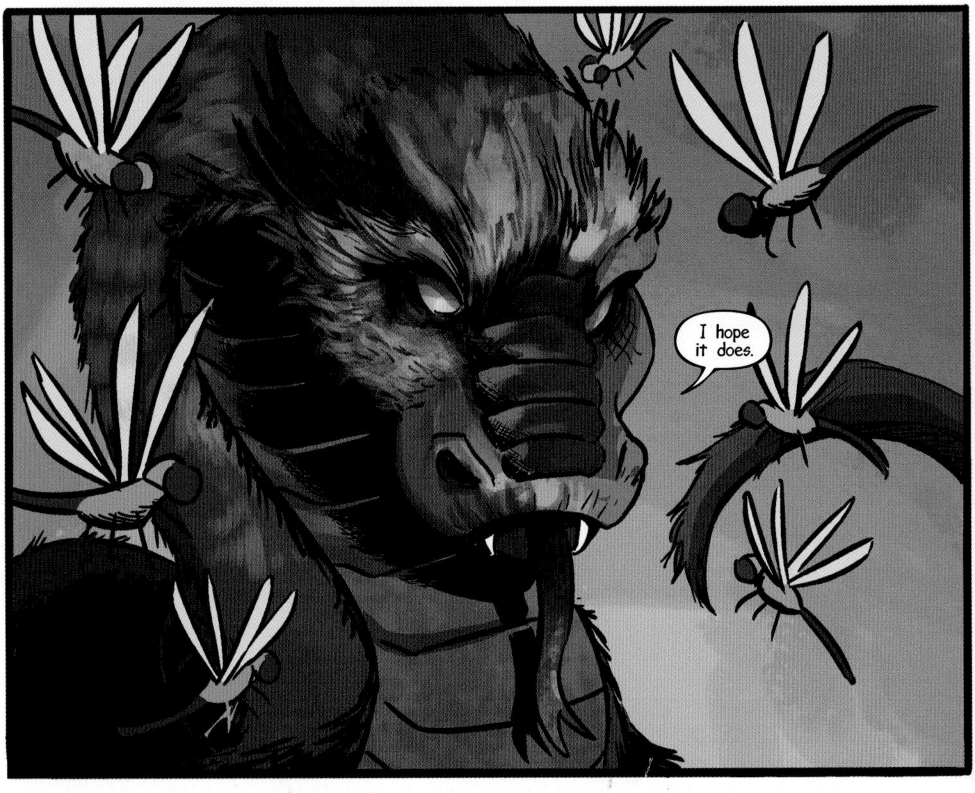
I hope it does.

CHAPTER FOUR

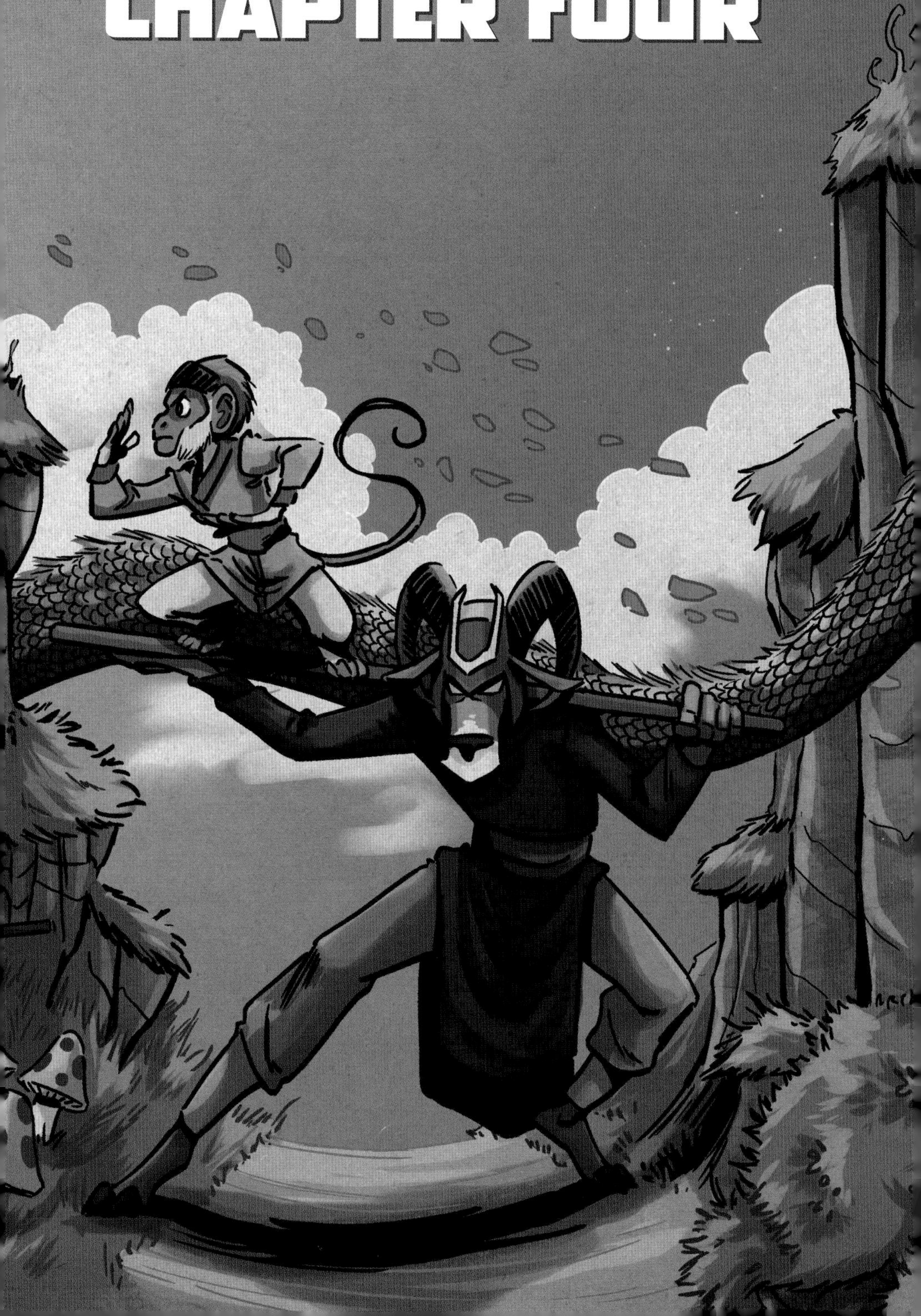

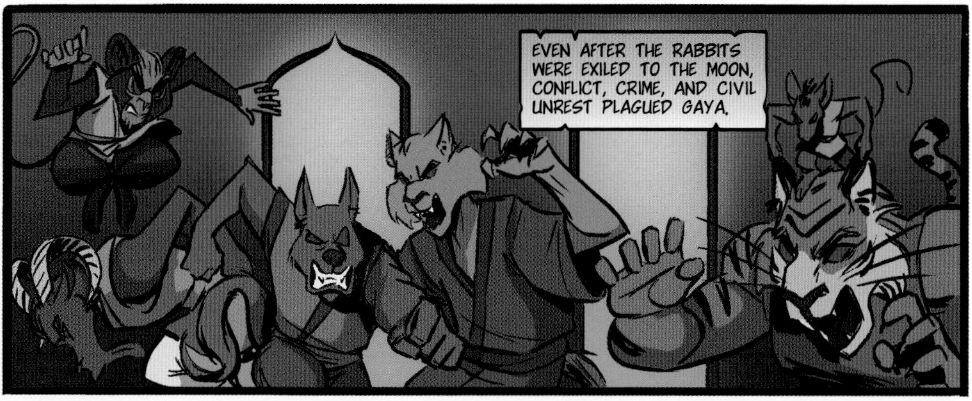
EVEN AFTER THE RABBITS WERE EXILED TO THE MOON, CONFLICT, CRIME, AND CIVIL UNREST PLAGUED GAYA.

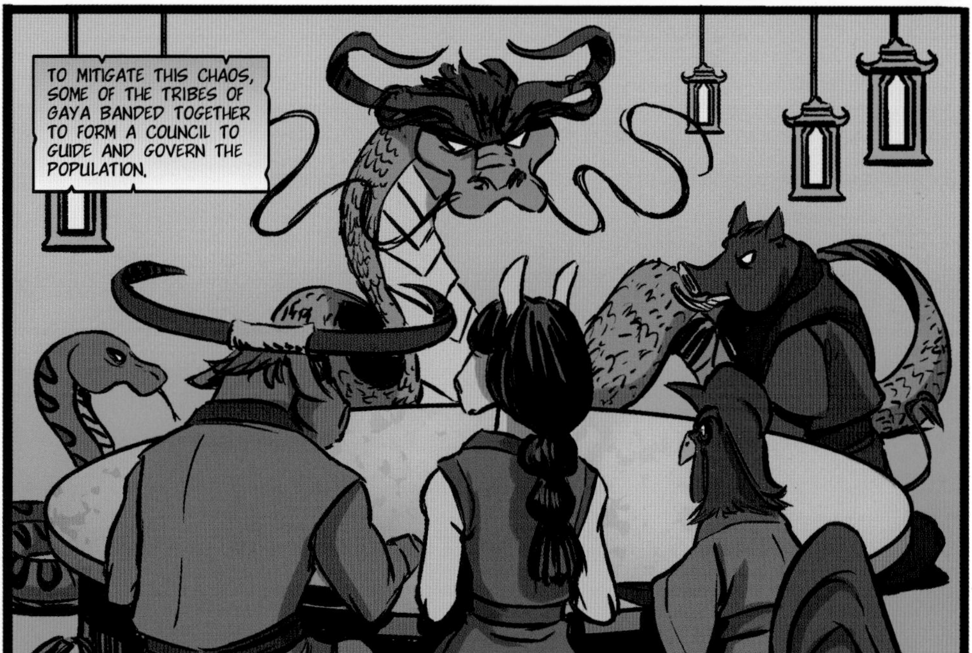
TO MITIGATE THIS CHAOS, SOME OF THE TRIBES OF GAYA BANDED TOGETHER TO FORM A COUNCIL TO GUIDE AND GOVERN THE POPULATION.

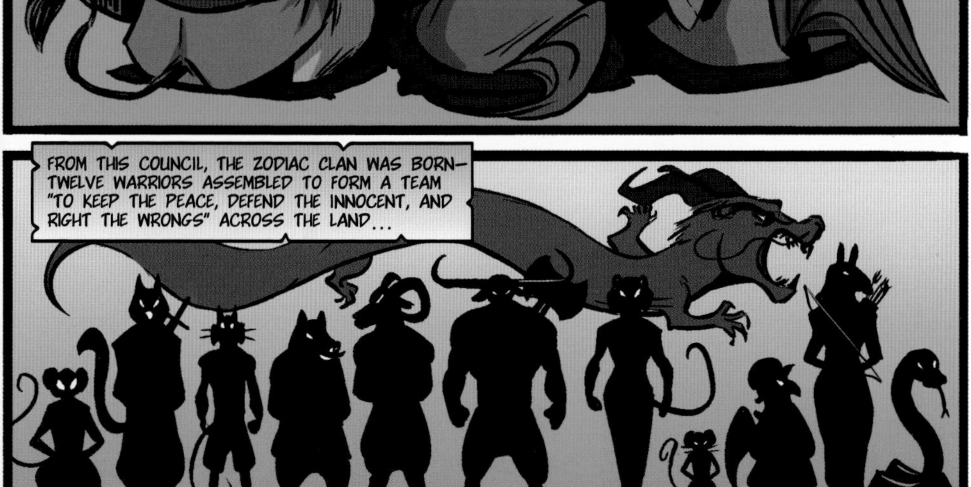
FROM THIS COUNCIL, THE ZODIAC CLAN WAS BORN— TWELVE WARRIORS ASSEMBLED TO FORM A TEAM "TO KEEP THE PEACE, DEFEND THE INNOCENT, AND RIGHT THE WRONGS" ACROSS THE LAND...

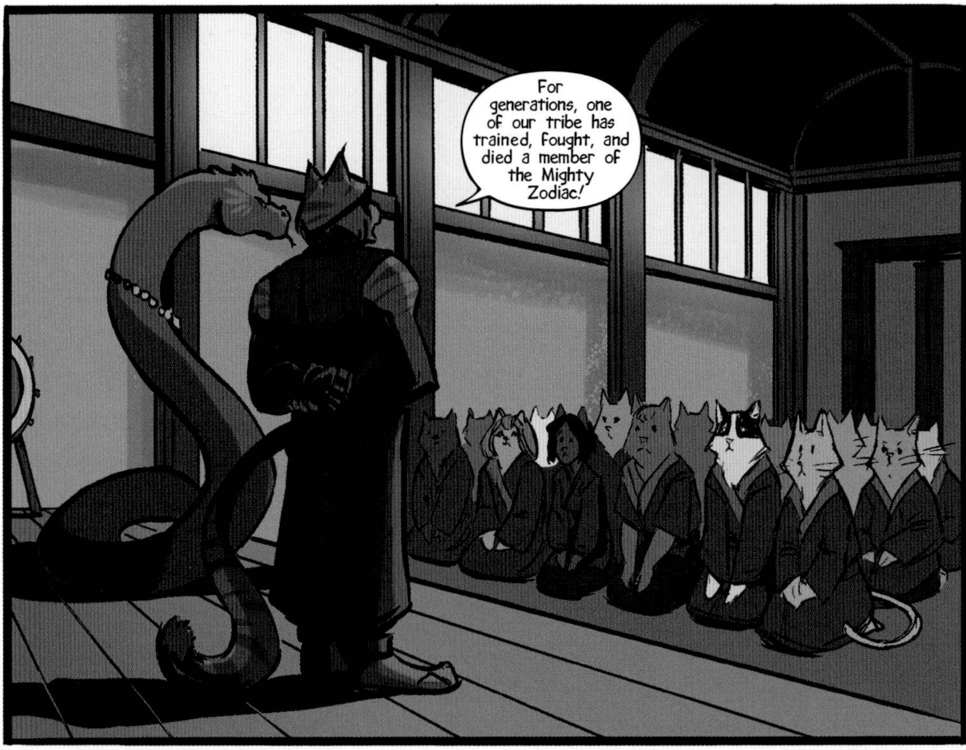
For generations, one of our tribe has trained, fought, and died a member of the Mighty Zodiac!

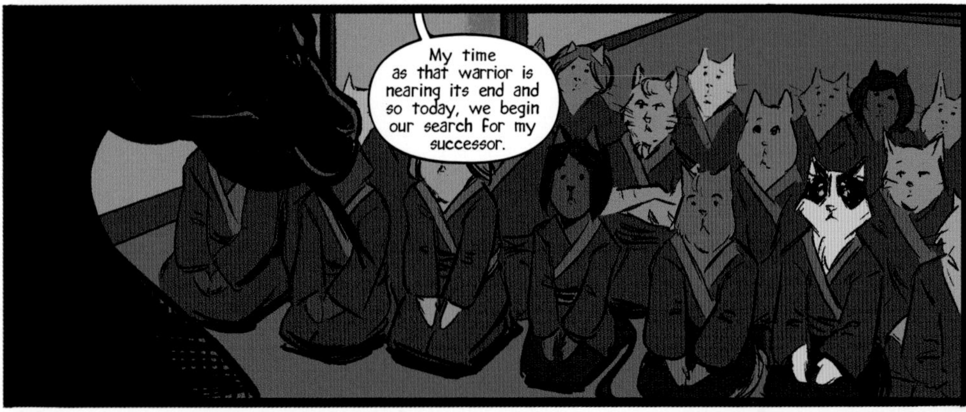
My time as that warrior is nearing its end and so today, we begin our search for my successor.

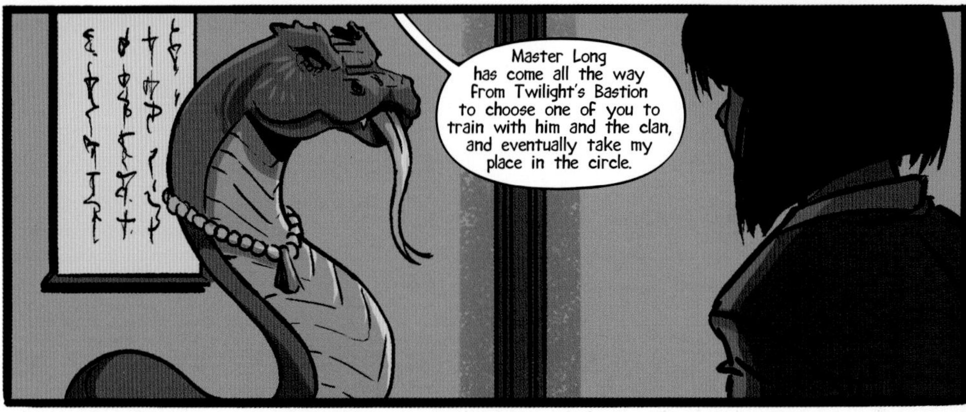
Master Long has come all the way from Twilight's Bastion to choose one of you to train with him and the clan, and eventually take my place in the circle.

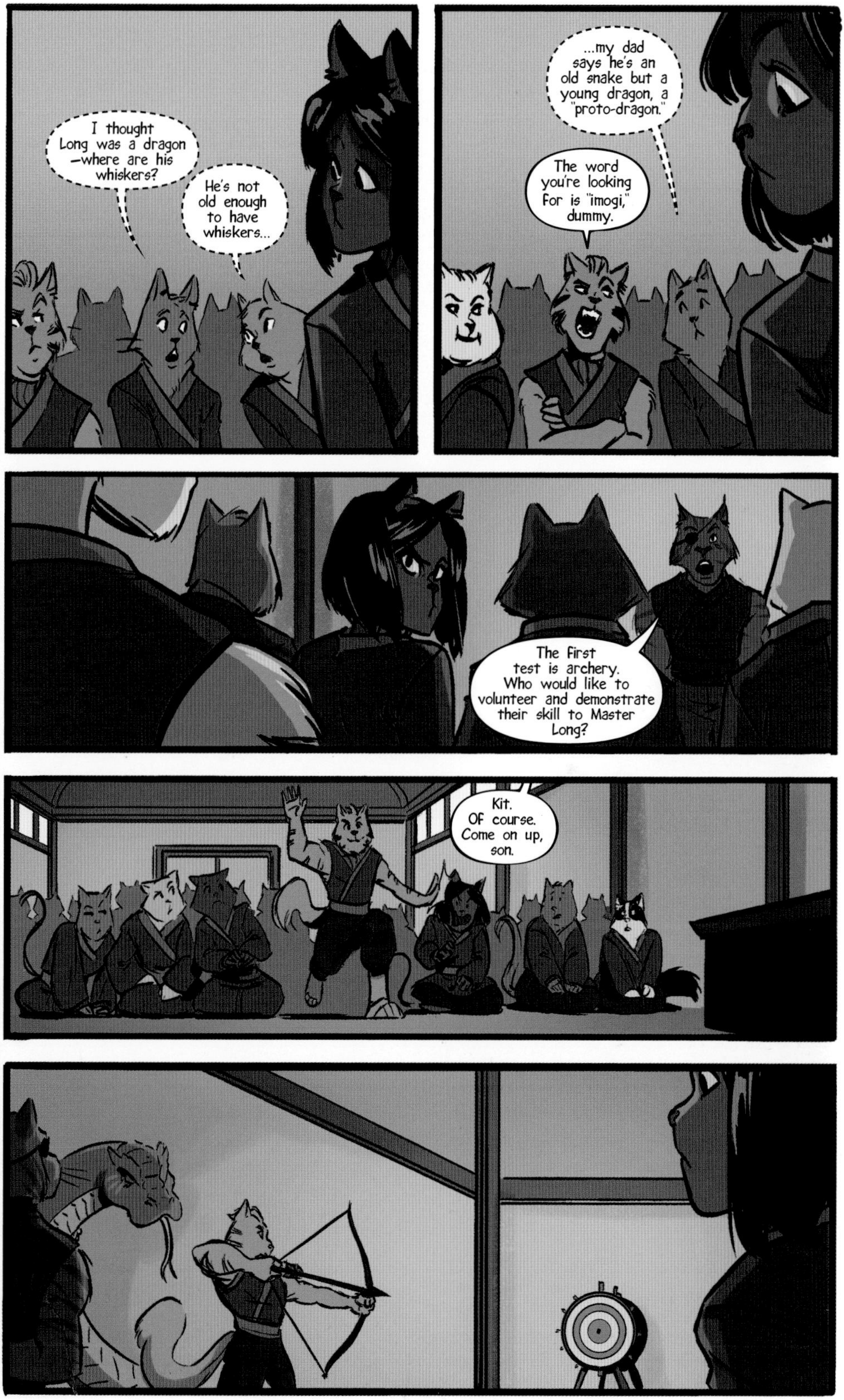
I thought Long was a dragon —where are his whiskers?
He's not old enough to have whiskers...
...my dad says he's an old snake but a young dragon, a "proto-dragon."
The word you're looking for is "imogi," dummy.
The first test is archery. Who would like to volunteer and demonstrate their skill to Master Long?
Kit. Of course. Come on up, son.

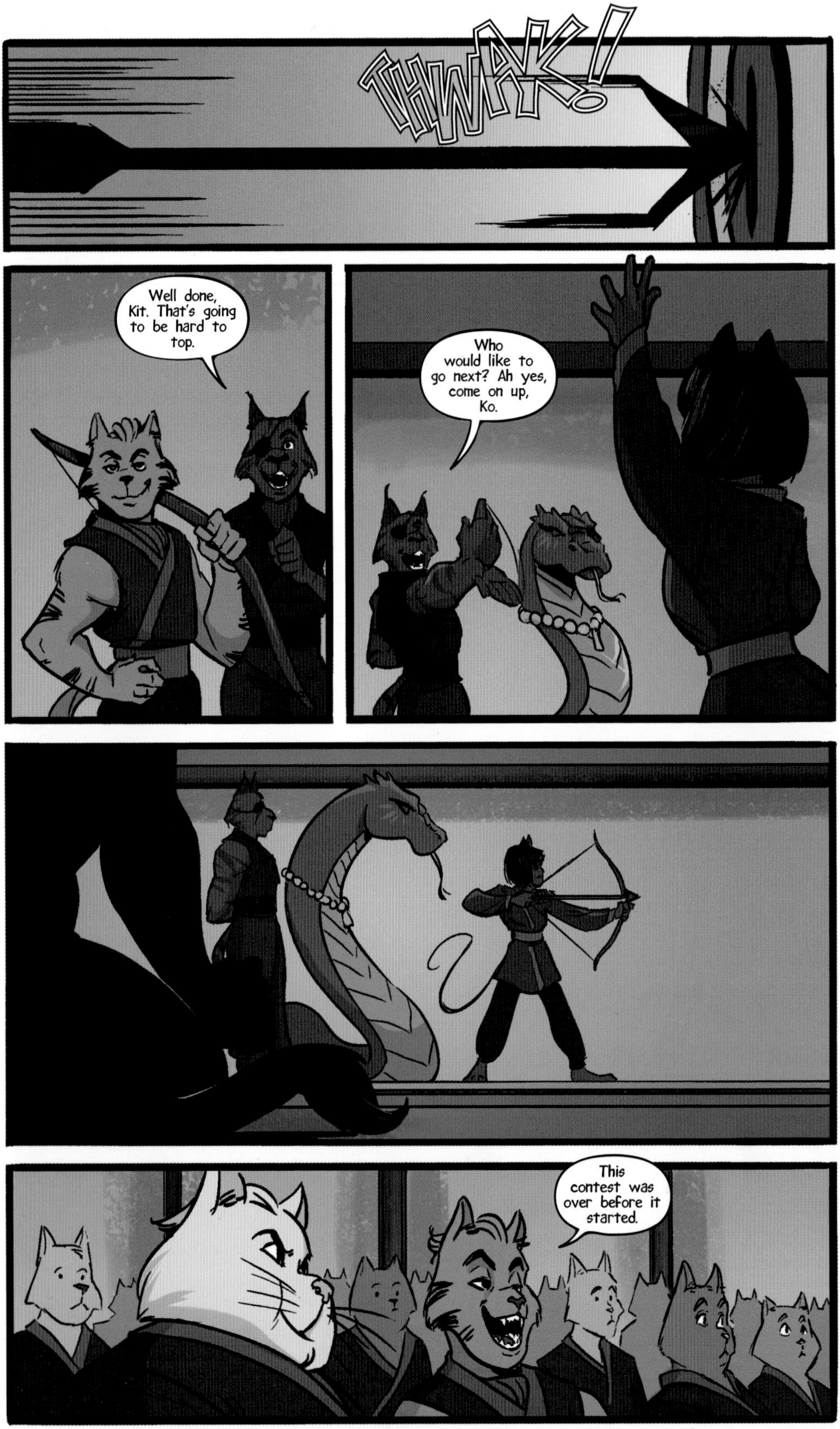
THWAK!
Well done, Kit. That's going to be hard to top.
Who would like to go next? Ah yes, come on up, Ko.
This contest was over before it started.

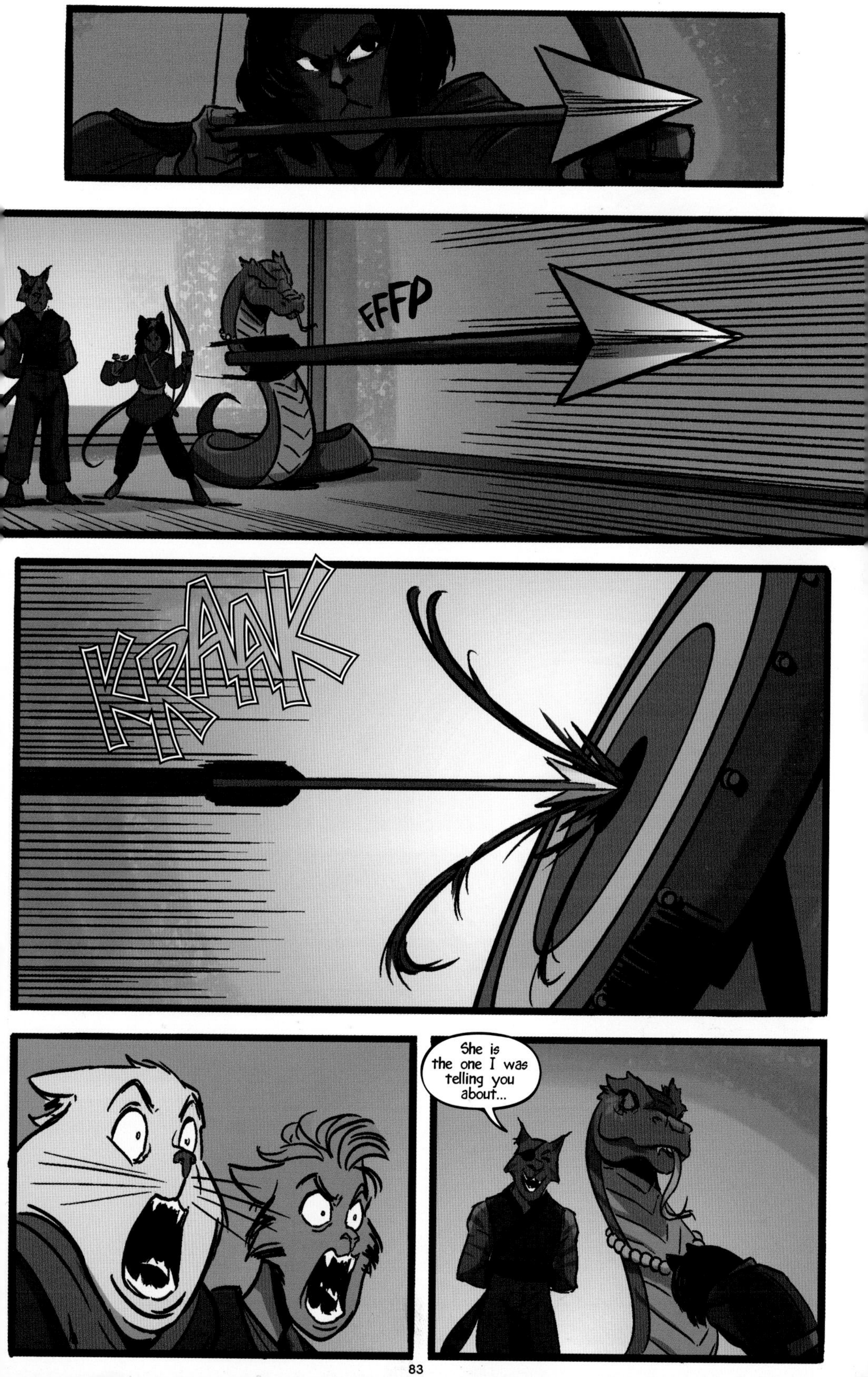
FFFP
KRAAAK
She is the one I was telling you about...

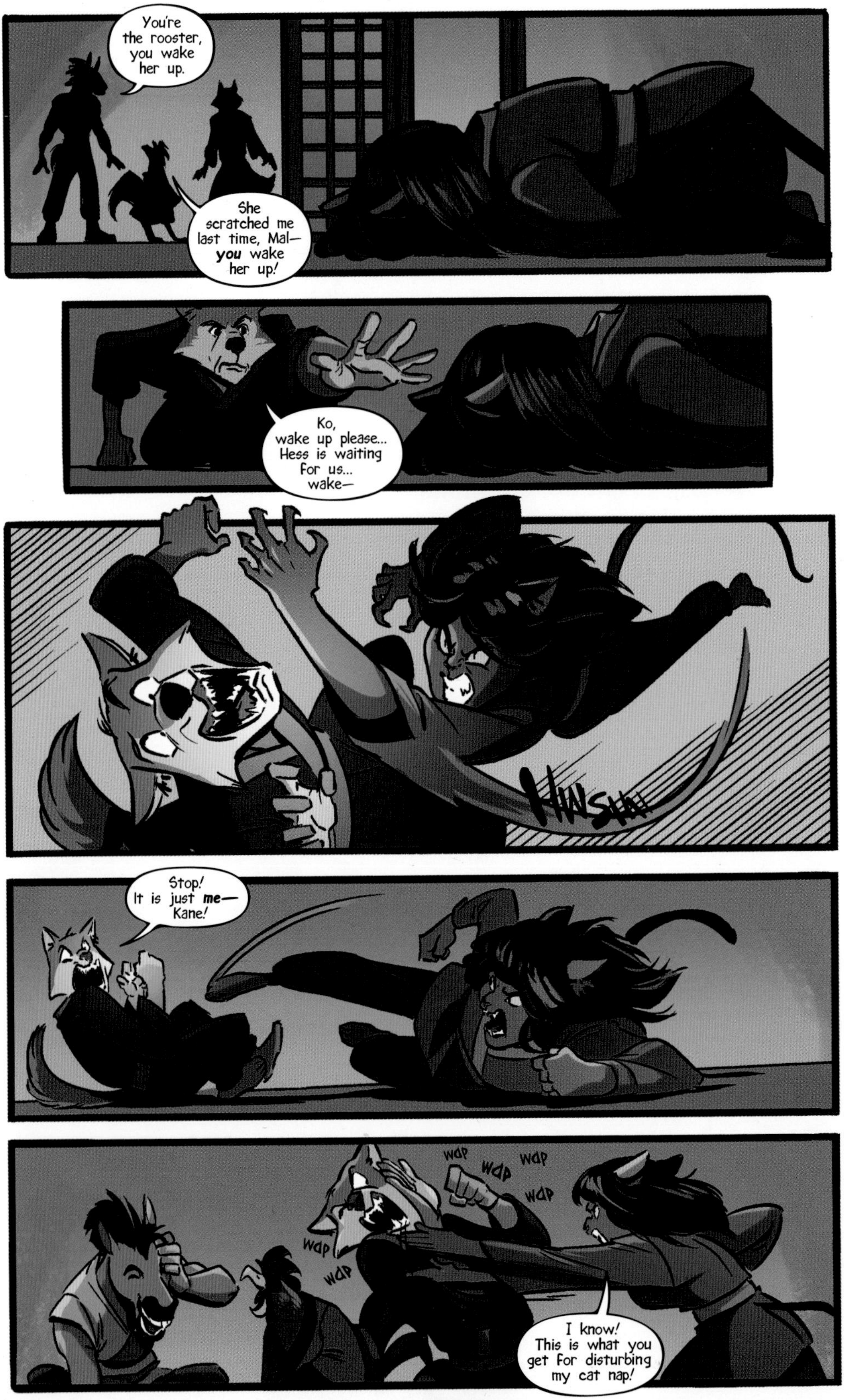
You're the rooster, you wake her up.
She scratched me last time, Mal— **you** wake her up!
Ko, wake up please... Hess is waiting for us... wake—
Stop! It is just **me**— Kane!
wap
wap
wap
wap
wap
wap
I know! This is what you get for disturbing my cat nap!

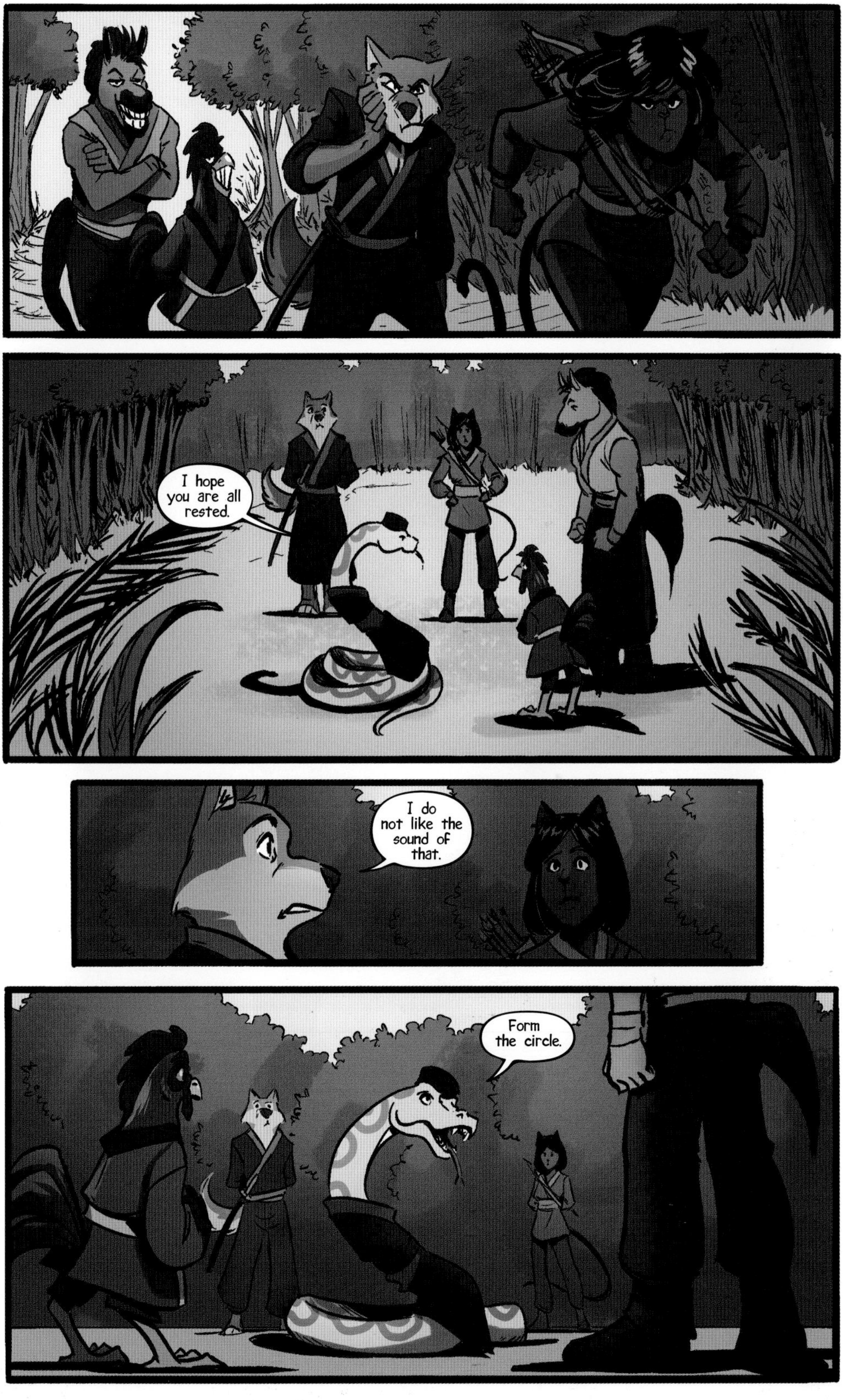
I hope you are all rested.
I do not like the sound of that.
Form the circle.

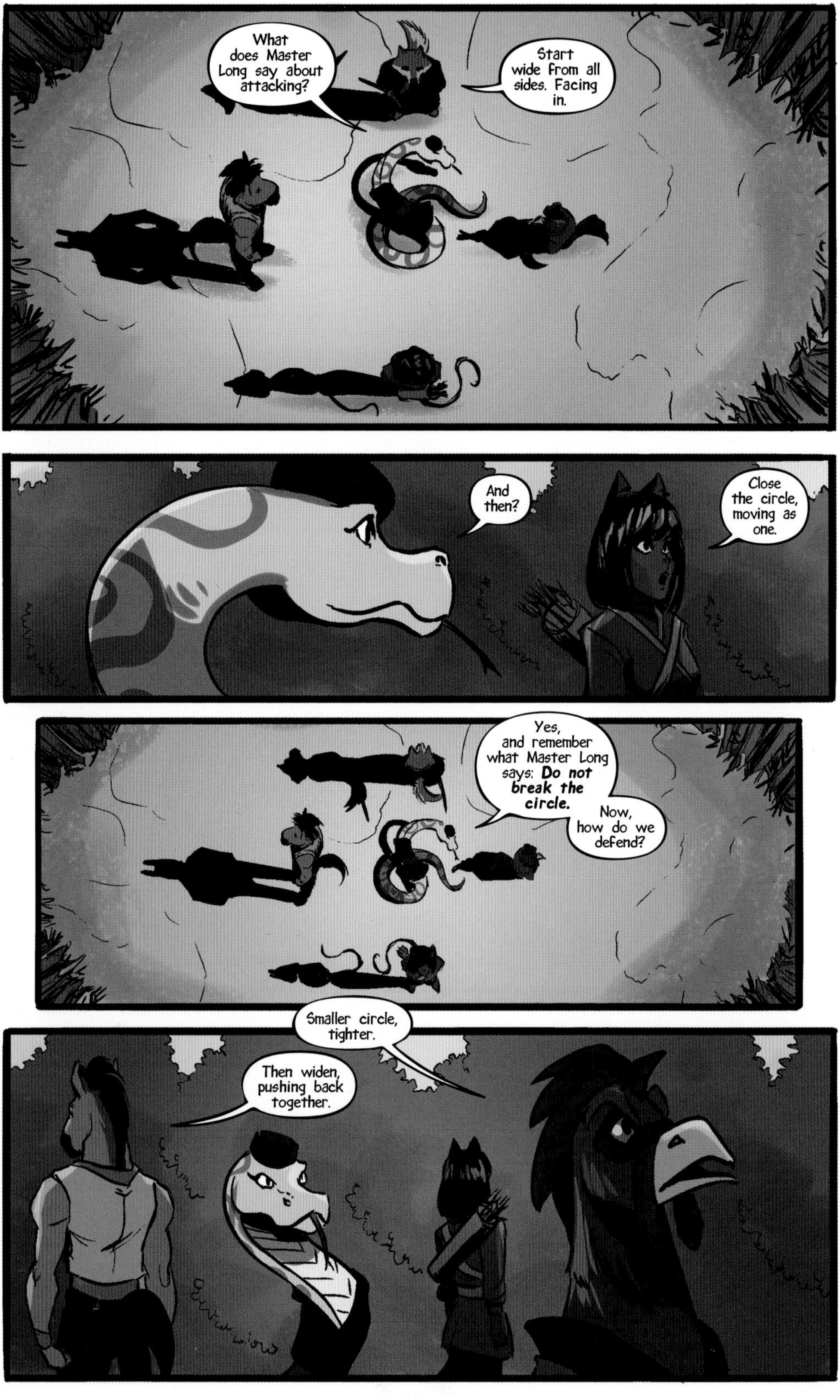
What does Master Long say about attacking?
Start wide from all sides. Facing in.
And then?
Close the circle, moving as one.
Yes, and remember what Master Long says: **Do not break the circle.**
Now, how do we defend?
Smaller circle, tighter.
Then widen, pushing back together.

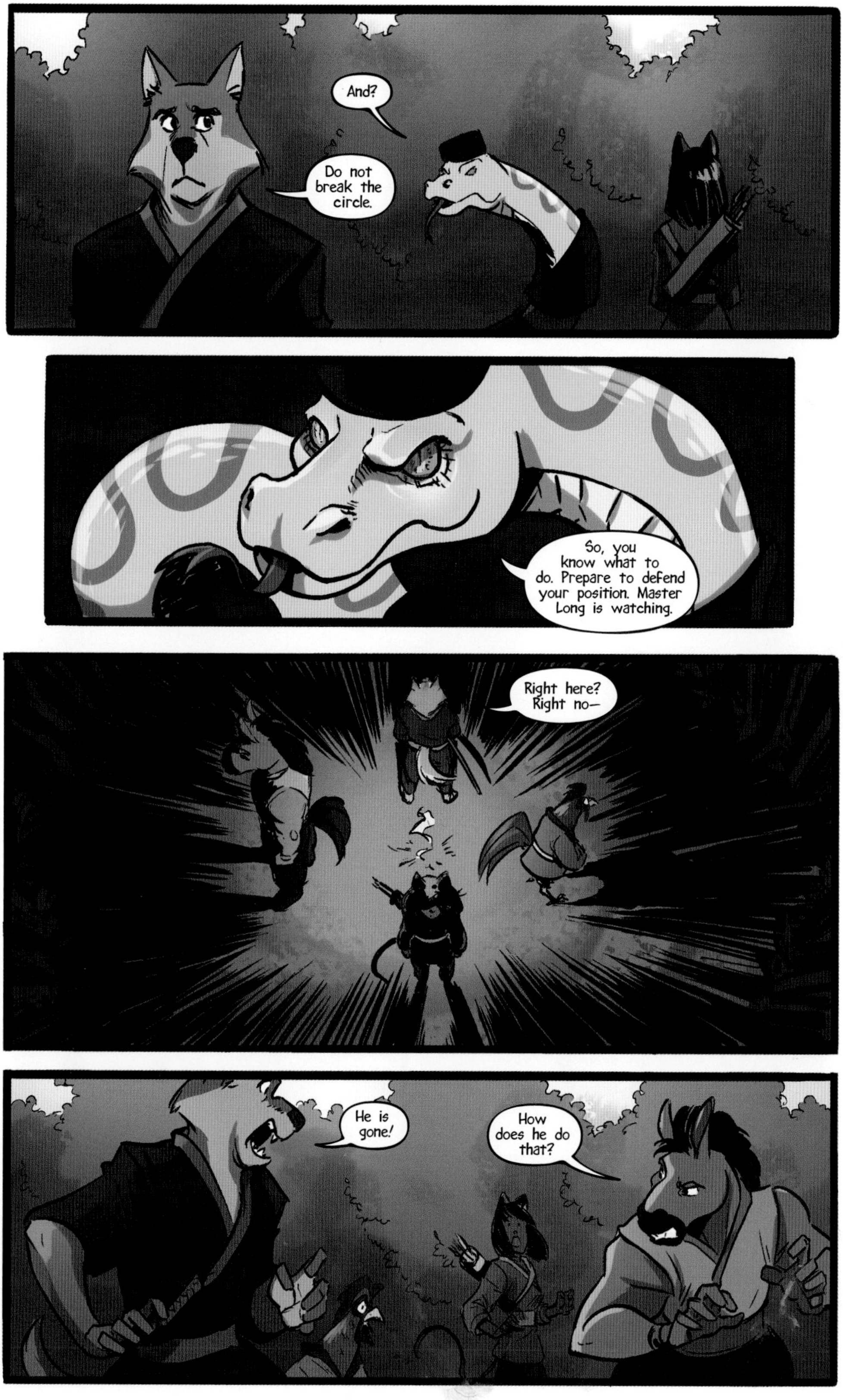
And?
Do not break the circle.
So, you know what to do. Prepare to defend your position. Master Long is watching.
Right here? Right no—
He is gone!
How does he do that?

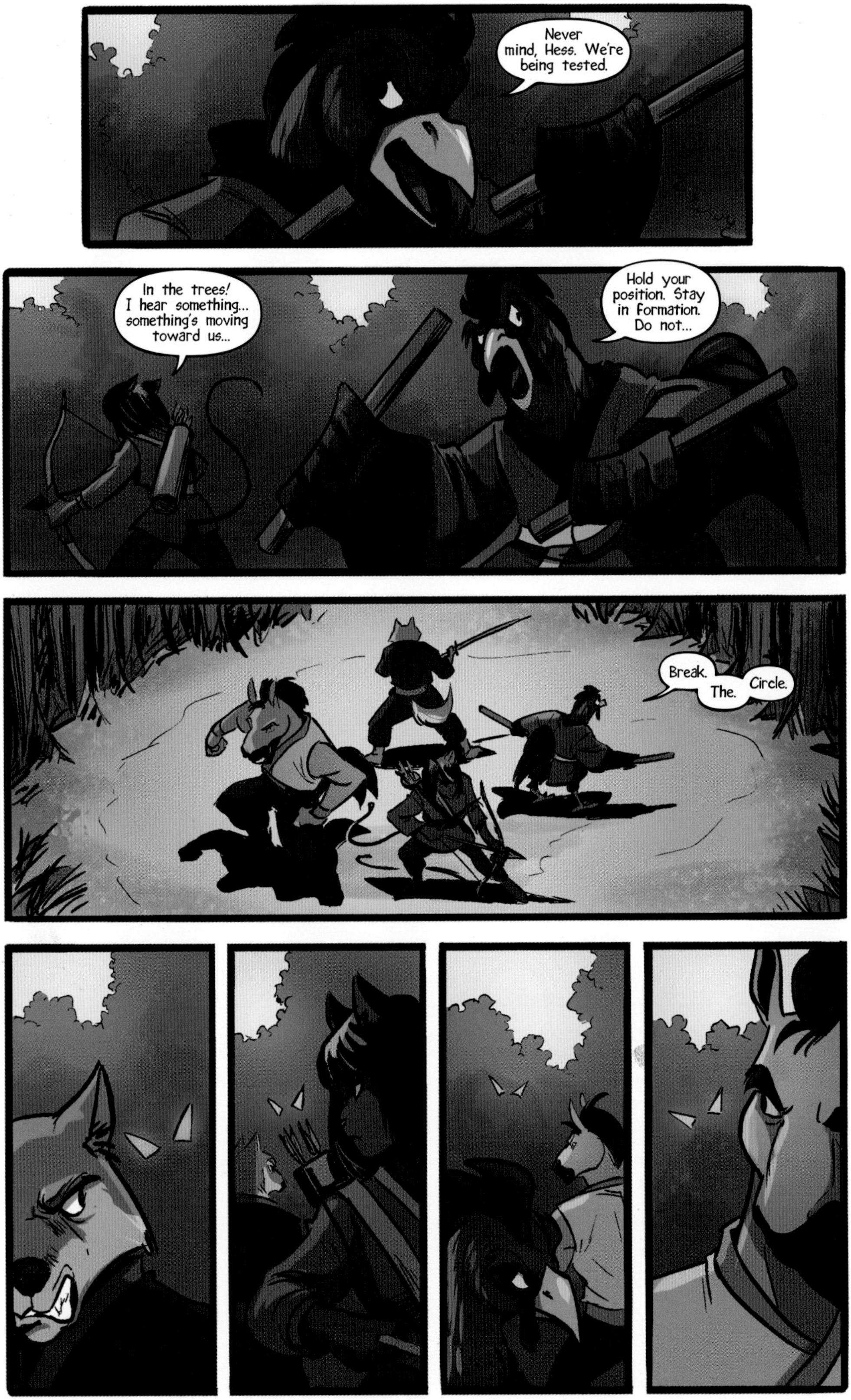
Never mind, Hess. We're being tested.
In the trees! I hear something... something's moving toward us...
Hold your position. Stay in formation. Do not...
Break. The. Circle.

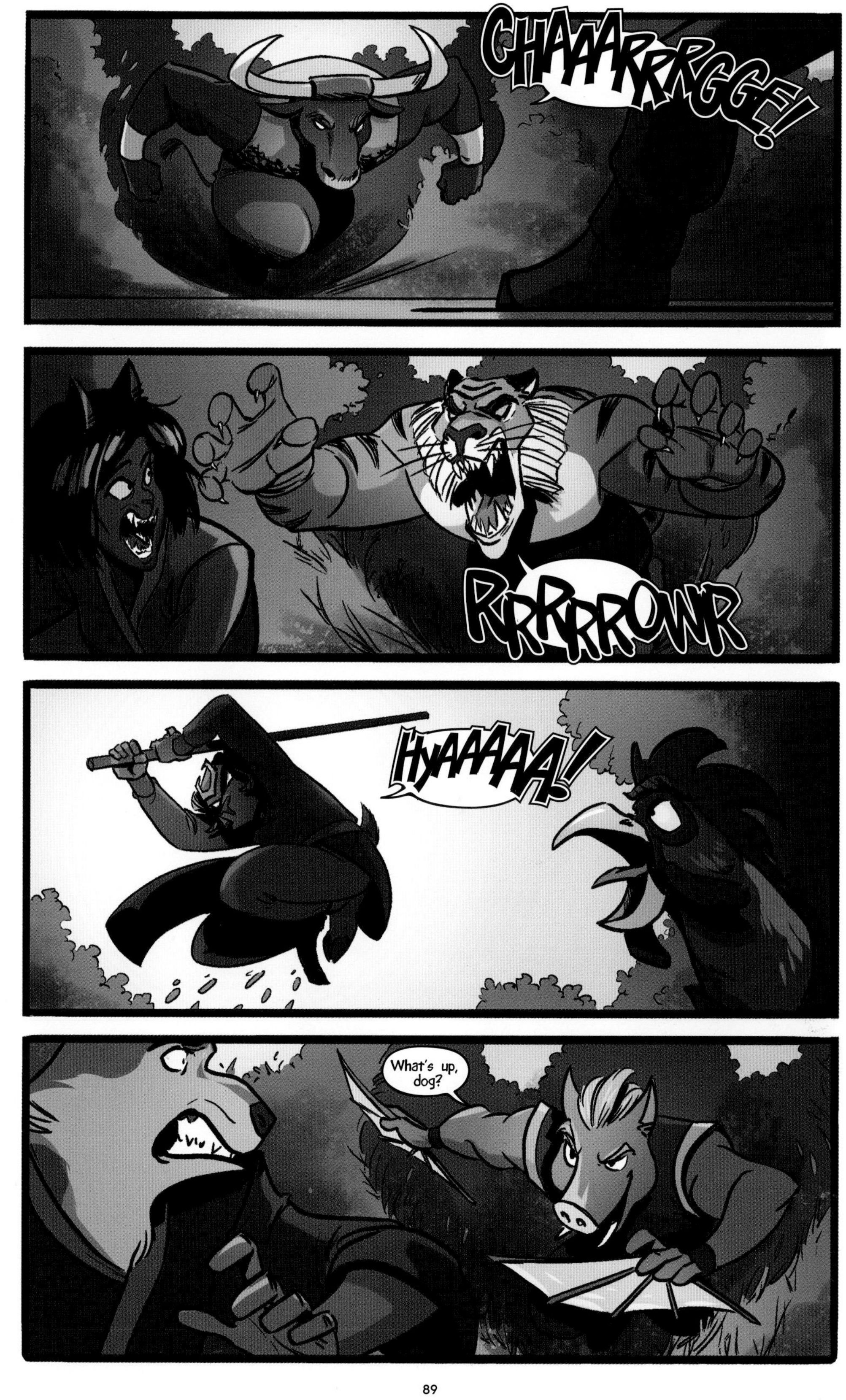
CHAAARRRGGE!
RRRRRROWR
HYAAAAA!
What's up, dog?

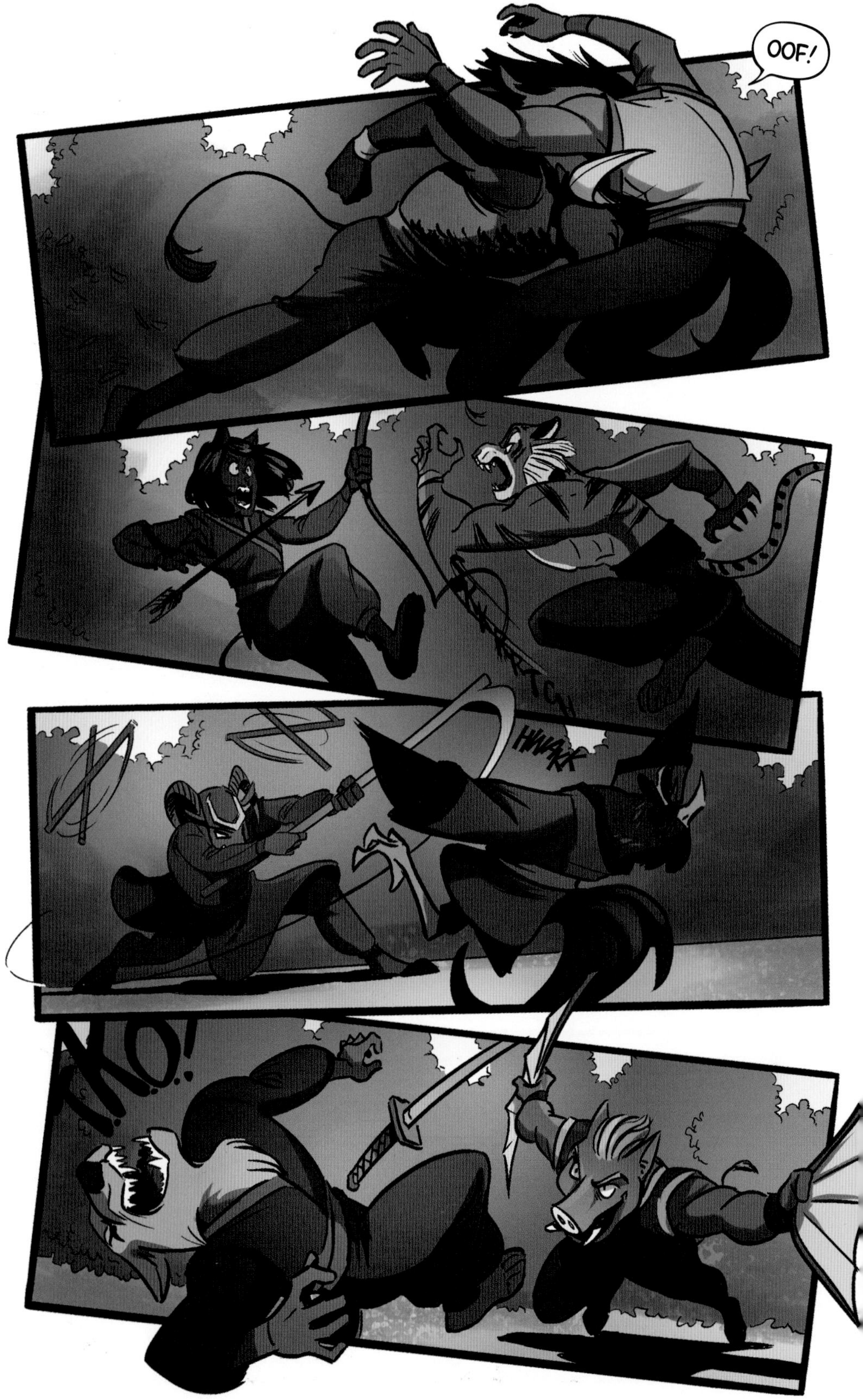
OOF!
HWAKK
NO!

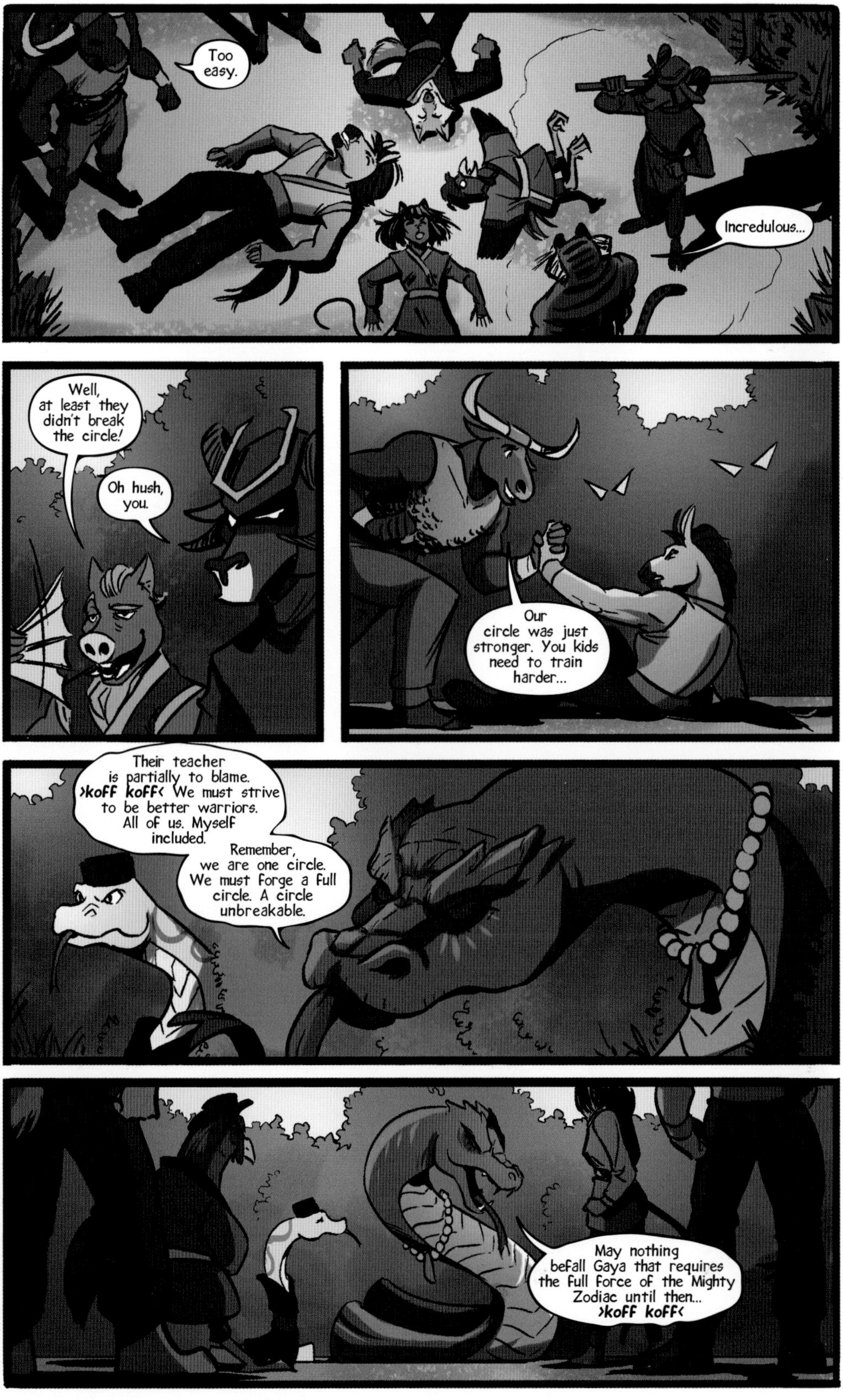
Too easy.
Incredulous...
Well, at least they didn't break the circle!
Oh hush, you.
Our circle was just stronger. You kids need to train harder...
Their teacher is partially to blame. **›koff koff‹** We must strive to be better warriors. All of us. Myself included.
Remember, we are one circle. We must forge a full circle. A circle unbreakable.
May nothing befall Gaya that requires the full force of the Mighty Zodiac until then... **›koff koff‹**

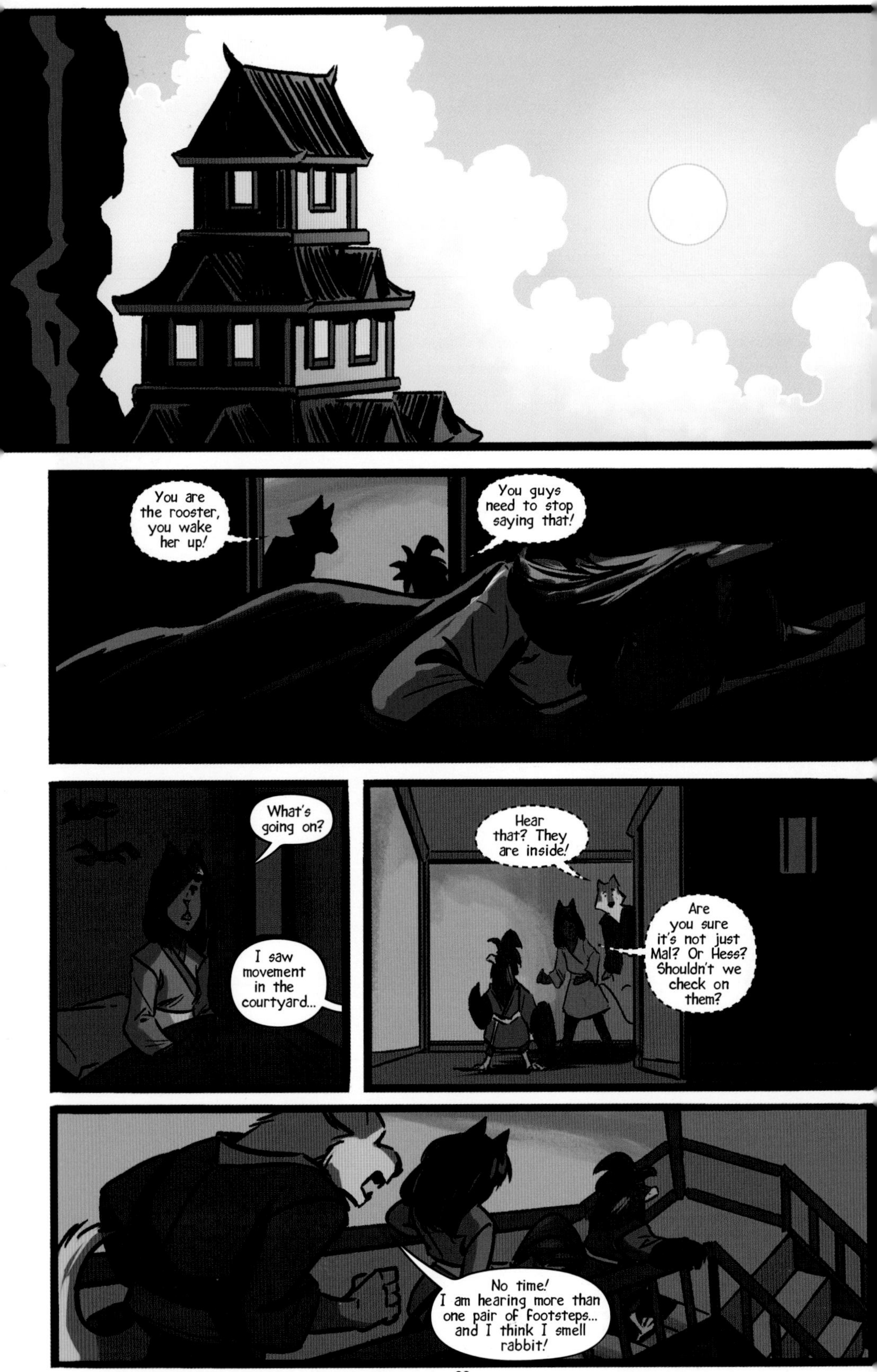
You are the rooster, you wake her up!
You guys need to stop saying that!
What's going on?
I saw movement in the courtyard...
Hear that? They are inside!
Are you sure it's not just Mal? Or Hess? Shouldn't we check on them?
No time! I am hearing more than one pair of footsteps... and I think I smell rabbit!

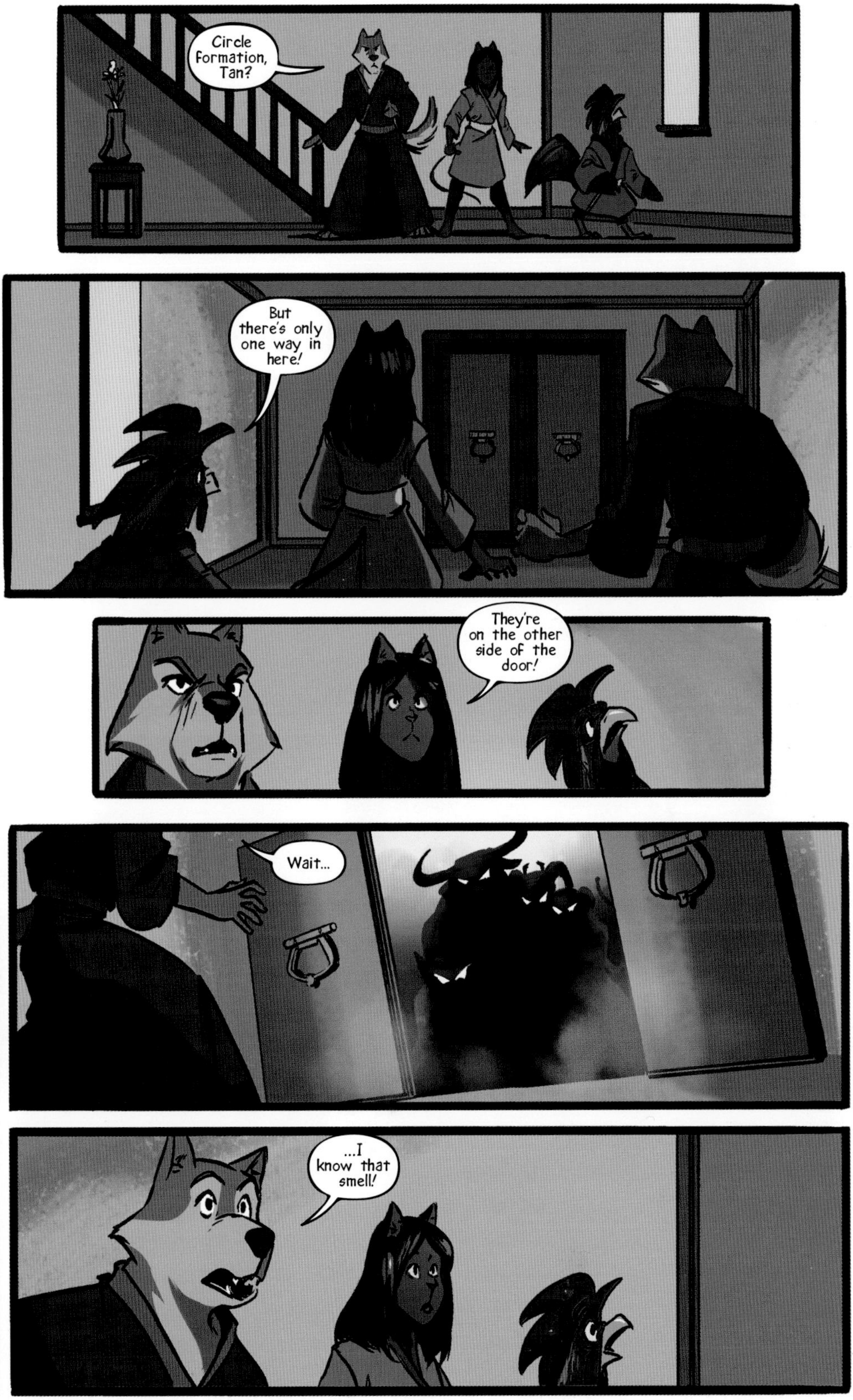
Circle formation, Tan?
But there's only one way in here!
They're on the other side of the door!
Wait...
...I know that smell!

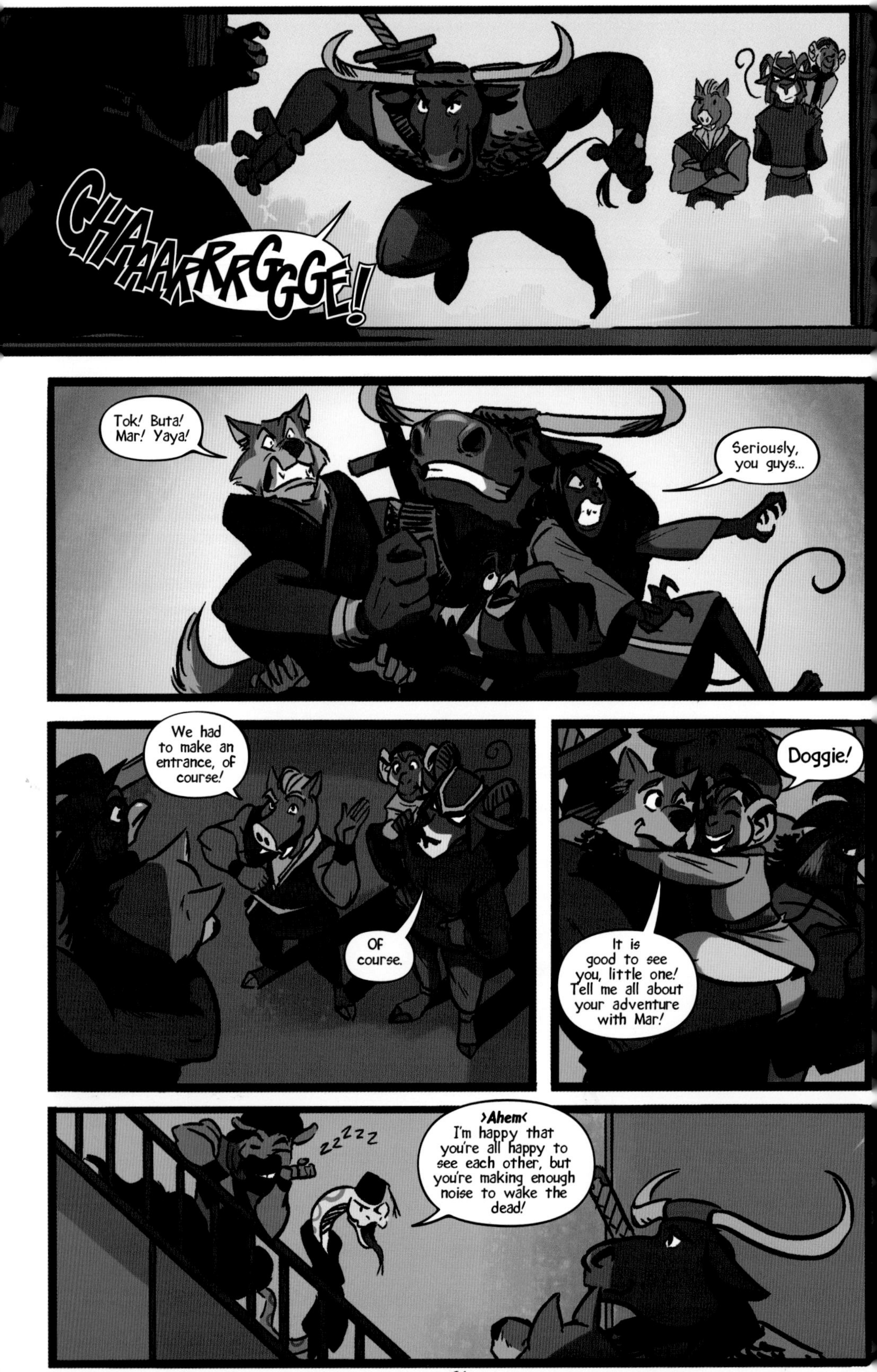
CHAAARRRGGGE!
Tok! Buta! Mar! Yaya!
Seriously, you guys...
We had to make an entrance, of course!
Of course.
Doggie!
It is good to see you, little one! Tell me all about your adventure with Mar!
zzzzz
>Ahem< I'm happy that you're all happy to see each other, but you're making enough noise to wake the dead!

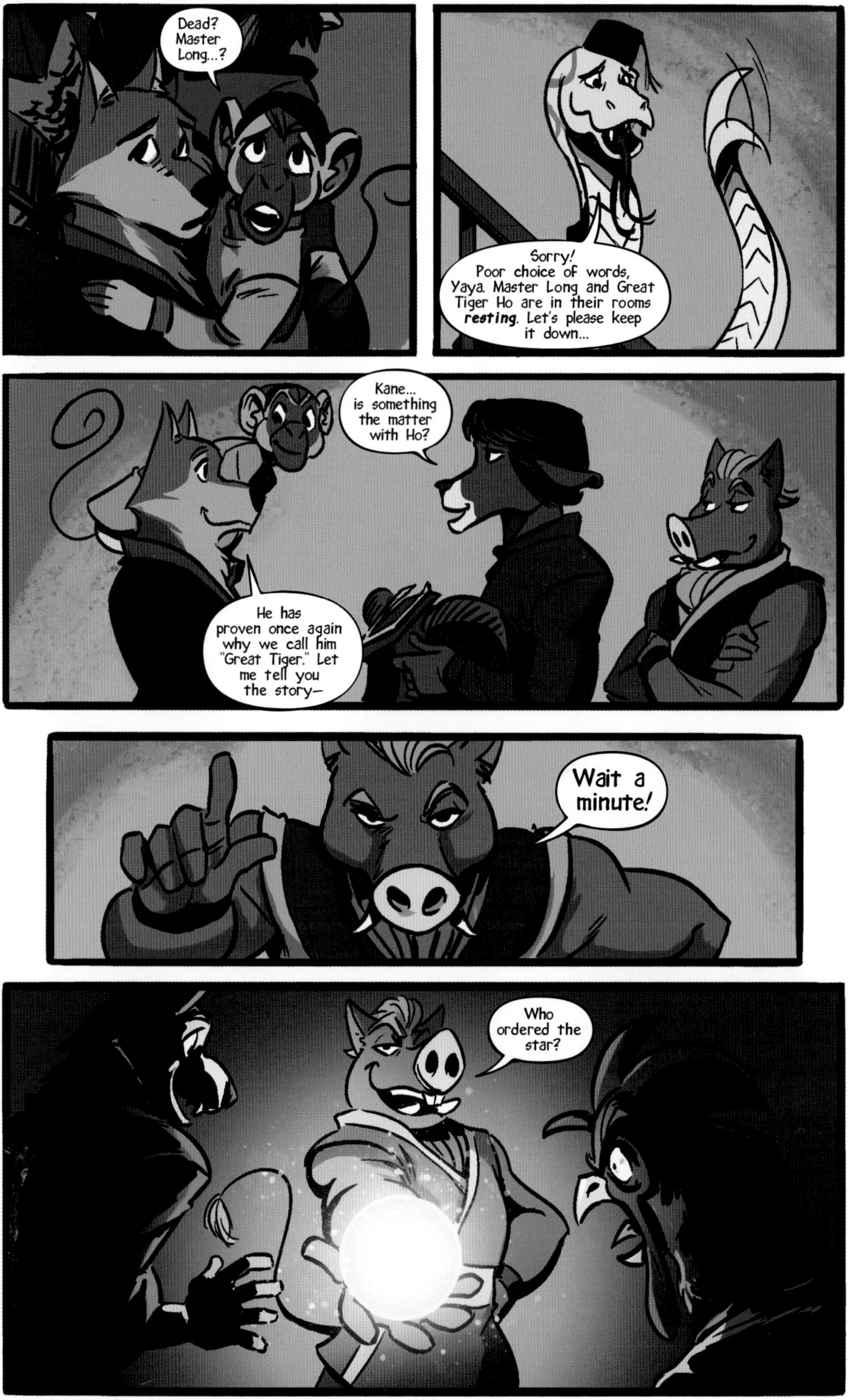
Dead? Master Long...?
Sorry! Poor choice of words, Yaya. Master Long and Great Tiger Ho are in their rooms **resting**. Let's please keep it down...
Kane... is something the matter with Ho?
He has proven once again why we call him "Great Tiger." Let me tell you the story—
Wait a minute!
Who ordered the star?

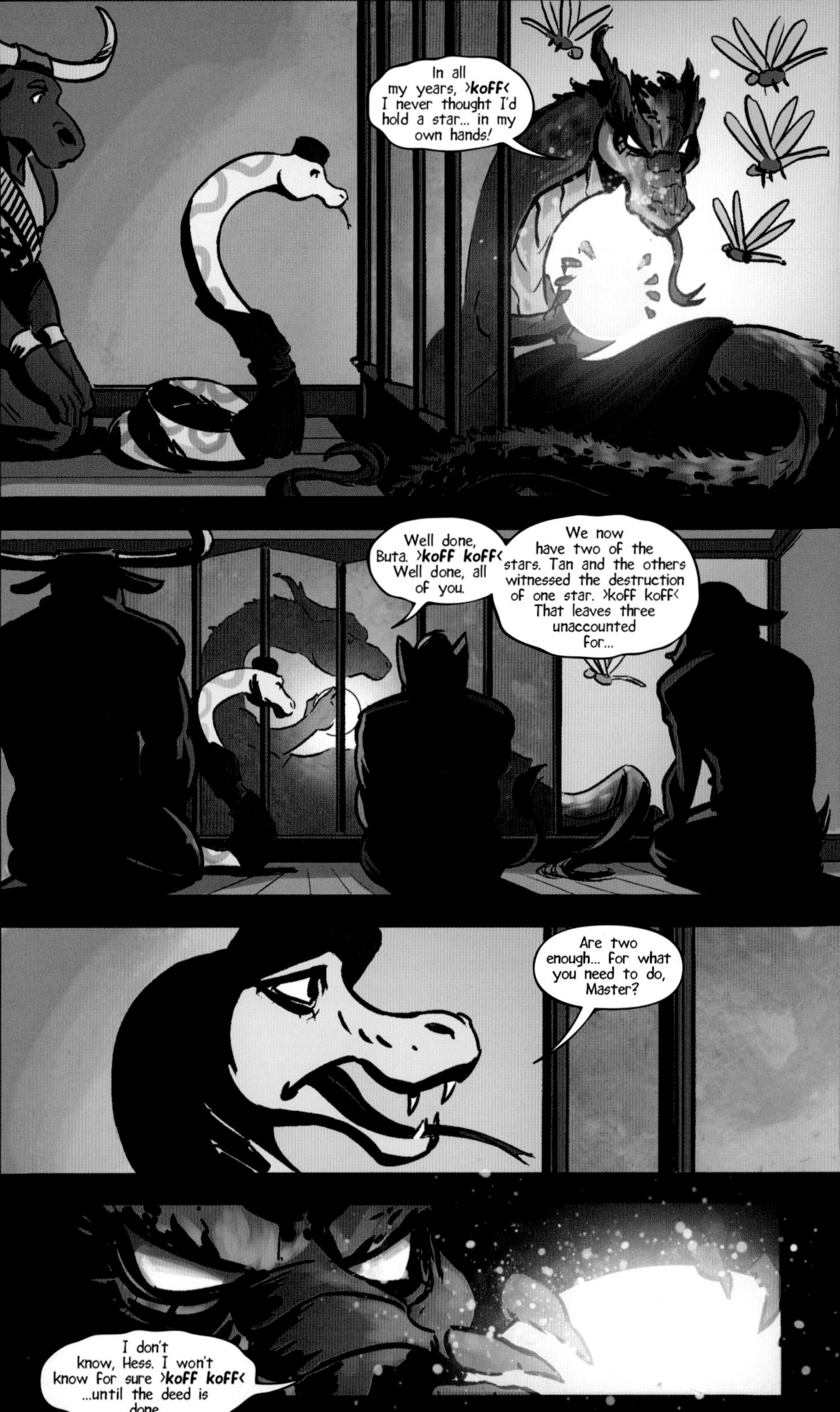
In all my years, >**koff**< I never thought I'd hold a star... in my own hands!
Well done, Buta. >**koff koff**< Well done, all of you.
We now have two of the stars. Tan and the others witnessed the destruction of one star. >koff koff< That leaves three unaccounted for...
Are two enough... for what you need to do, Master?
I don't know, Hess. I won't know for sure >**koff koff**< ...until the deed is done.

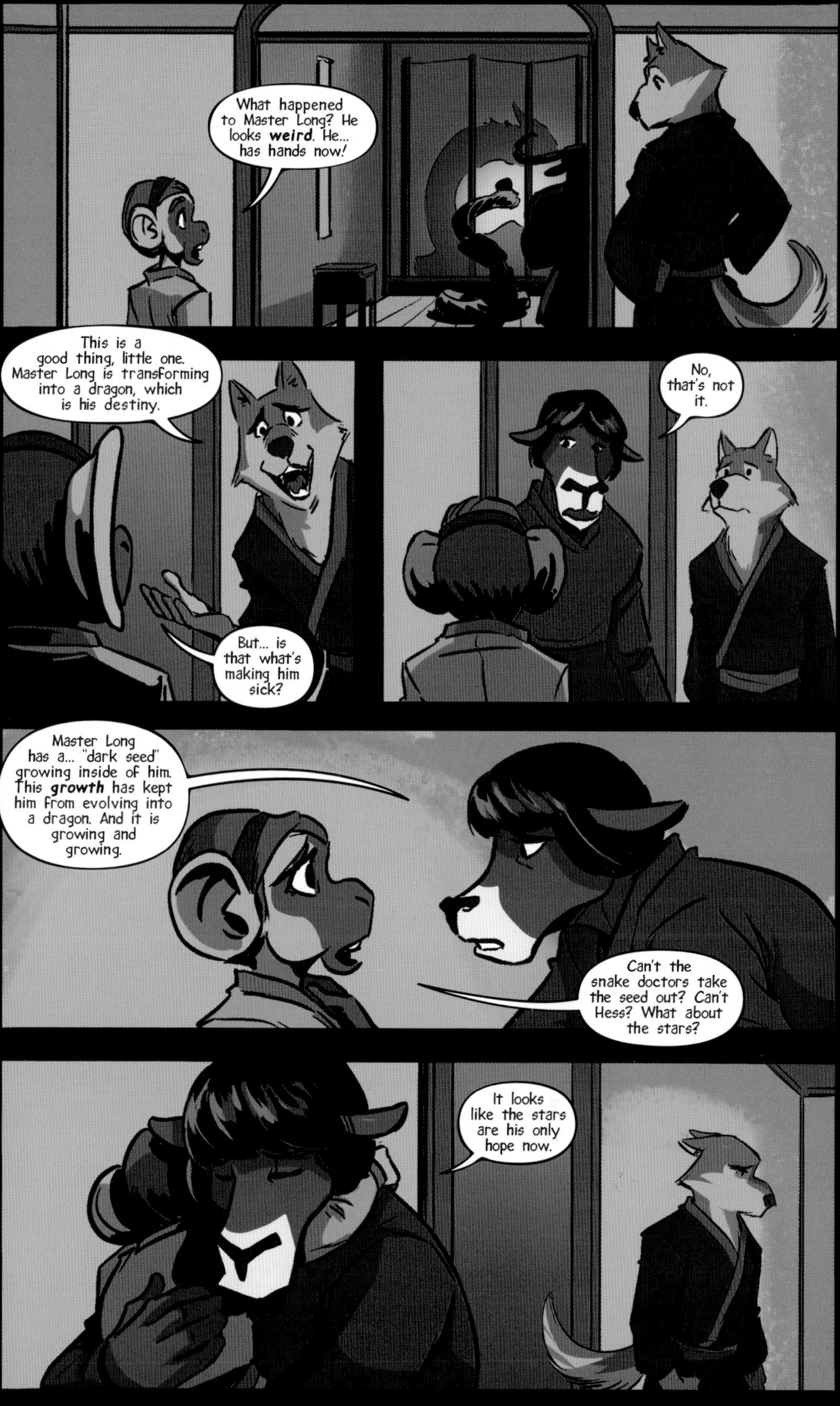
What happened to Master Long? He looks **weird**. He... has hands now!
This is a good thing, little one. Master Long is transforming into a dragon, which is his destiny.
But... is that what's making him sick?
No, that's not it.
Master Long has a... "dark seed" growing inside of him. This **growth** has kept him from evolving into a dragon. And it is growing and growing.
Can't the snake doctors take the seed out? Can't Hess? What about the stars?
It looks like the stars are his only hope now.

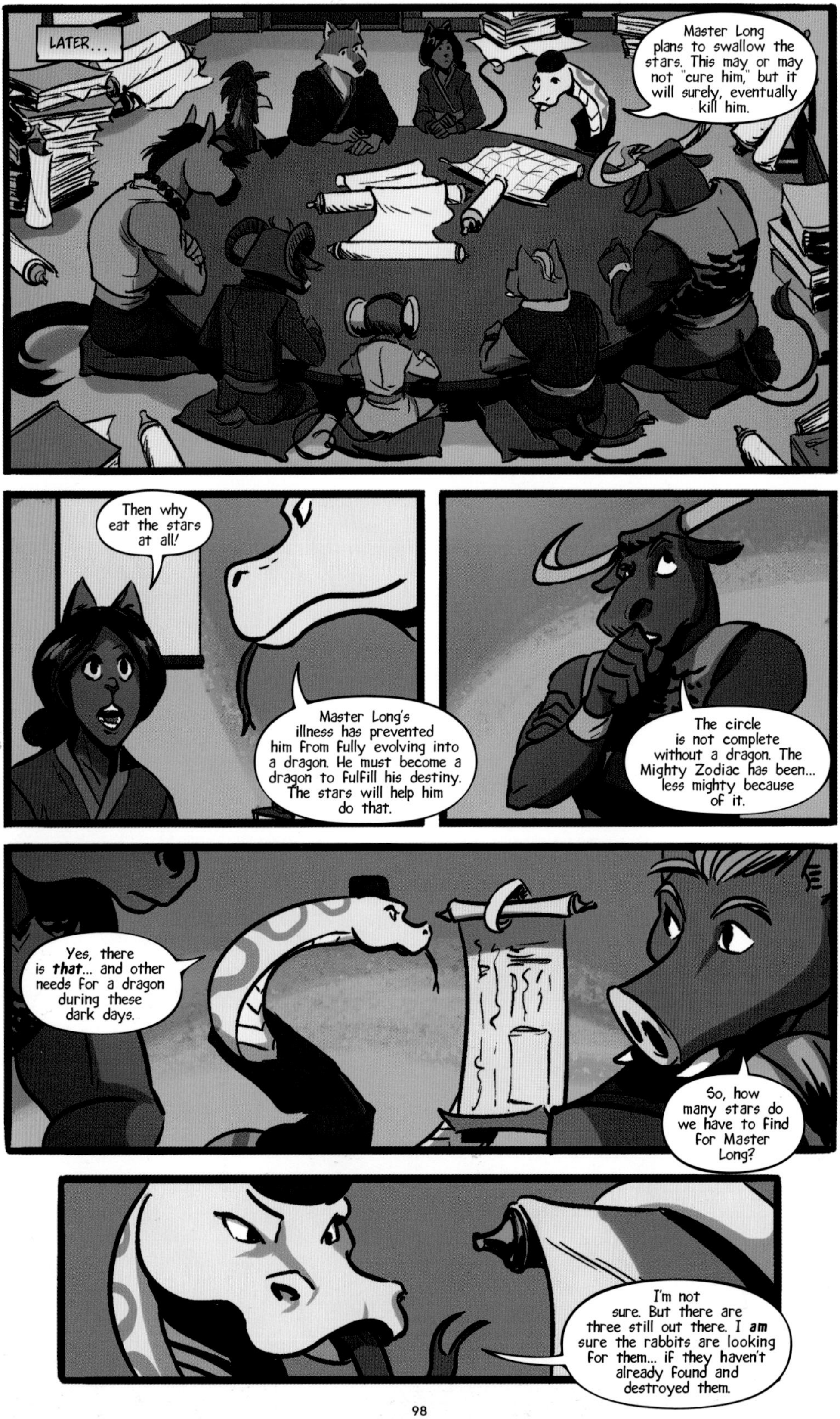
LATER...
Master Long plans to swallow the stars. This may or may not "cure him," but it will surely, eventually kill him.
Then why eat the stars at all!
Master Long's illness has prevented him from fully evolving into a dragon. He must become a dragon to fulfill his destiny. The stars will help him do that.
The circle is not complete without a dragon. The Mighty Zodiac has been... less mighty because of it.
Yes, there is ***that***... and other needs for a dragon during these dark days.
So, how many stars do we have to find for Master Long?
I'm not sure. But there are three still out there. I ***am*** sure the rabbits are looking for them... if they haven't already found and destroyed them.

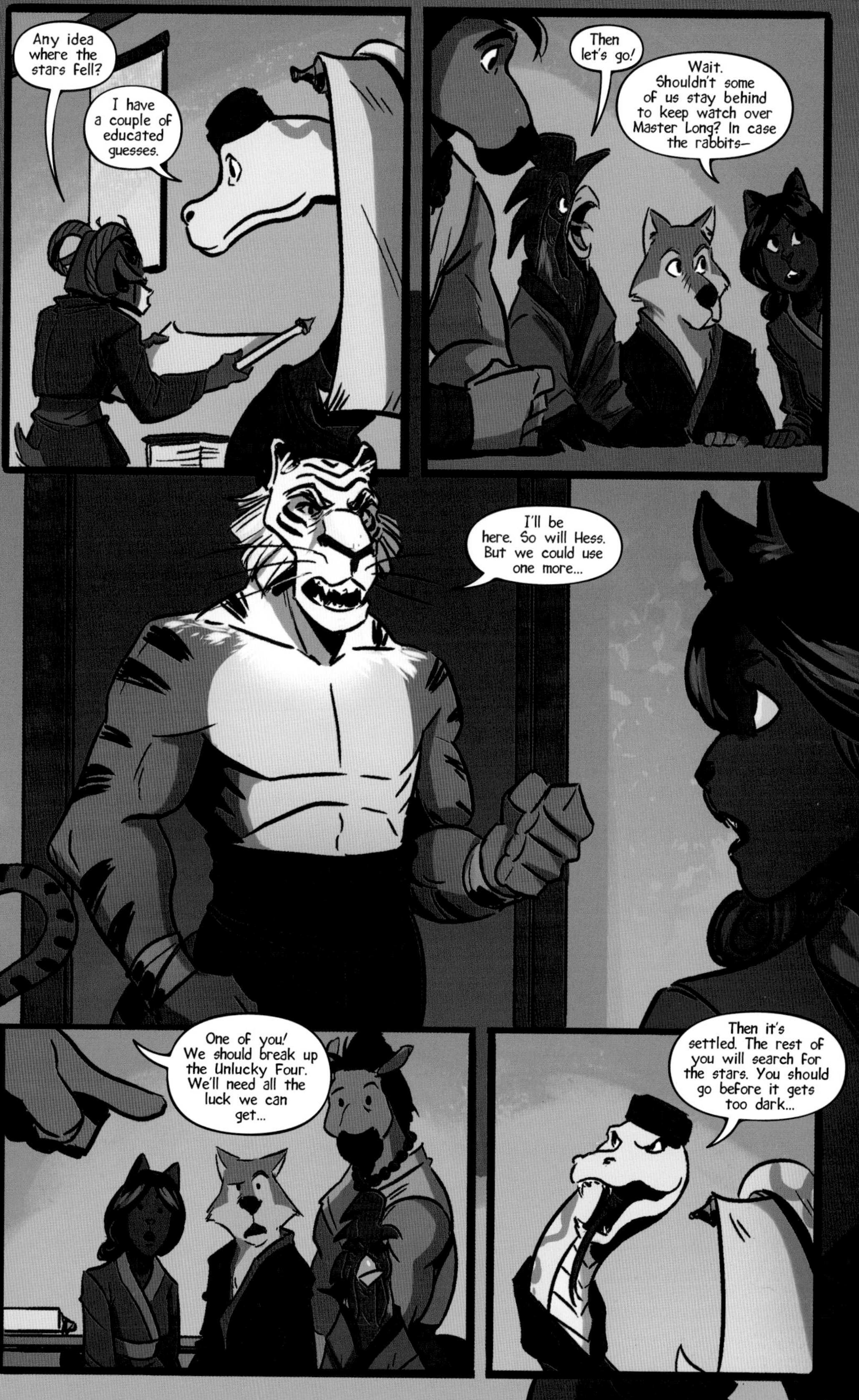
Any idea where the stars fell?
I have a couple of educated guesses.
Then let's go!
Wait. Shouldn't some of us stay behind to keep watch over Master Long? In case the rabbits—
I'll be here. So will Hess. But we could use one more...
One of you! We should break up the Unlucky Four. We'll need all the luck we can get...
Then it's settled. The rest of you will search for the stars. You should go before it gets too dark...

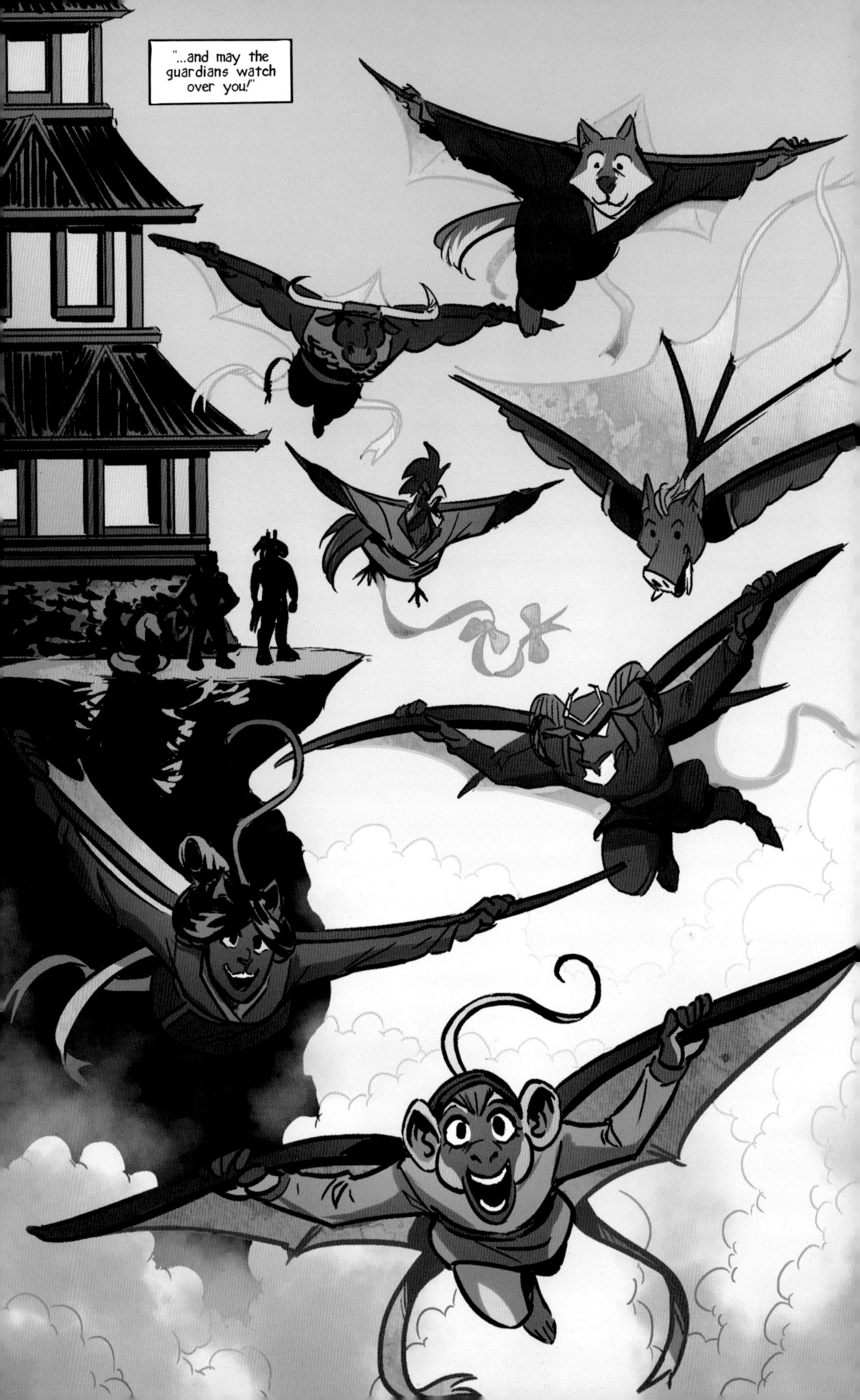
"...and may the guardians watch over you!"

CHAPTER FIVE

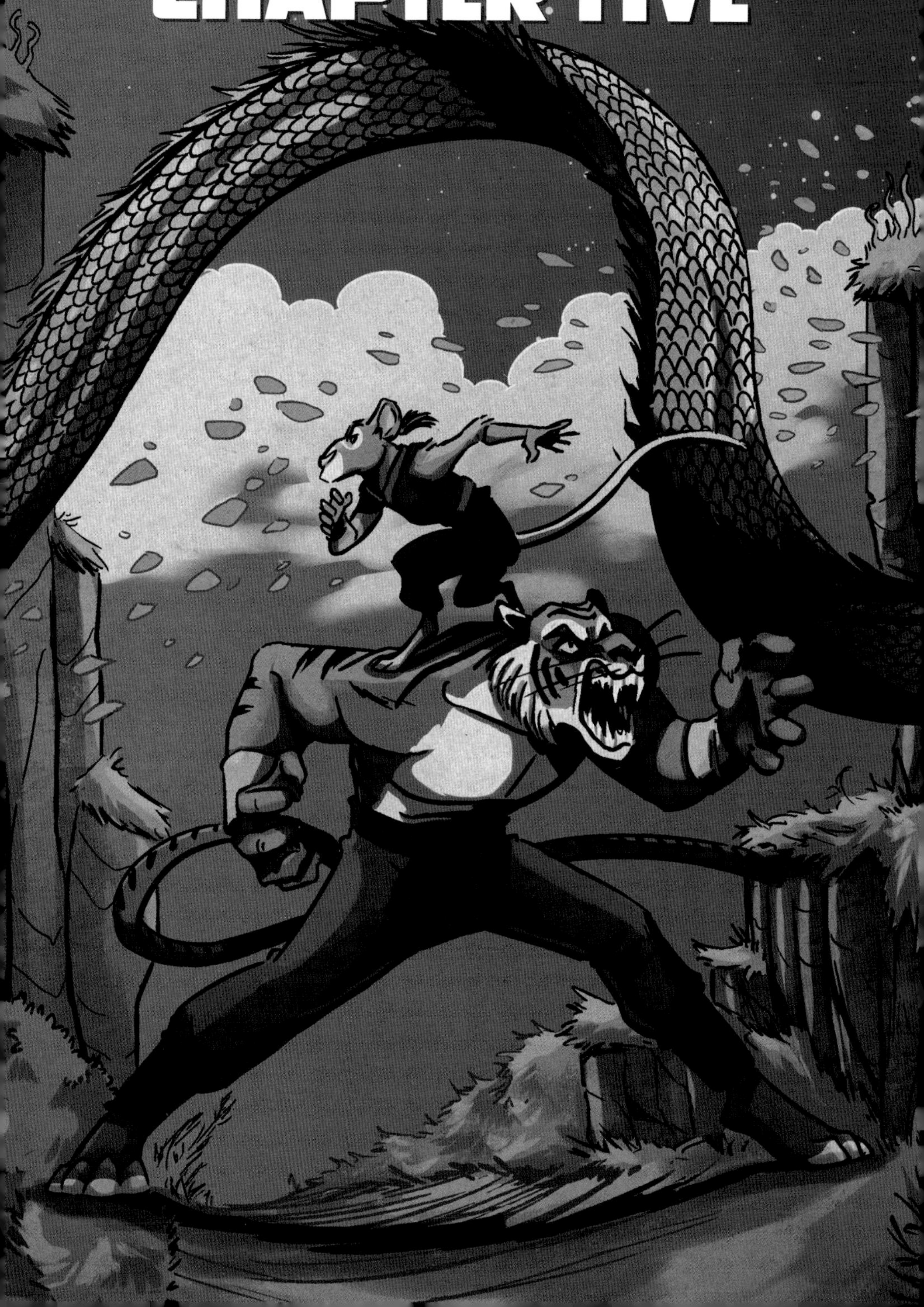

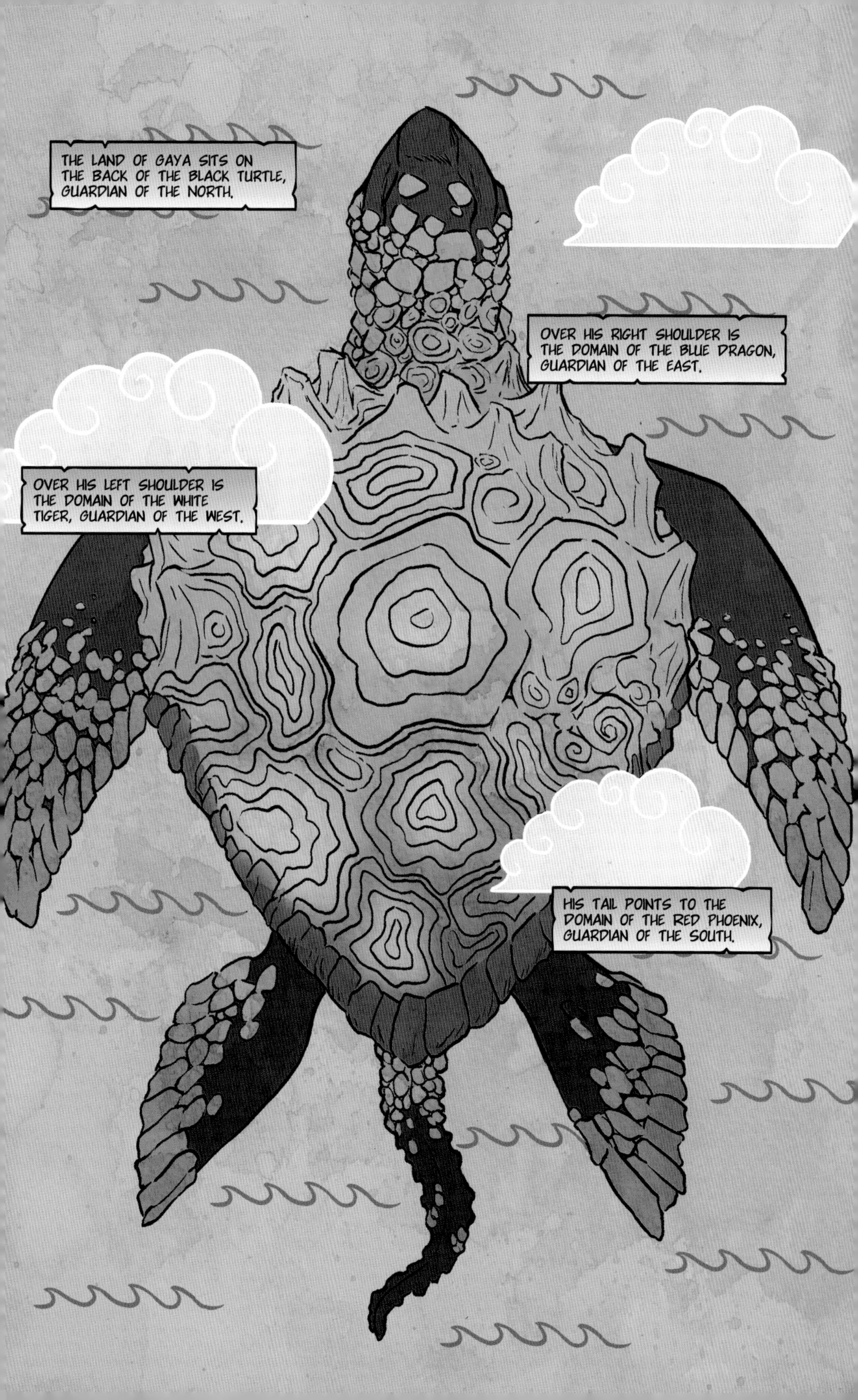
THE LAND OF GAYA SITS ON THE BACK OF THE BLACK TURTLE, GUARDIAN OF THE NORTH.
OVER HIS RIGHT SHOULDER IS THE DOMAIN OF THE BLUE DRAGON, GUARDIAN OF THE EAST.
OVER HIS LEFT SHOULDER IS THE DOMAIN OF THE WHITE TIGER, GUARDIAN OF THE WEST.
HIS TAIL POINTS TO THE DOMAIN OF THE RED PHOENIX, GUARDIAN OF THE SOUTH.

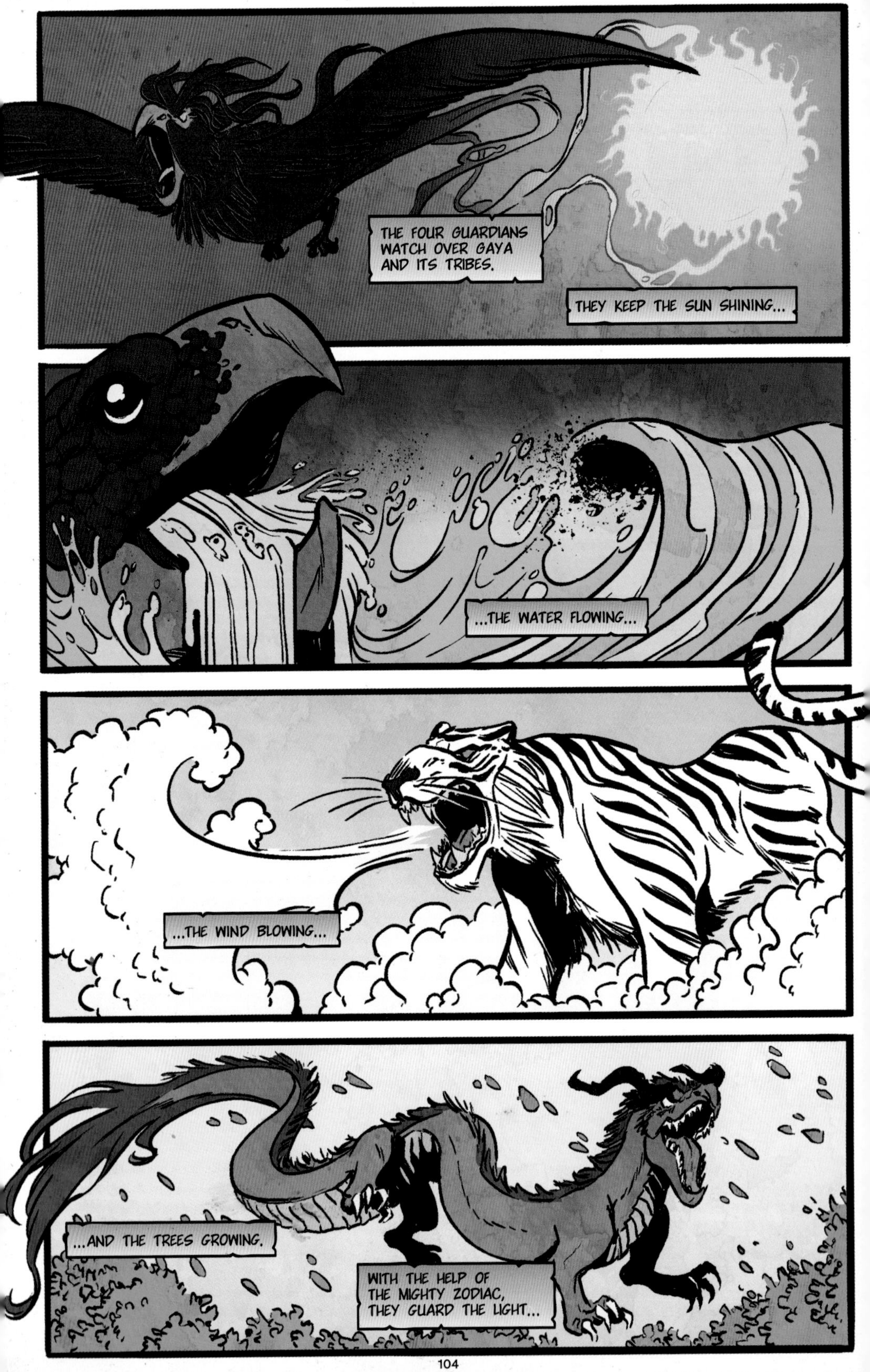
THE FOUR GUARDIANS WATCH OVER GAYA AND ITS TRIBES.
THEY KEEP THE SUN SHINING...
...THE WATER FLOWING...
...THE WIND BLOWING...
...AND THE TREES GROWING.
WITH THE HELP OF THE MIGHTY ZODIAC, THEY GUARD THE LIGHT...

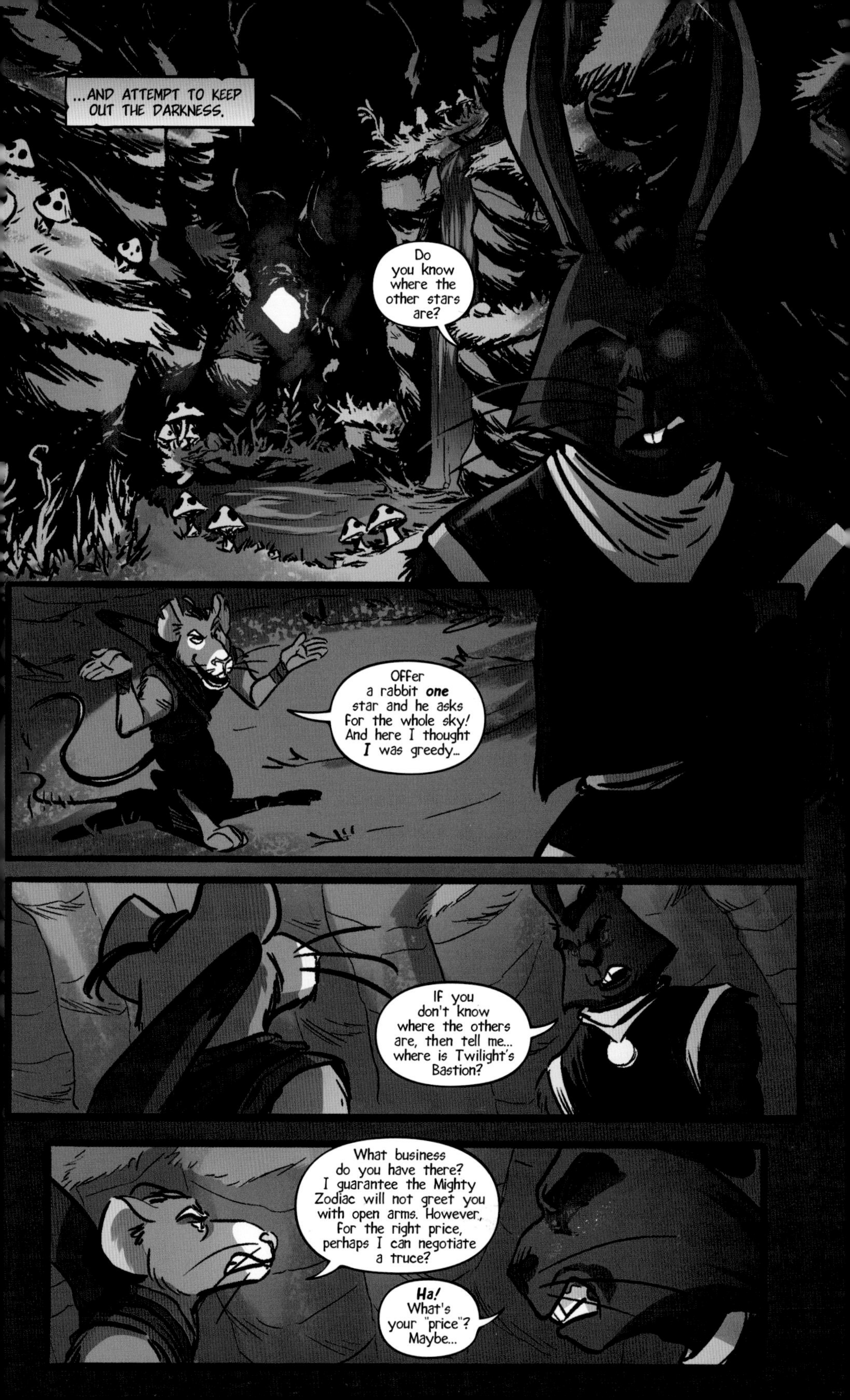
...AND ATTEMPT TO KEEP OUT THE DARKNESS.
Do you know where the other stars are?
Offer a rabbit **one** star and he asks for the whole sky! And here I thought *I* was greedy...
If you don't know where the others are, then tell me... where is Twilight's Bastion?
What business do you have there? I guarantee the Mighty Zodiac will not greet you with open arms. However, for the right price, perhaps I can negotiate a truce?
Ha! What's your "price"? Maybe...

...one star? The one you had hidden in that cave!

Nooo!

Detain the rodent. He might be useful later. As for this star, destroy it *now.*

Destroy it?! Are you crazy! Do you not know the power it possesses...

I know that Long needs the stars.

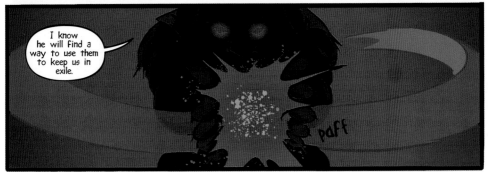

I know he will find a way to use them to keep us in exile.

paff

The stars are light. We are darkness. This is a light and darkness war for which there can never be a truce!

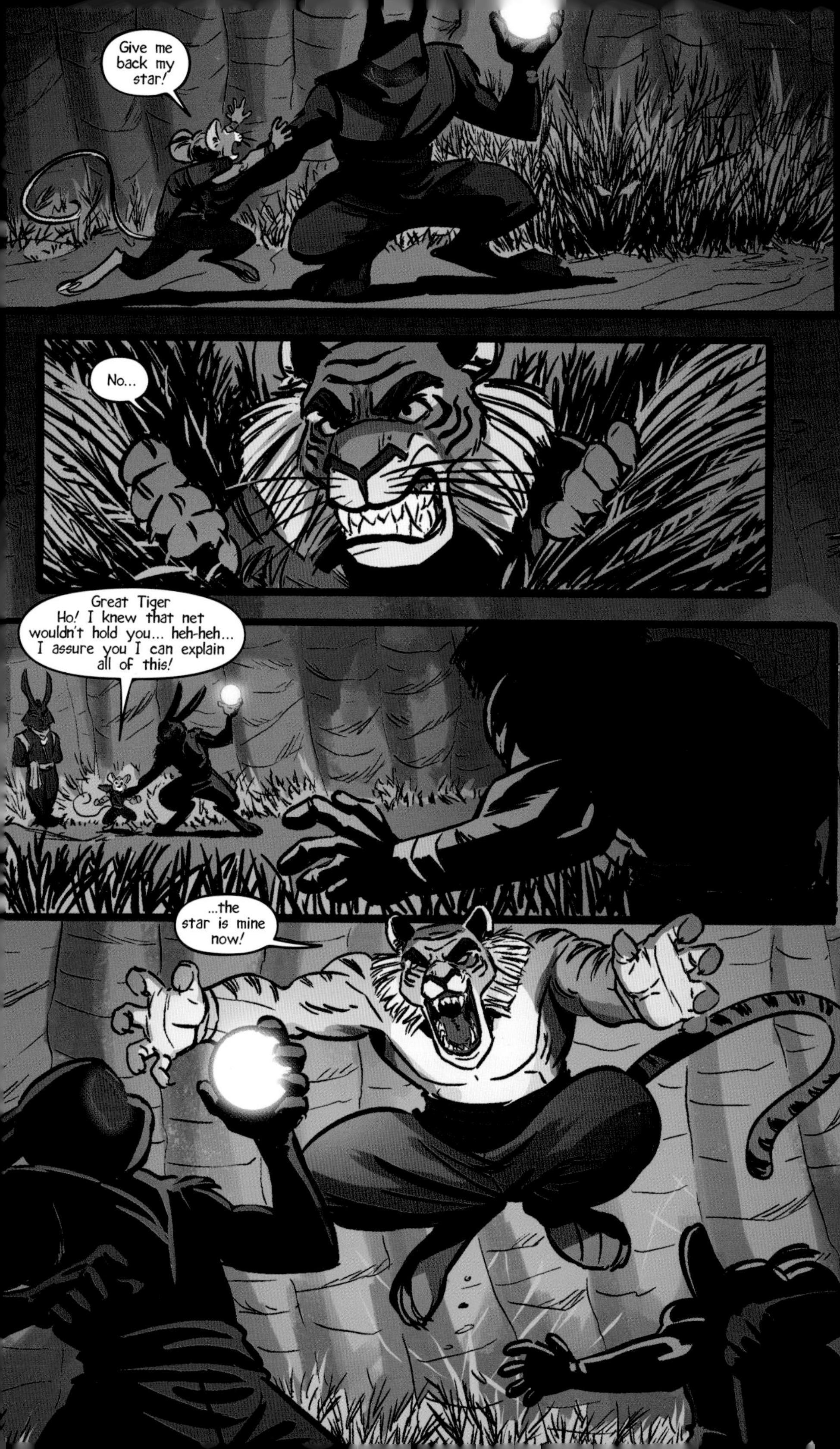
Give me back my star!
No...
Great Tiger Ho! I knew that net wouldn't hold you... heh-heh... I assure you I can explain all of this!
...the star is mine now!

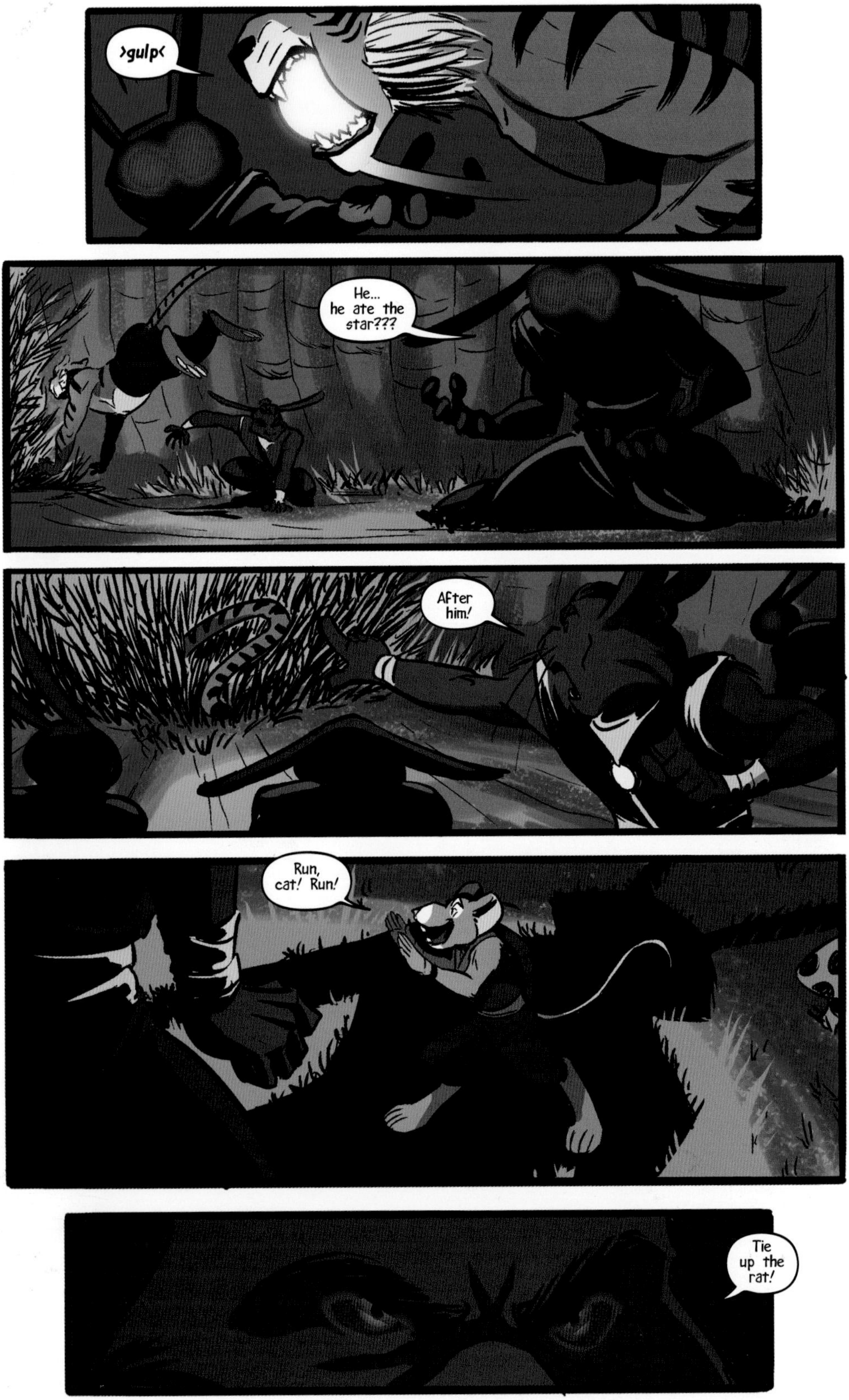
>gulp<
He... he ate the star???
After him!
Run, cat! Run!
Tie up the rat!

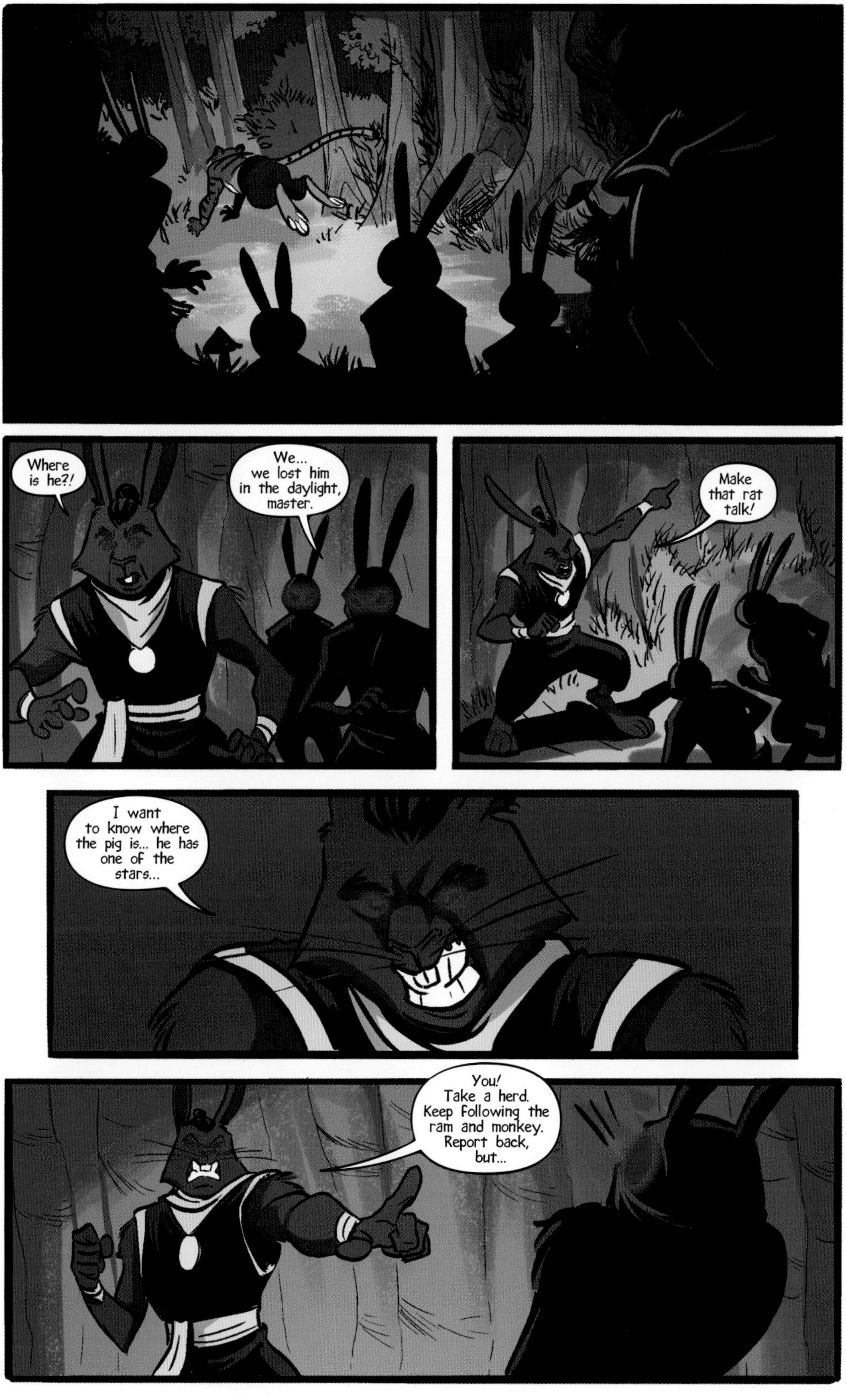
Where is he?!
We... we lost him in the daylight, master.
Make that rat talk!
I want to know where the pig is... he has one of the stars...
You! Take a herd. Keep following the ram and monkey. Report back, but...

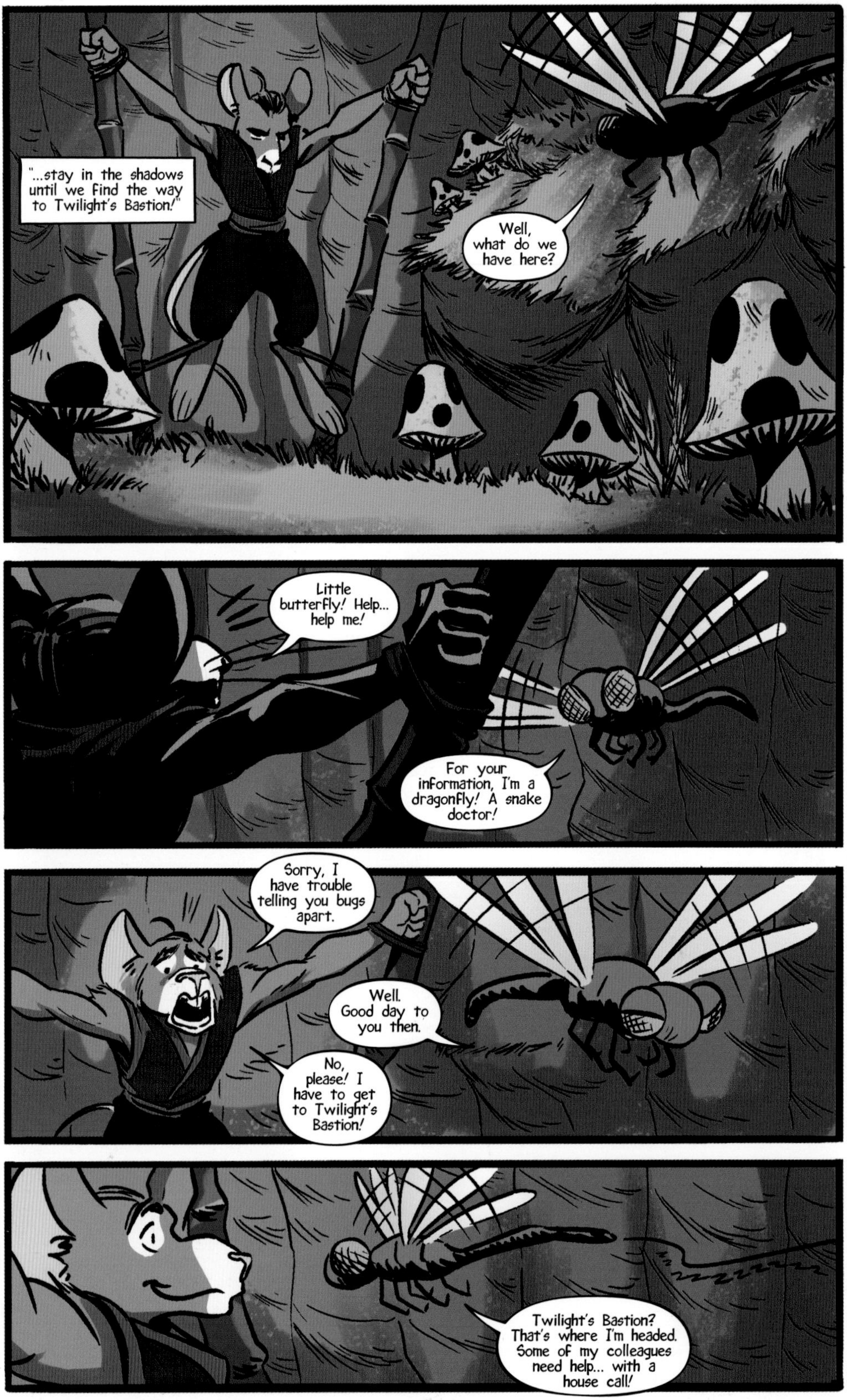
"...stay in the shadows until we find the way to Twilight's Bastion!"
Well, what do we have here?
Little butterfly! Help... help me!
For your information, I'm a dragonfly! A snake doctor!
Sorry, I have trouble telling you bugs apart.
Well. Good day to you then.
No, please! I have to get to Twilight's Bastion!
Twilight's Bastion? That's where I'm headed. Some of my colleagues need help... with a house call!

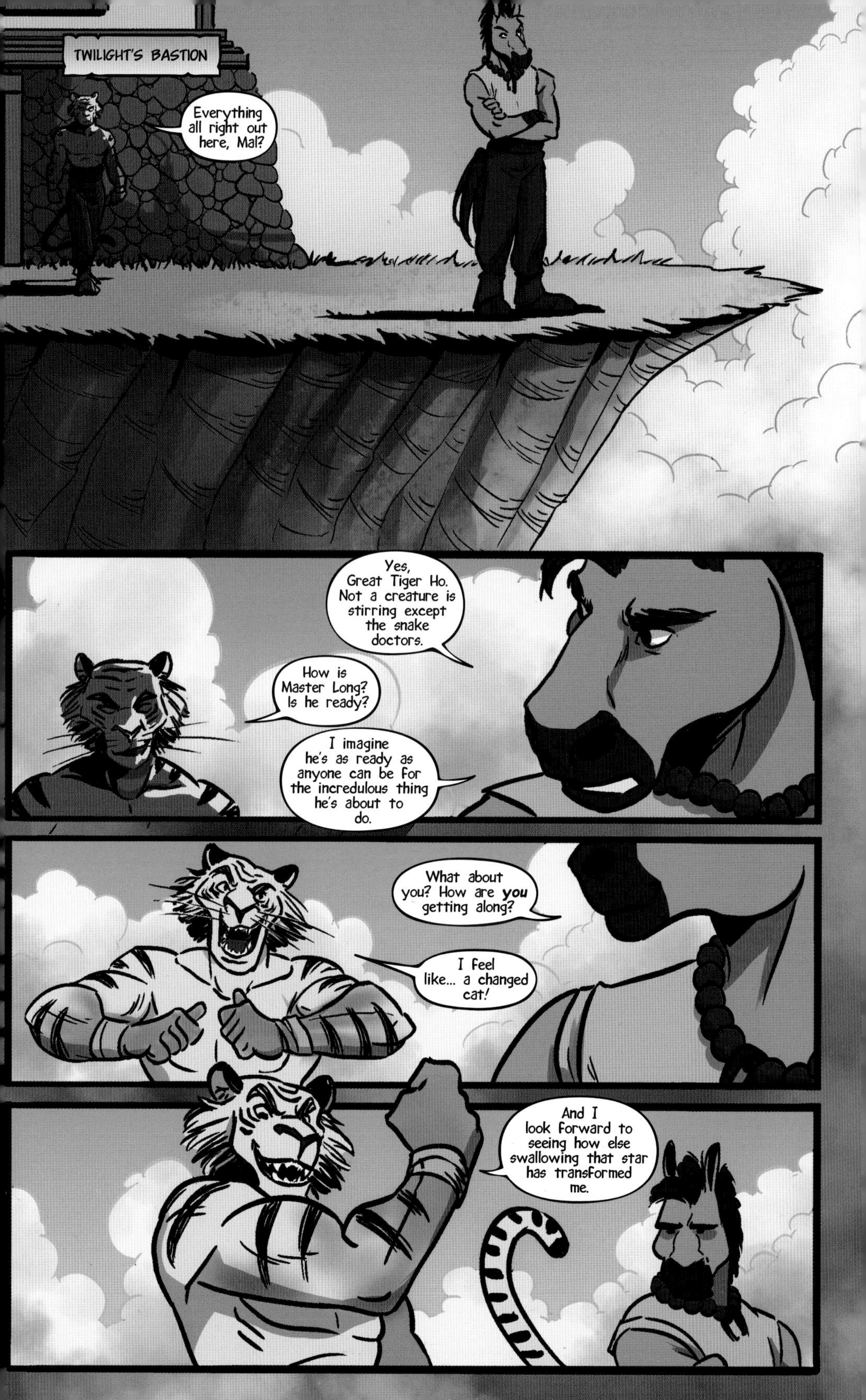
TWILIGHT'S BASTION
Everything all right out here, Mal?
Yes, Great Tiger Ho. Not a creature is stirring except the snake doctors.
How is Master Long? Is he ready?
I imagine he's as ready as anyone can be for the incredulous thing he's about to do.
What about you? How are **you** getting along?
I feel like... a changed cat!
And I look forward to seeing how else swallowing that star has transformed me.

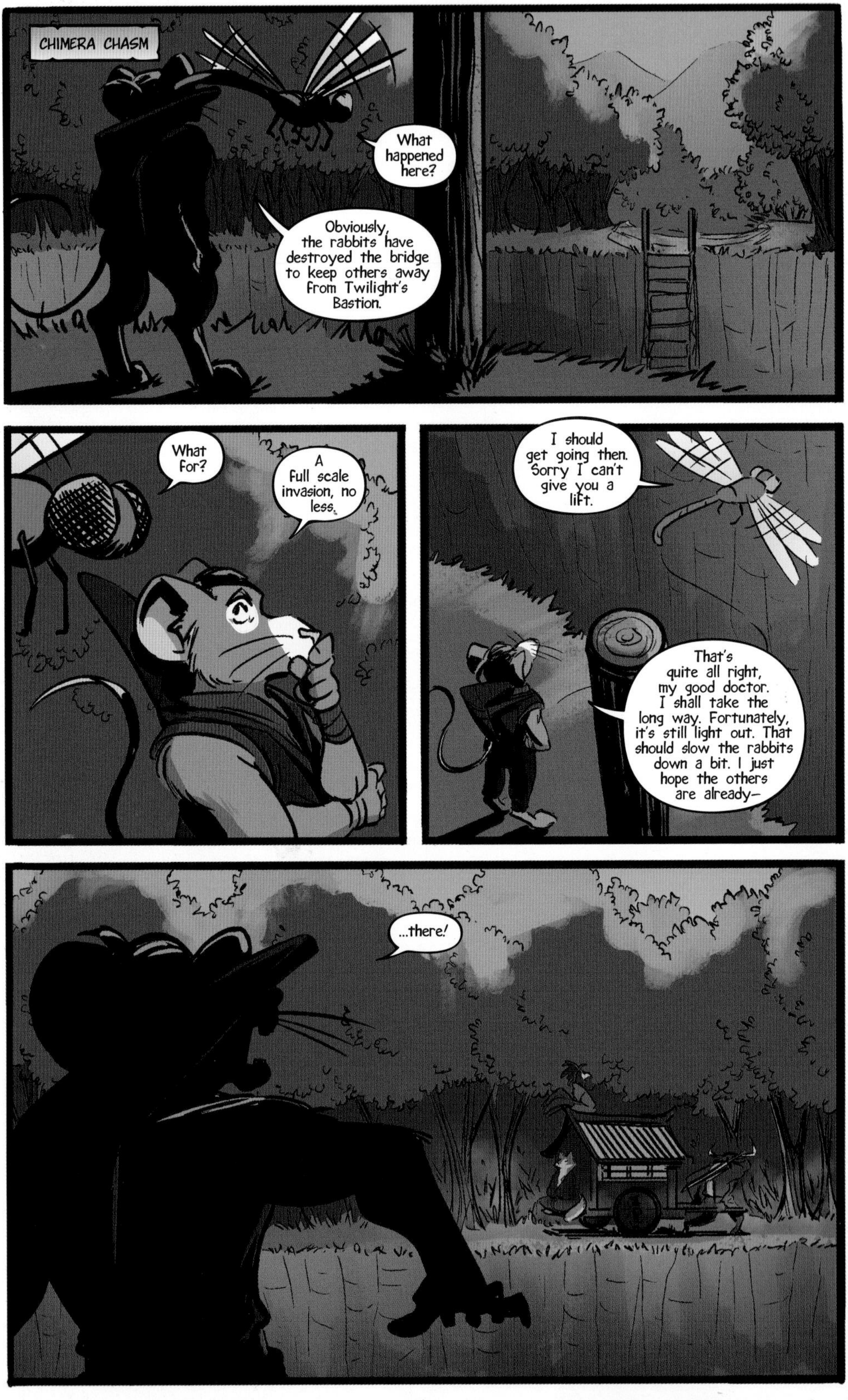
CHIMERA CHASM
What happened here?
Obviously, the rabbits have destroyed the bridge to keep others away from Twilight's Bastion.
What for?
A full scale invasion, no less.
I should get going then. Sorry I can't give you a lift.
That's quite all right, my good doctor. I shall take the long way. Fortunately, it's still light out. That should slow the rabbits down a bit. I just hope the others are already—
...there!

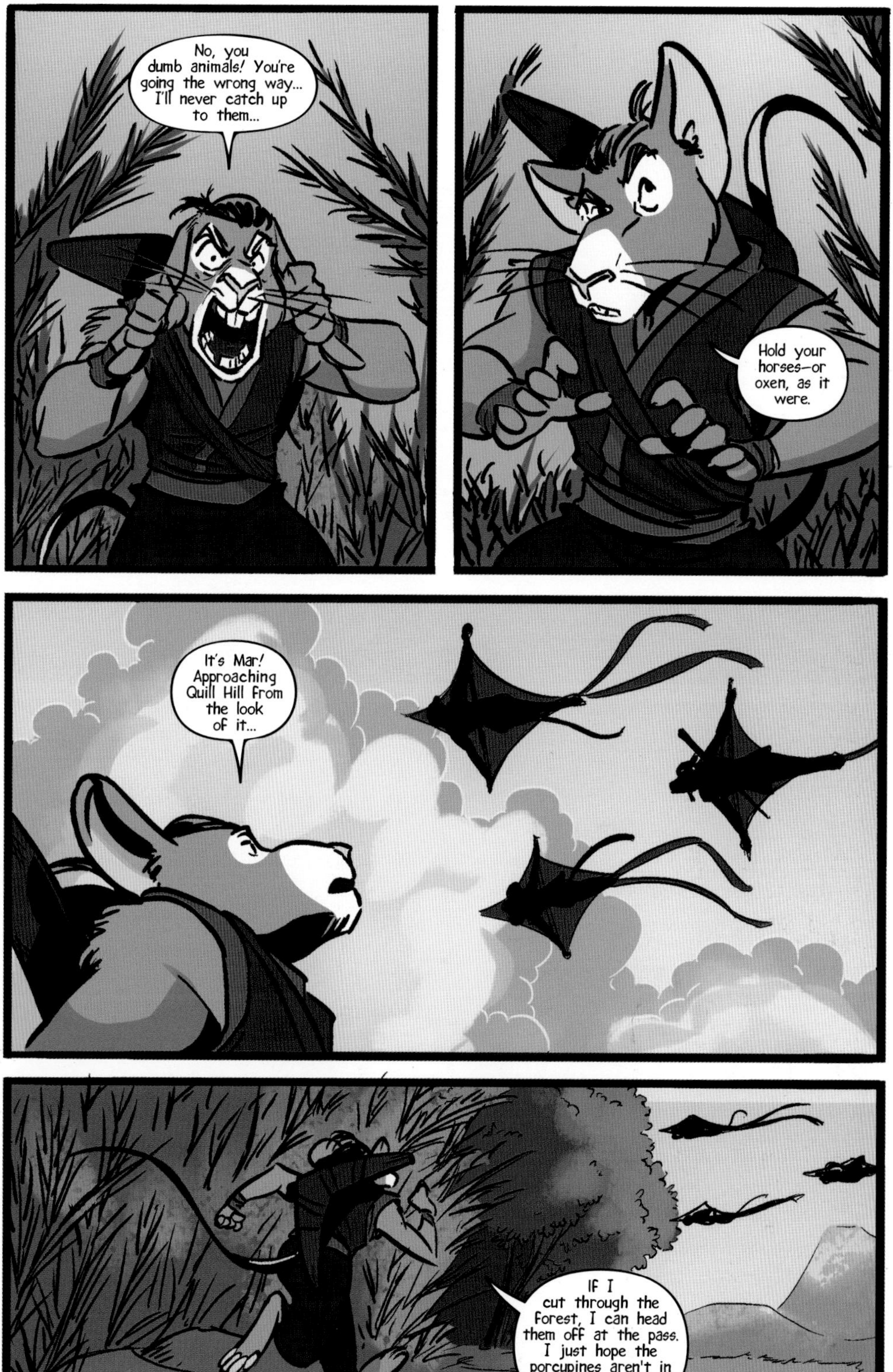
No, you dumb animals! You're going the wrong way... I'll never catch up to them...
Hold your horses—or oxen, as it were.
It's Mar! Approaching Quill Hill from the look of it...
If I cut through the forest, I can head them off at the pass. I just hope the porcupines aren't in a prickly mood today!

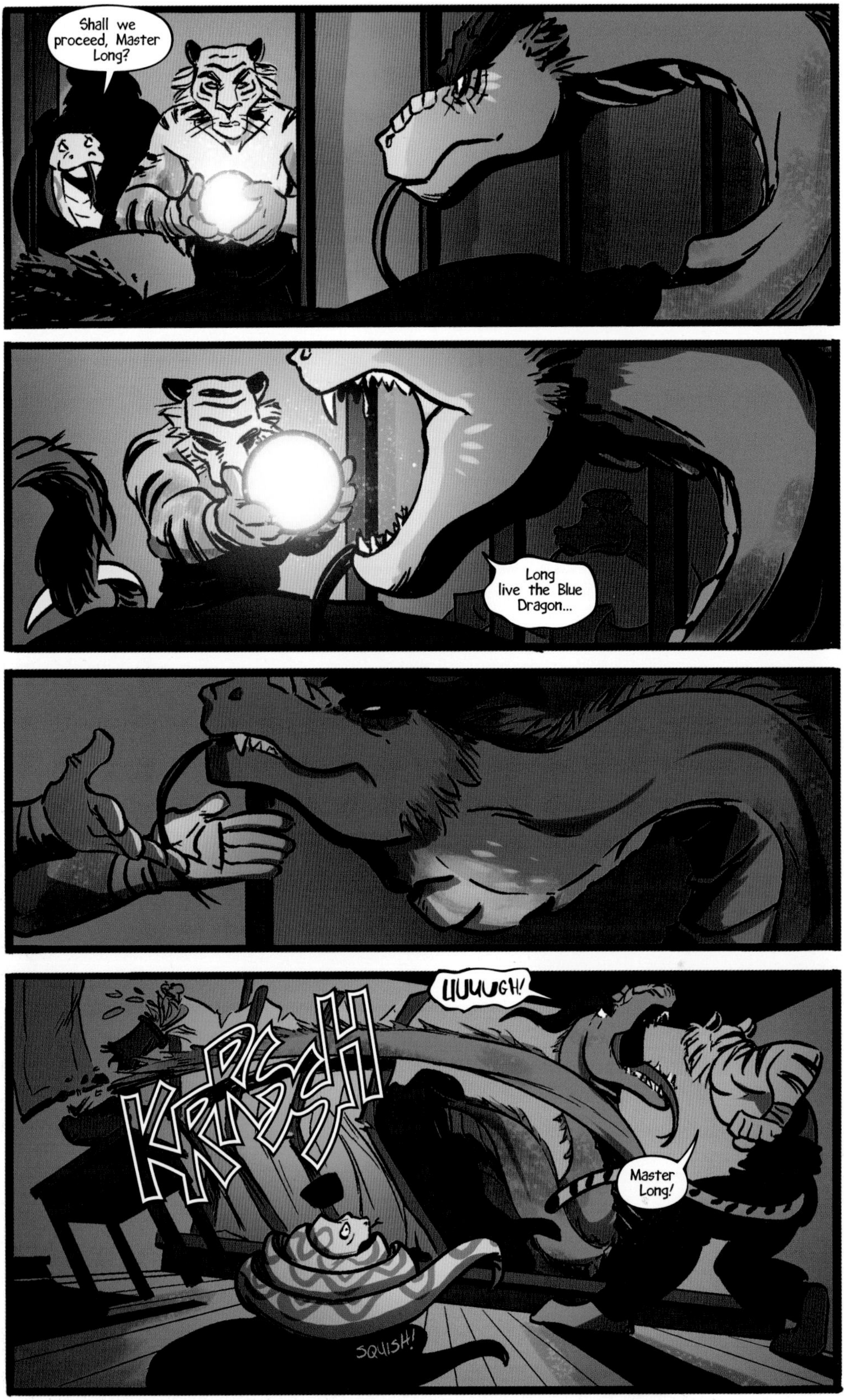
Shall we proceed, Master Long?
Long live the Blue Dragon...
UUUUGH!
Master Long!
SQUISH!

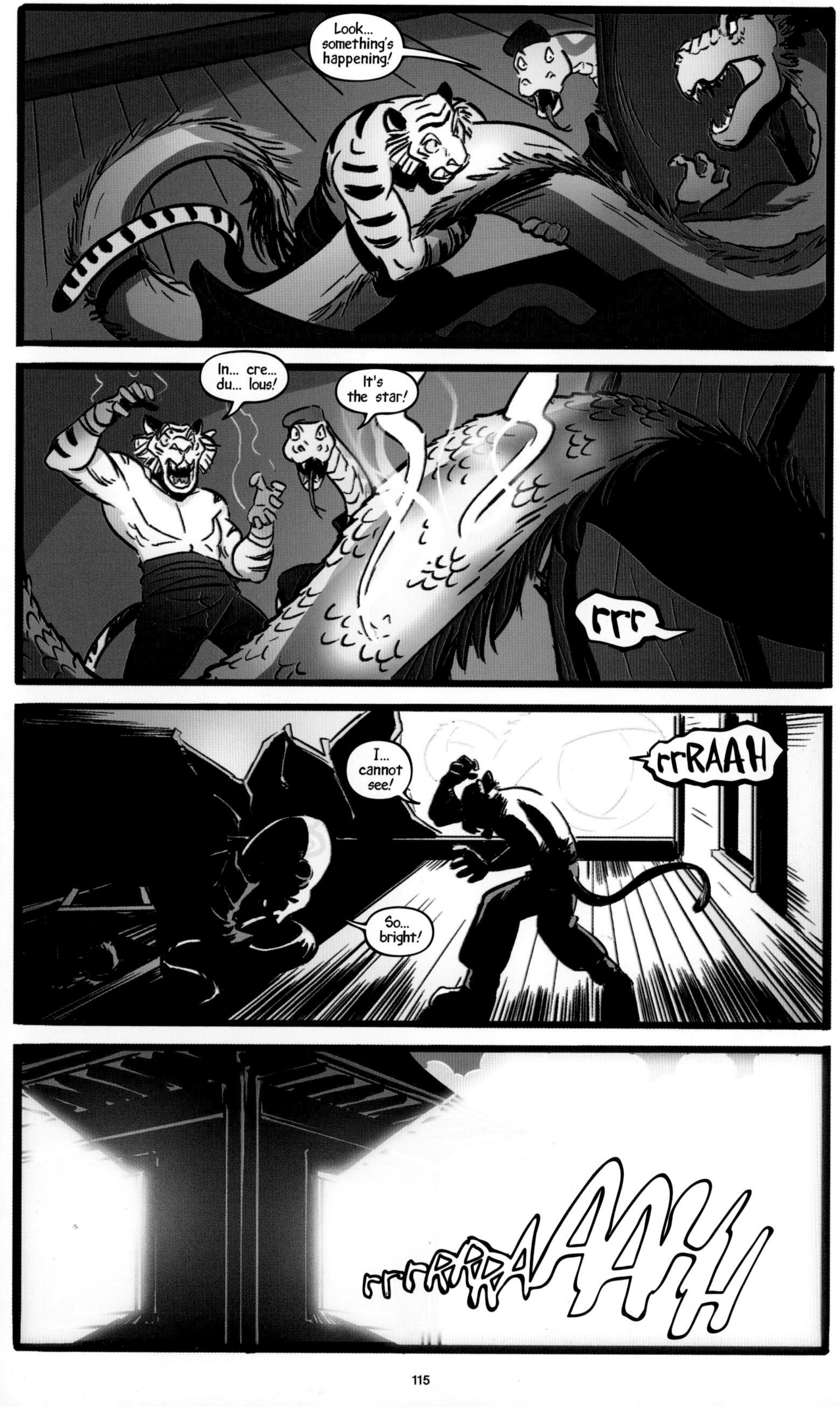
Look... something's happening!
In... cre... du... lous!
It's the star!
rrr
I... cannot see!
rrRAAH
So... bright!
rrrrRRRRAAAH

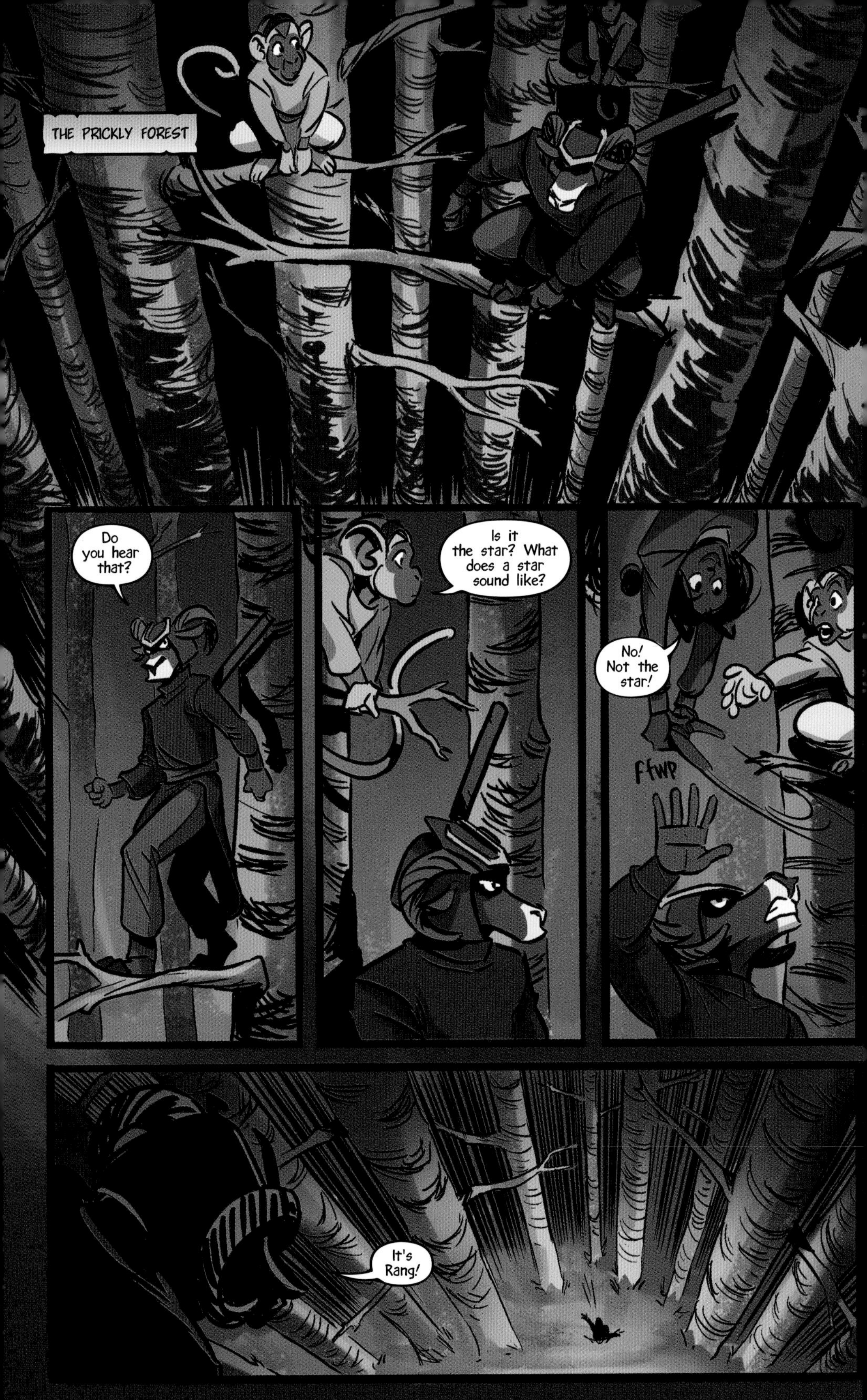
THE PRICKLY FOREST
Do you hear that?
Is it the star? What does a star sound like?
No! Not the star!
ffwp
It's Rang!

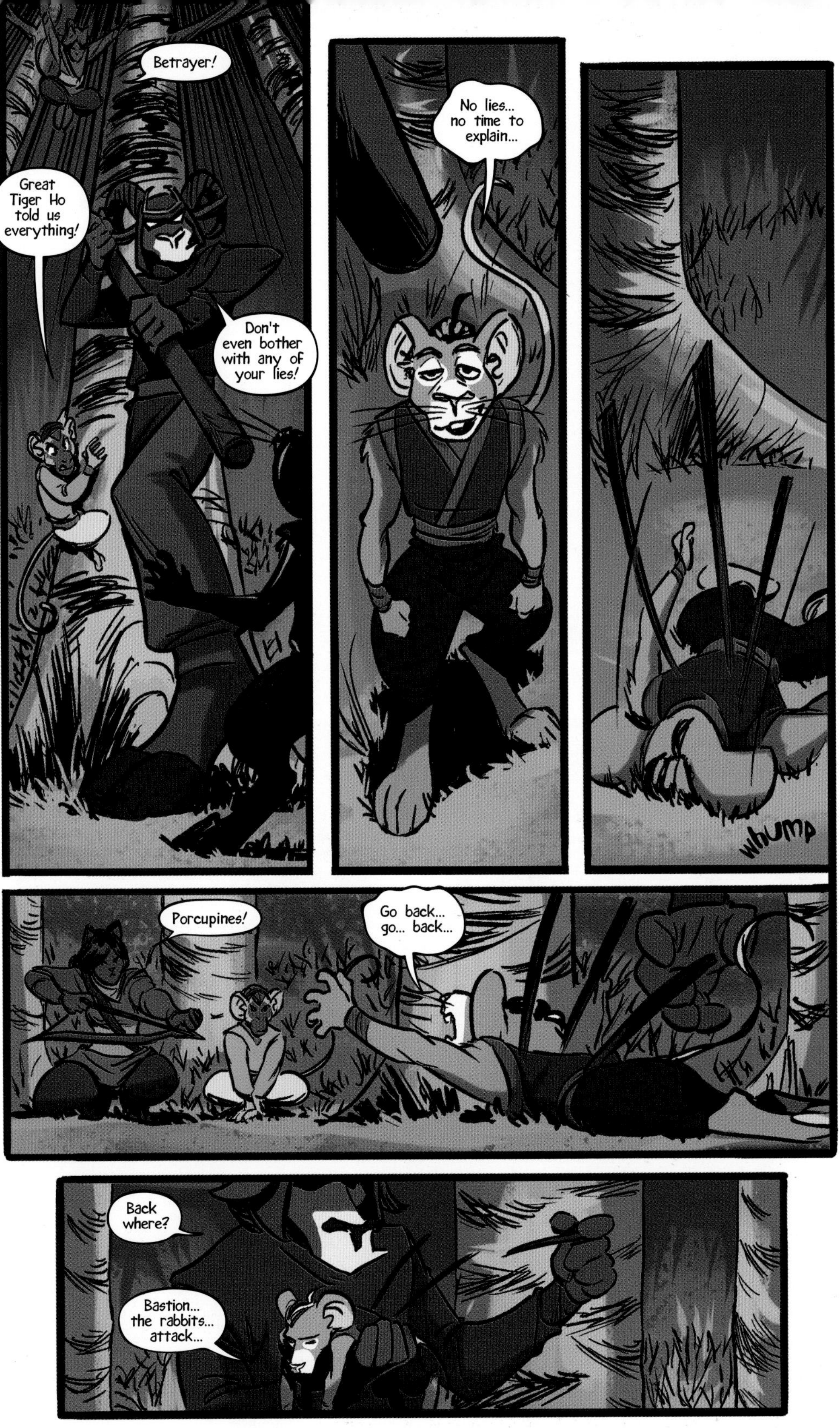
Betrayer!
Great Tiger Ho told us everything!
Don't even bother with any of your lies!
No lies... no time to explain...
whump
Porcupines!
Go back... go... back...
Back where?
Bastion... the rabbits... attack...

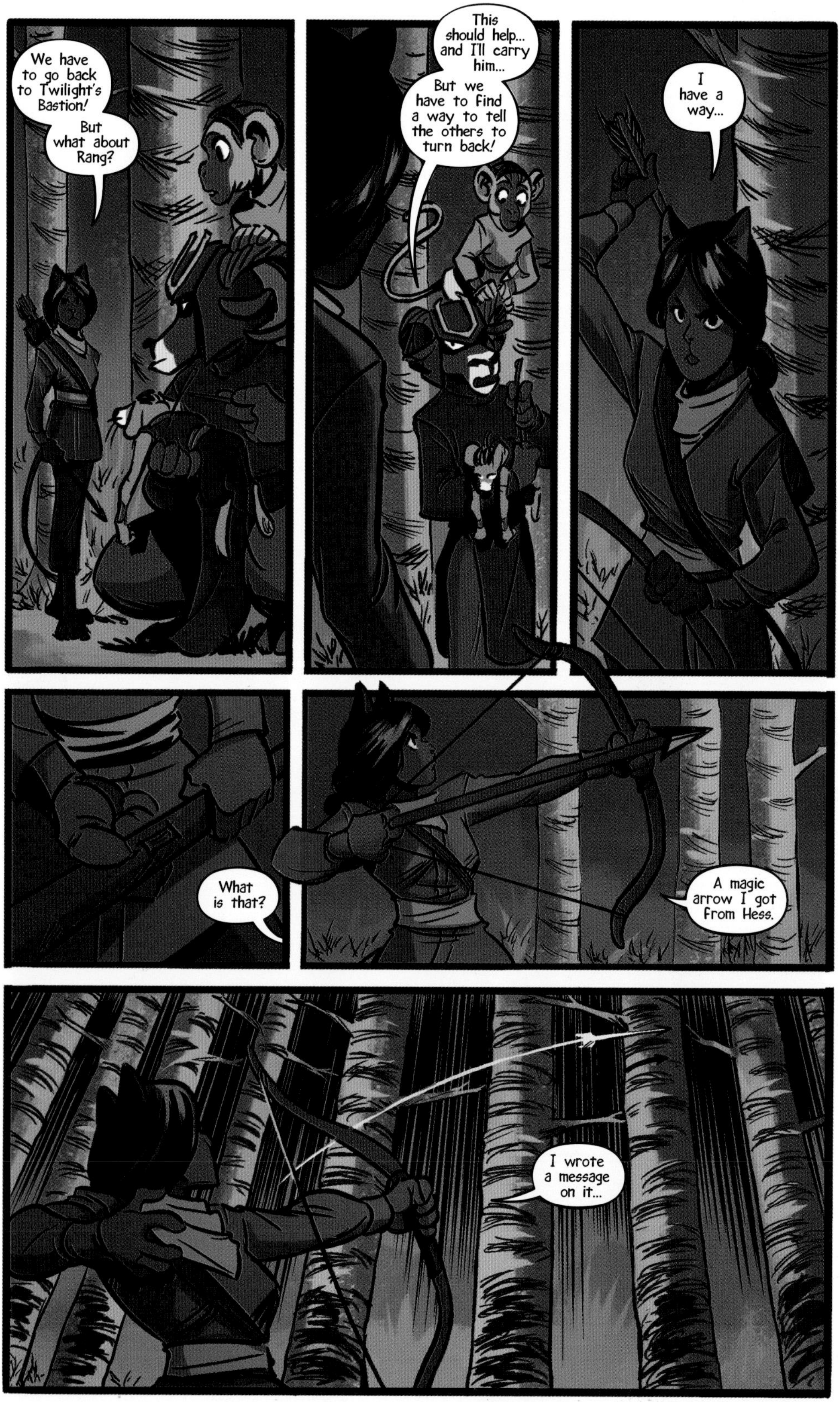
We have to go back to Twilight's Bastion!
But what about Rang?
This should help... and I'll carry him...
But we have to find a way to tell the others to turn back!
I have a way...
What is that?
A magic arrow I got from Hess.
I wrote a message on it...

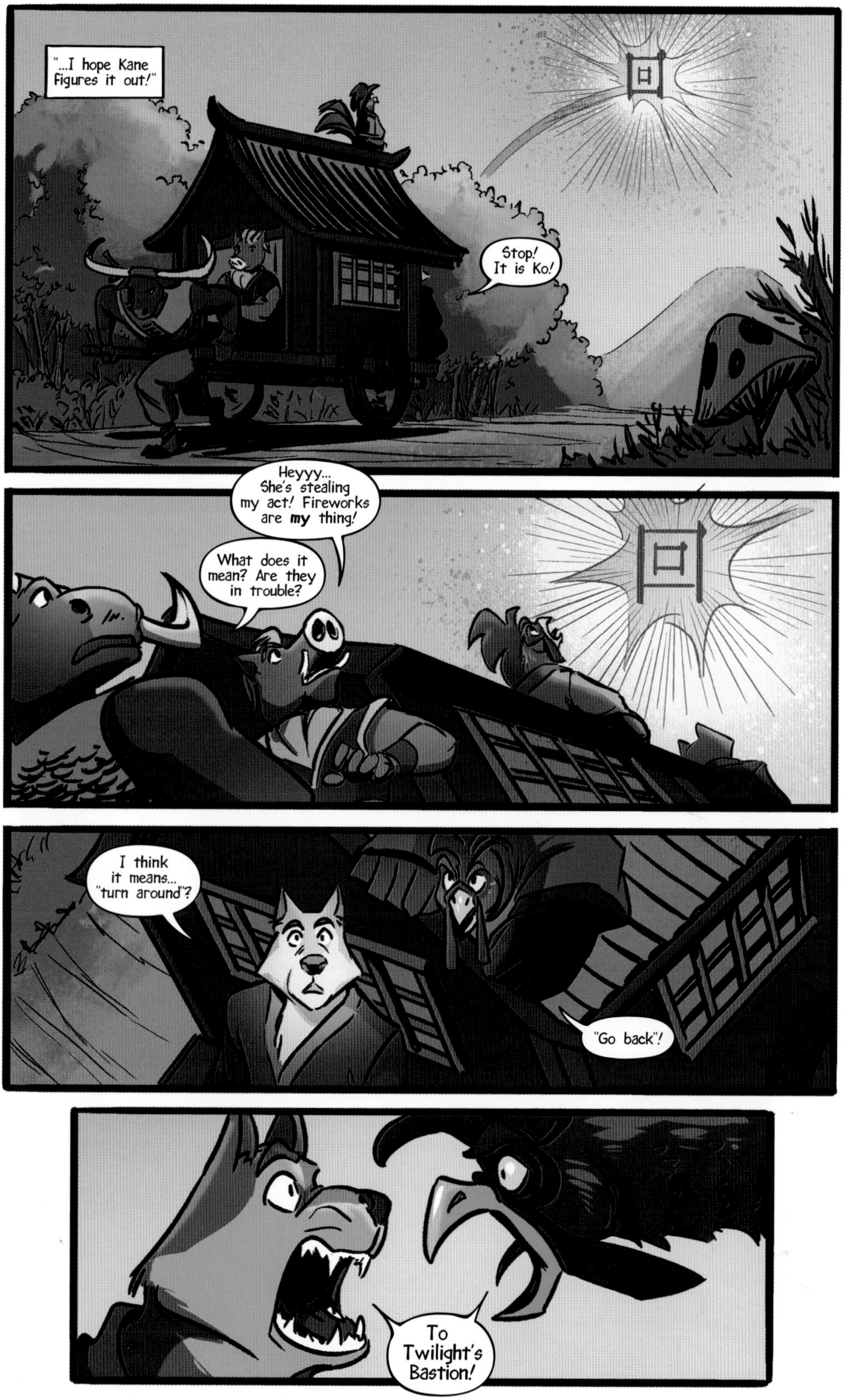
"...I hope Kane Figures it out!"
Stop! It is Ko!
Heyyy... She's stealing my act! Fireworks are **my** thing!
What does it mean? Are they in trouble?
I think it means... "turn around"?
"Go back"!
To Twilight's Bastion!

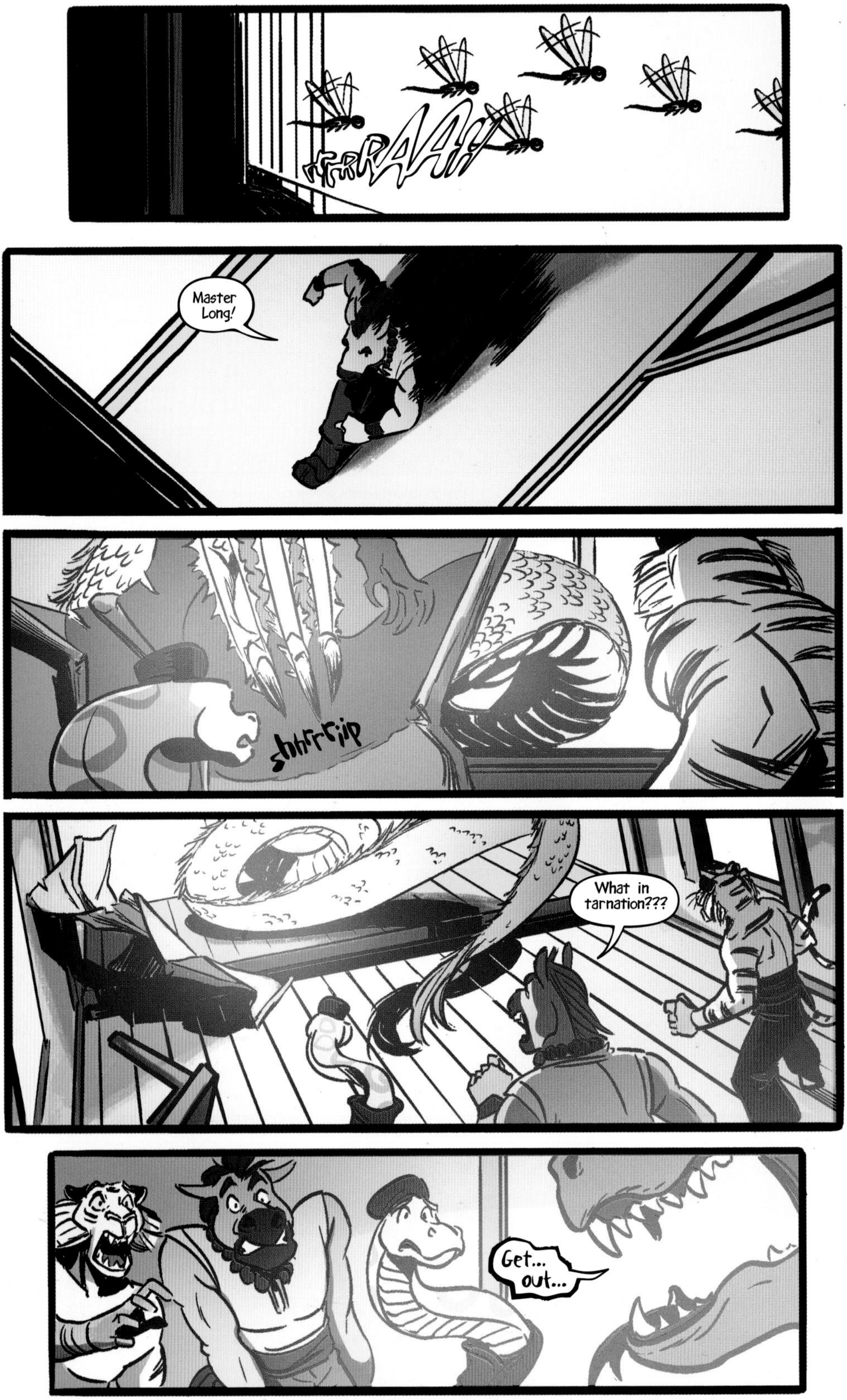
rrrrRAAAH
Master Long!
shhrrrip
What in tarnation???
Get... out...

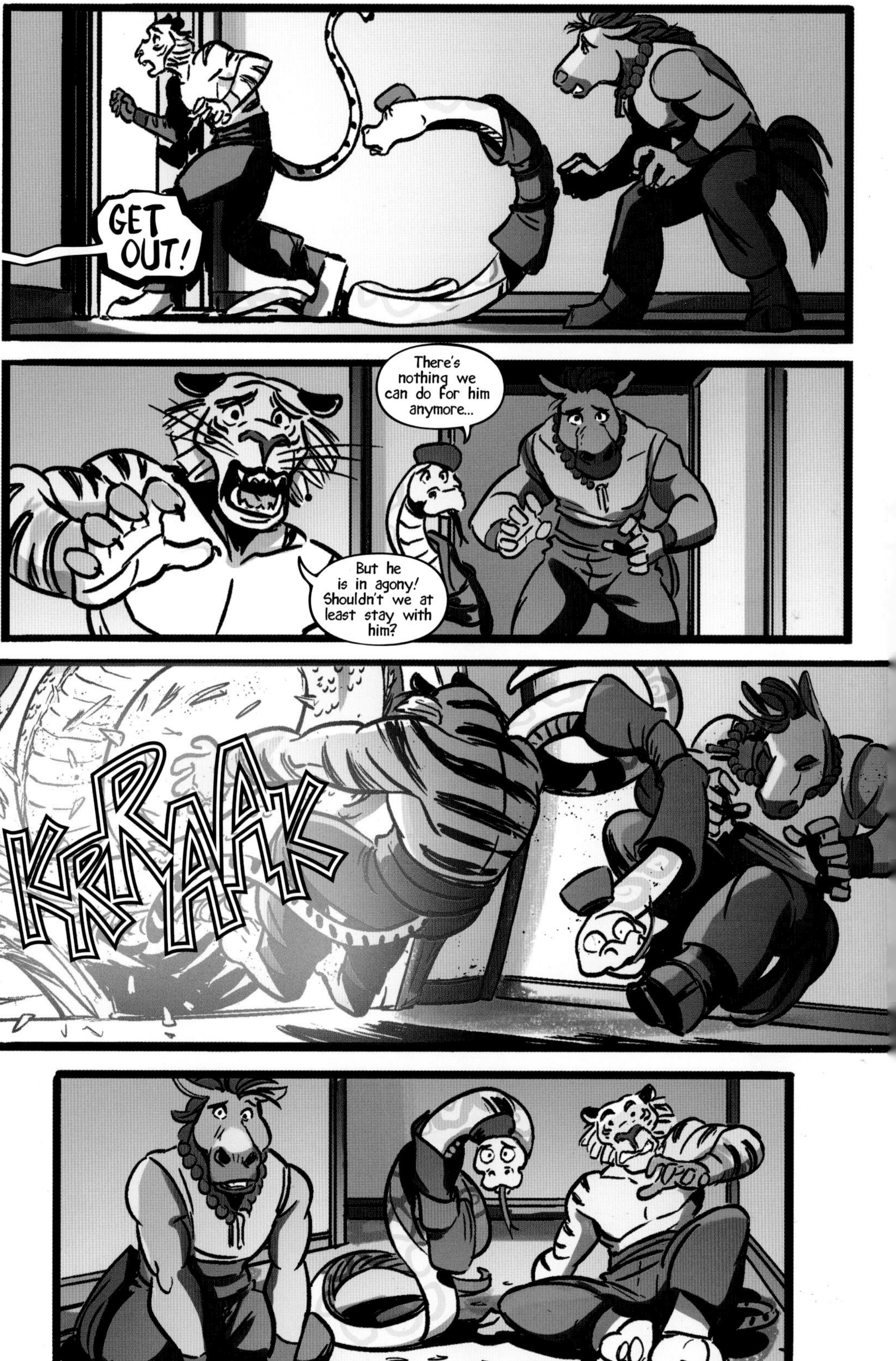
GET OUT!
There's nothing we can do for him anymore...
But he is in agony! Shouldn't we at least stay with him?
KRRAAAK

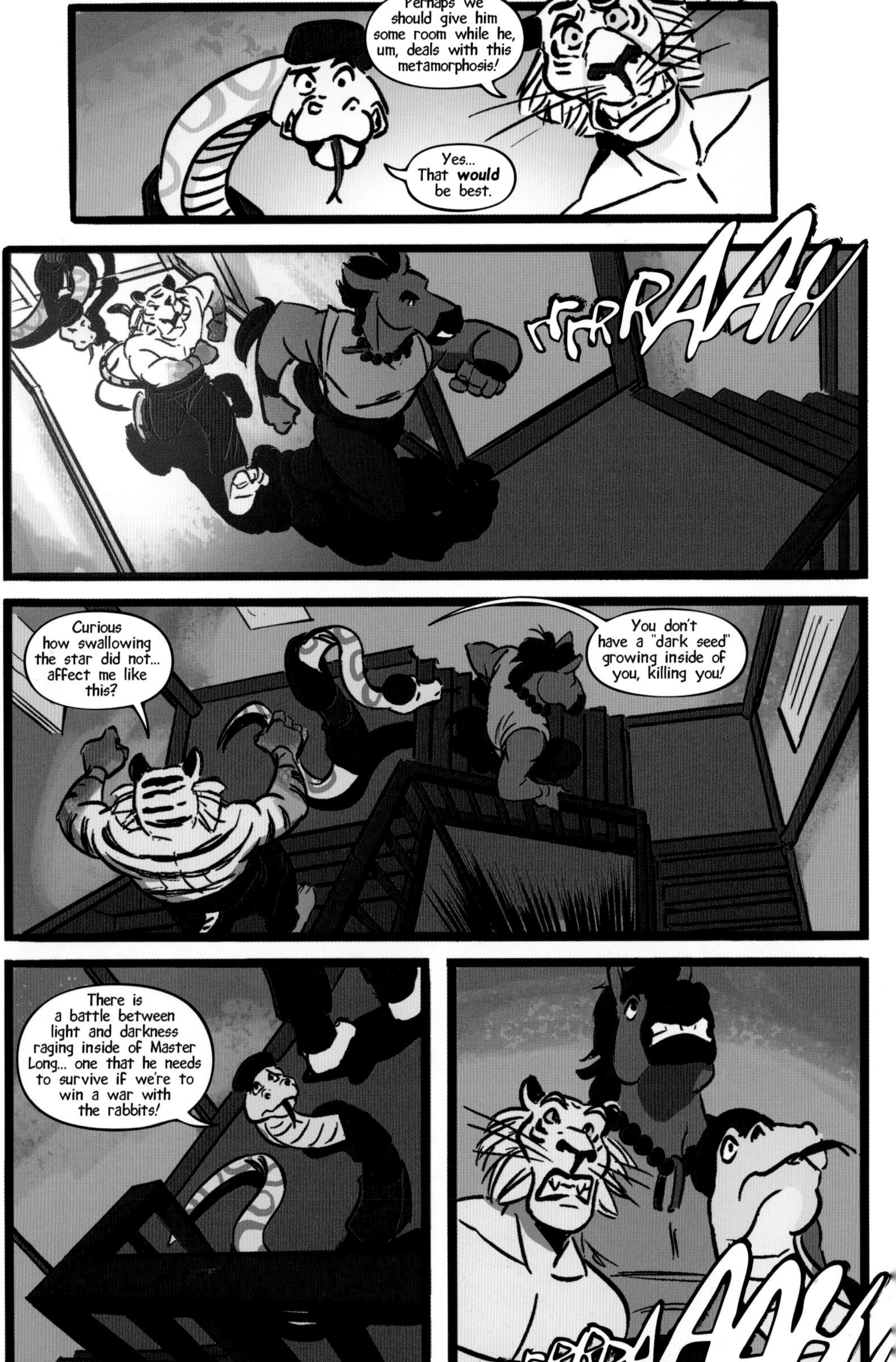
Perhaps we should give him some room while he, um, deals with this metamorphosis!
Yes... That **would** be best.
rrrRRAAAH
Curious how swallowing the star did not... affect me like this?
You don't have a "dark seed" growing inside of you, killing you!
There is a battle between light and darkness raging inside of Master Long... one that he needs to survive if we're to win a war with the rabbits!
rrrRRRRAAAAH

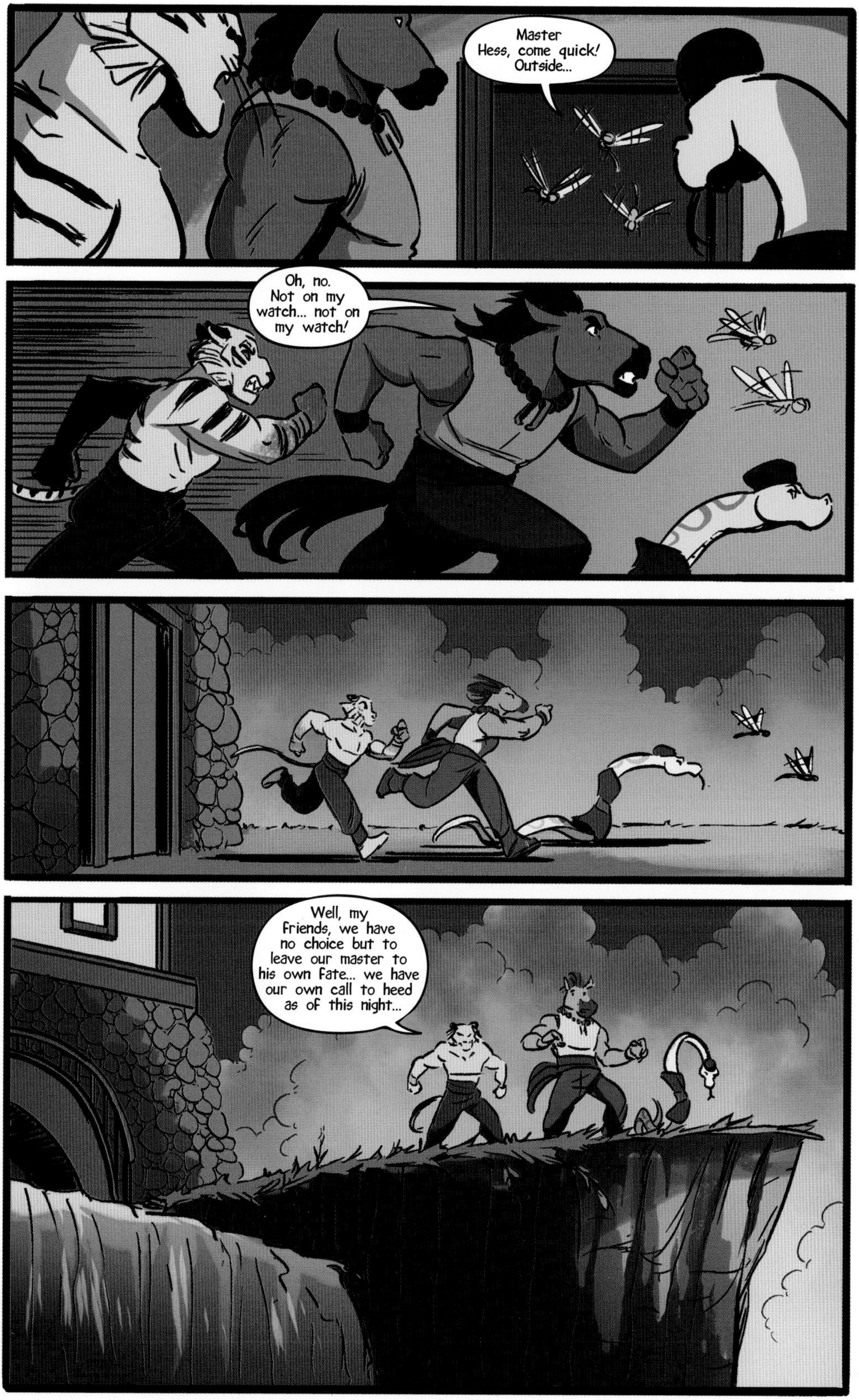
Master Hess, come quick! Outside...
Oh, no. Not on my watch... not on my watch!
Well, my friends, we have no choice but to leave our master to his own fate... we have our own call to heed as of this night...

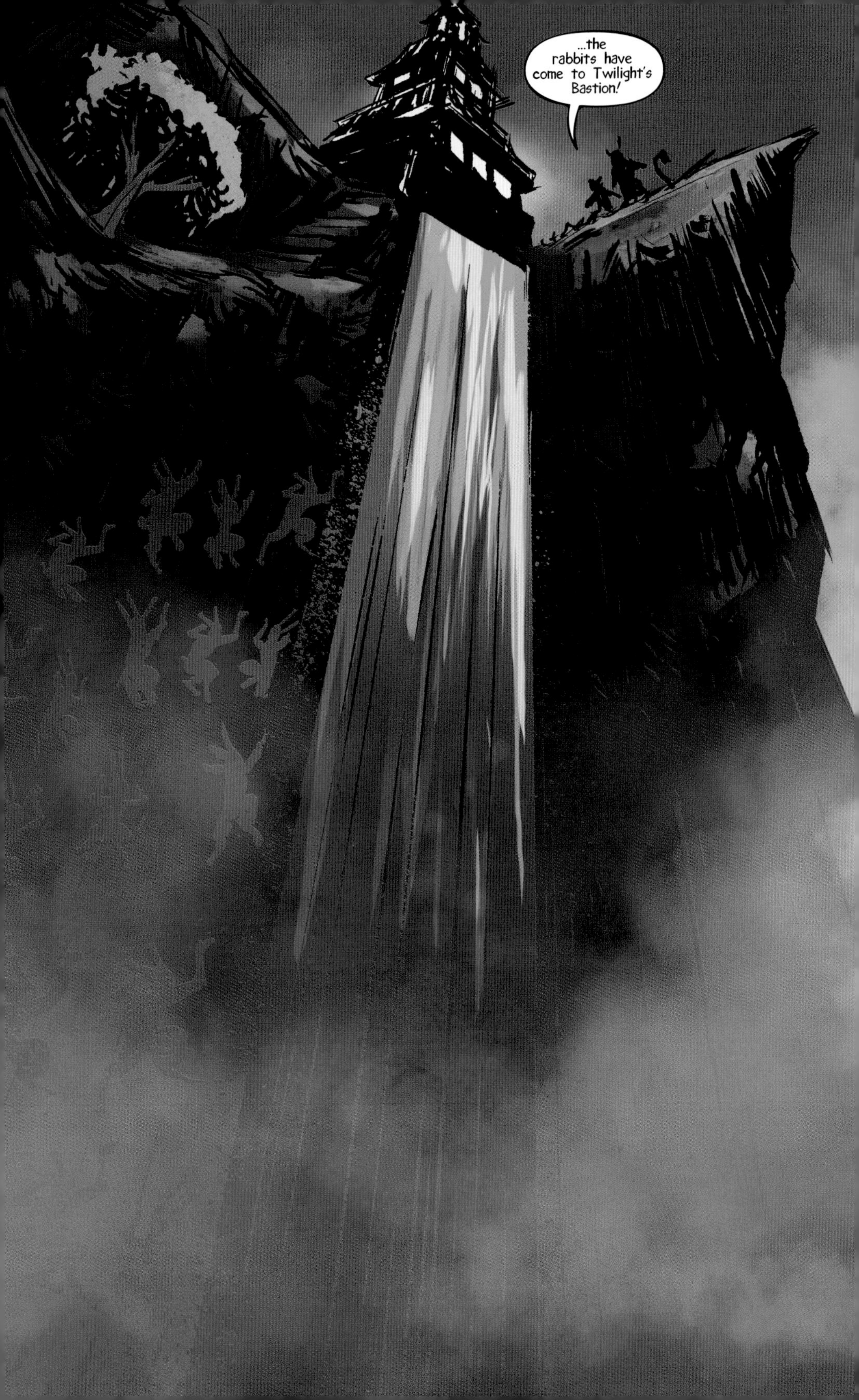
...the rabbits have come to Twilight's Bastion!

CHAPTER SIX

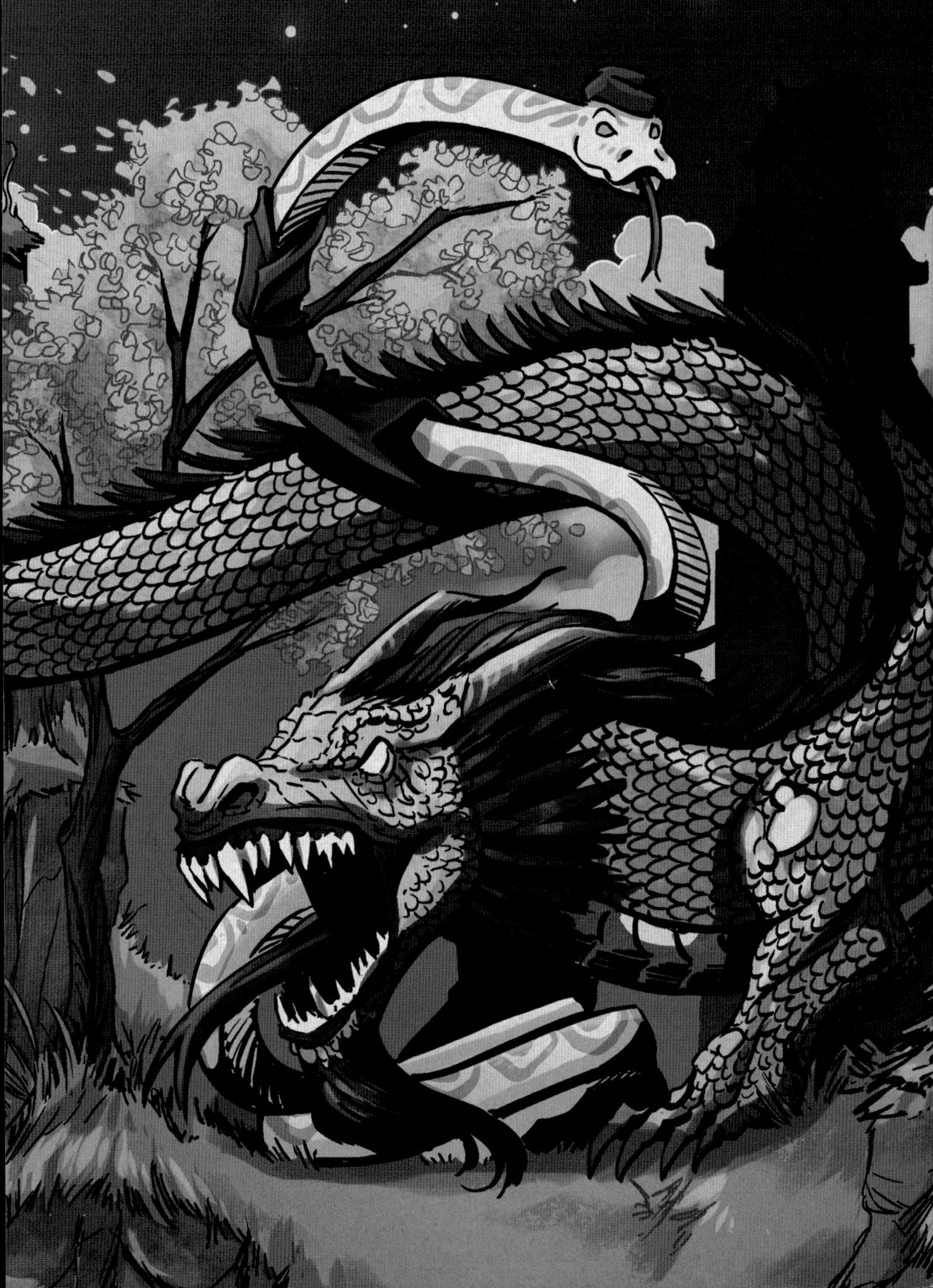

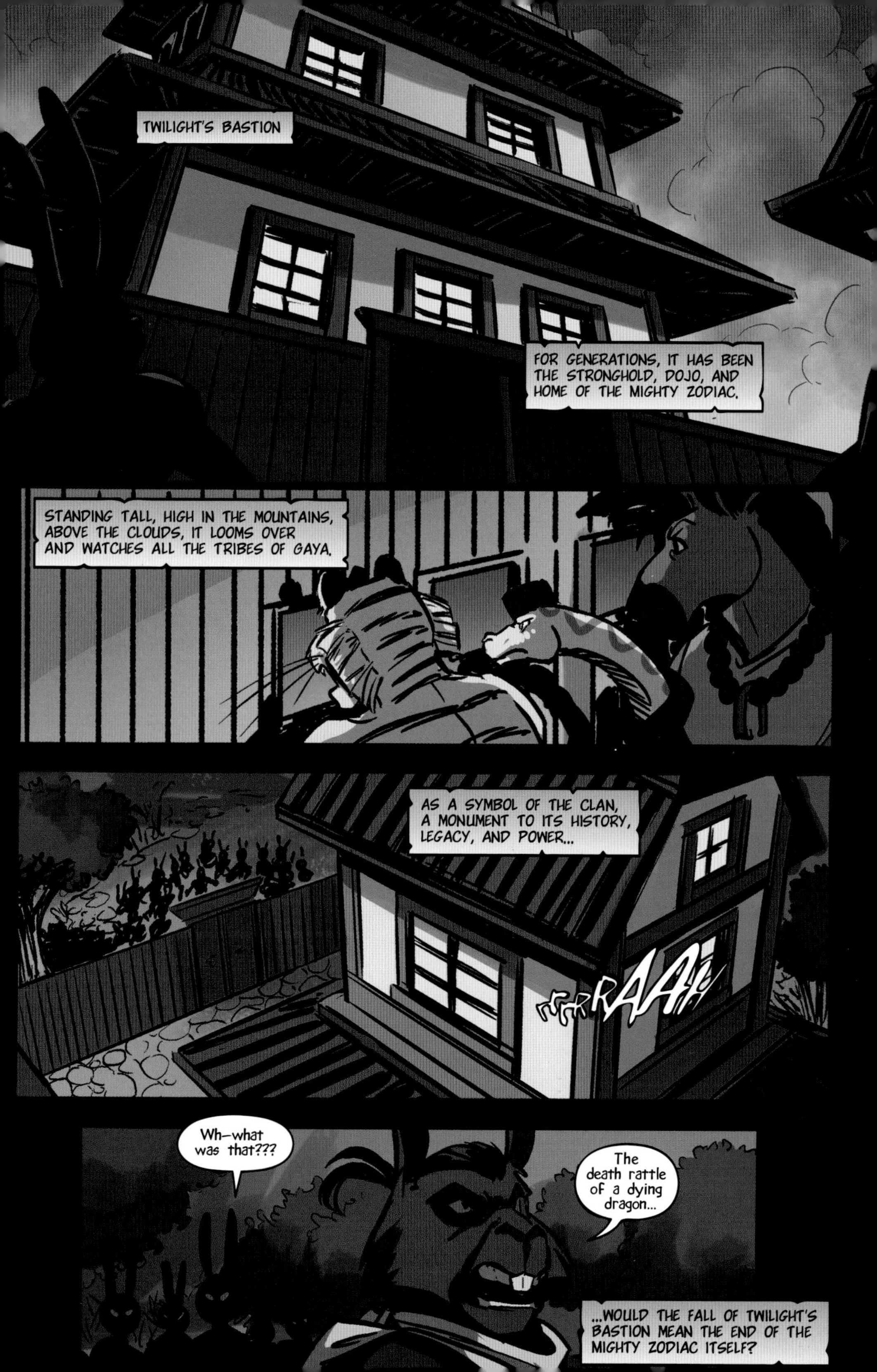
TWILIGHT'S BASTION
FOR GENERATIONS, IT HAS BEEN THE STRONGHOLD, DOJO, AND HOME OF THE MIGHTY ZODIAC.
STANDING TALL, HIGH IN THE MOUNTAINS, ABOVE THE CLOUDS, IT LOOMS OVER AND WATCHES ALL THE TRIBES OF GAYA.
AS A SYMBOL OF THE CLAN, A MONUMENT TO ITS HISTORY, LEGACY, AND POWER...
rrrrRAAAH
Wh–what was that???
The death rattle of a dying dragon...
...WOULD THE FALL OF TWILIGHT'S BASTION MEAN THE END OF THE MIGHTY ZODIAC ITSELF?

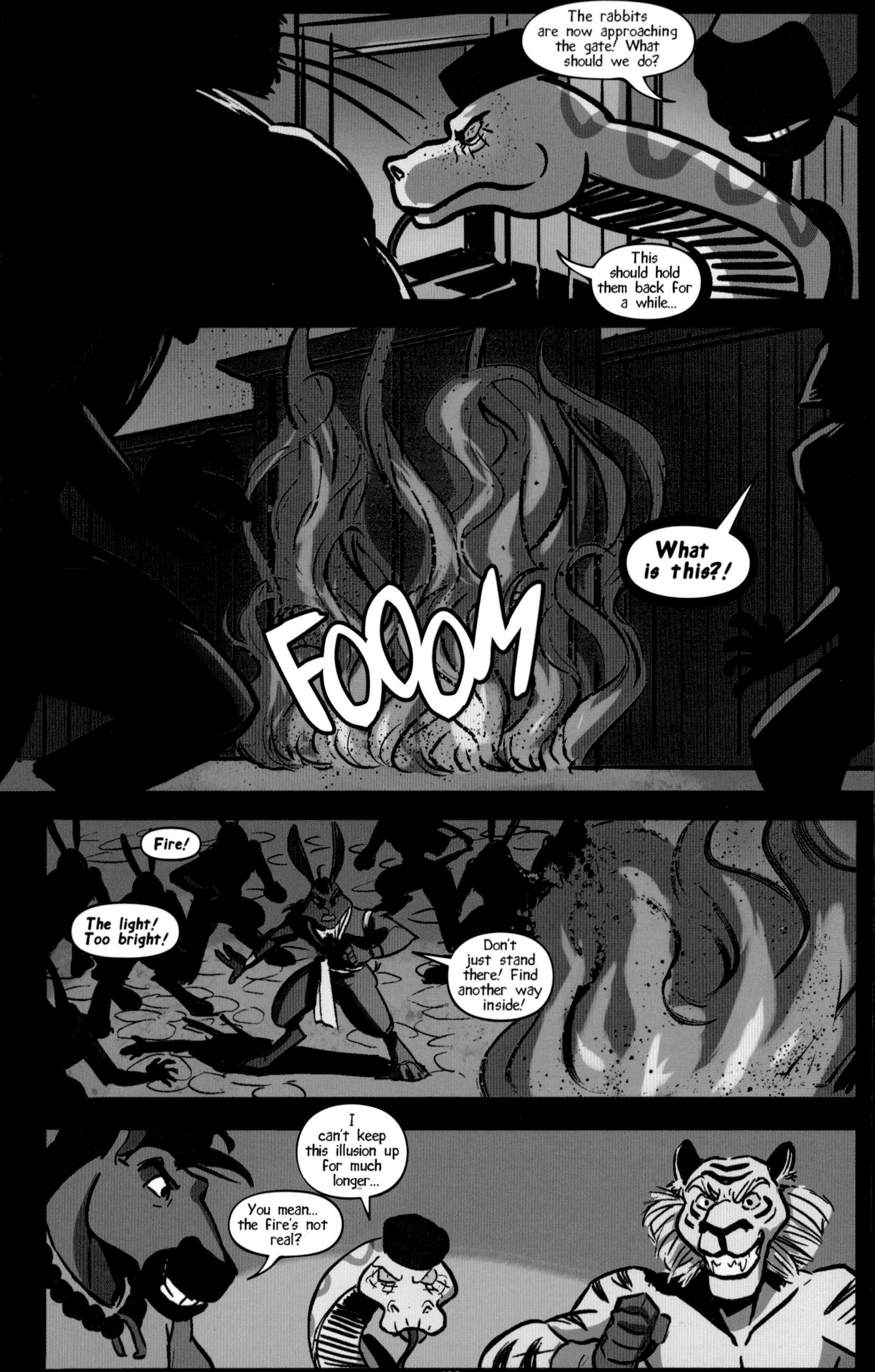
The rabbits are now approaching the gate! What should we do?
This should hold them back for a while...
FOOOM
What is this?!
Fire!
The light! Too bright!
Don't just stand there! Find another way inside!
I can't keep this illusion up for much longer...
You mean... the fire's not real?

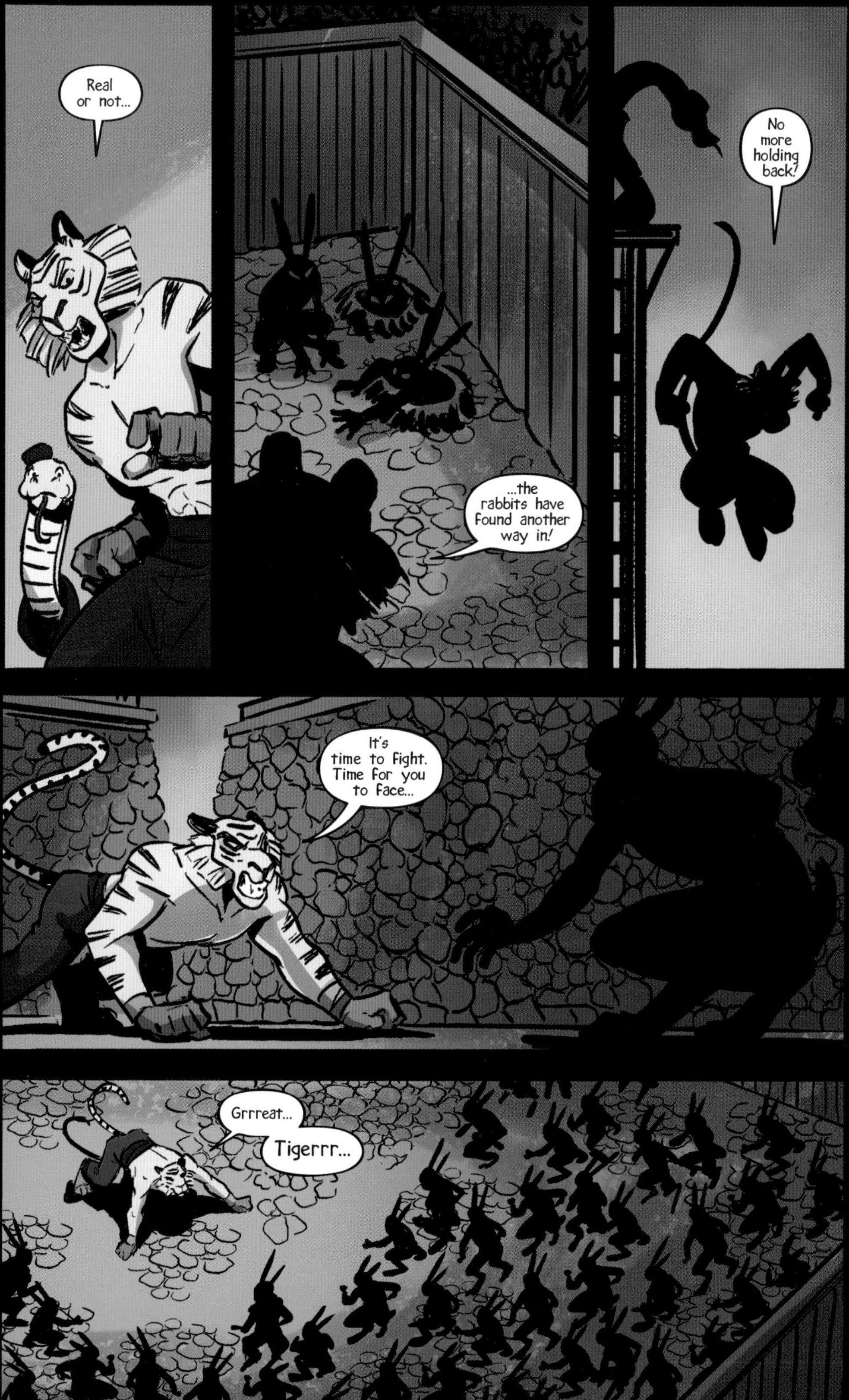
Real or not...
...the rabbits have found another way in!
No more holding back!
It's time to fight. Time for you to face...
Grrreat...
Tigerrr...

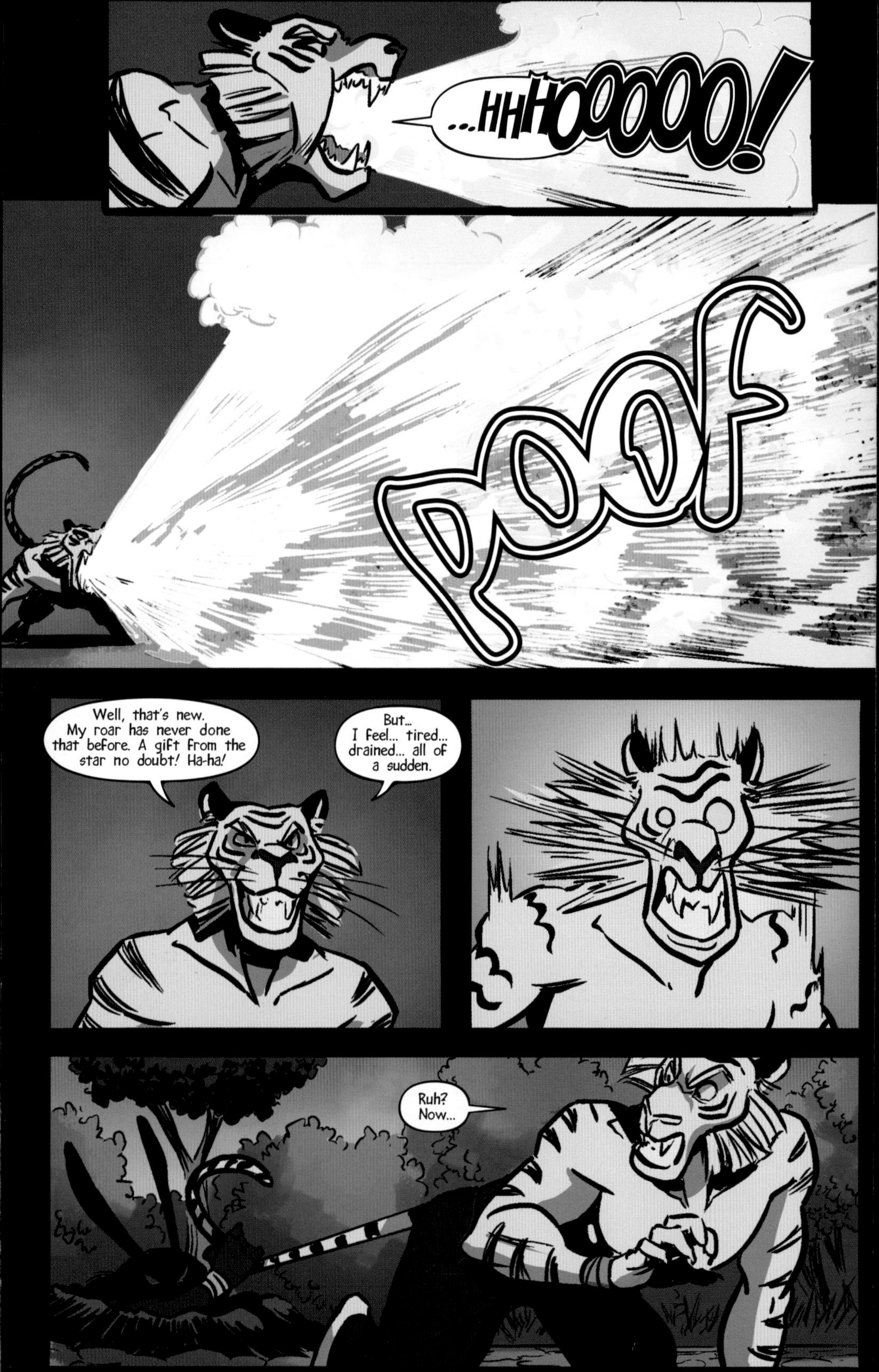
...HHHOOOOOO!
POOF
Well, that's new. My roar has never done that before. A gift from the star no doubt! Ha-ha!
But... I feel... tired... drained... all of a sudden.
Ruh? Now...

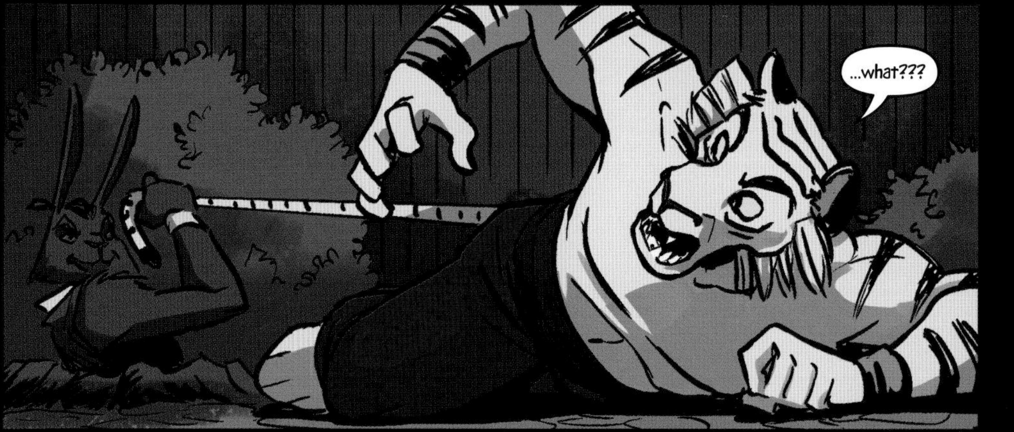
...what???

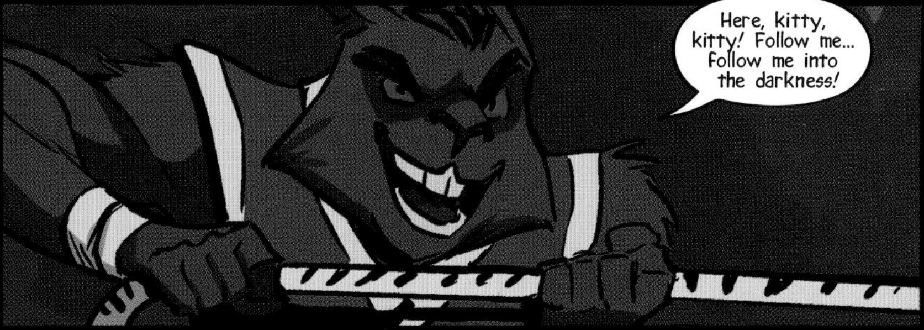
Here, kitty, kitty! Follow me... follow me into the darkness!

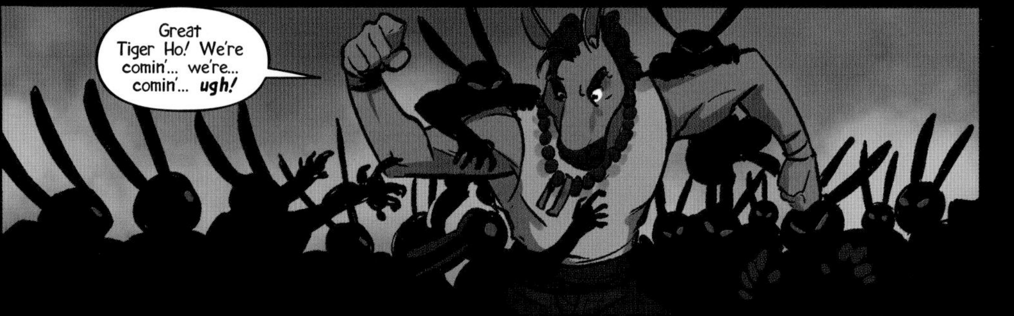
Great Tiger Ho! We're comin'... we're... comin'... **ugh!**

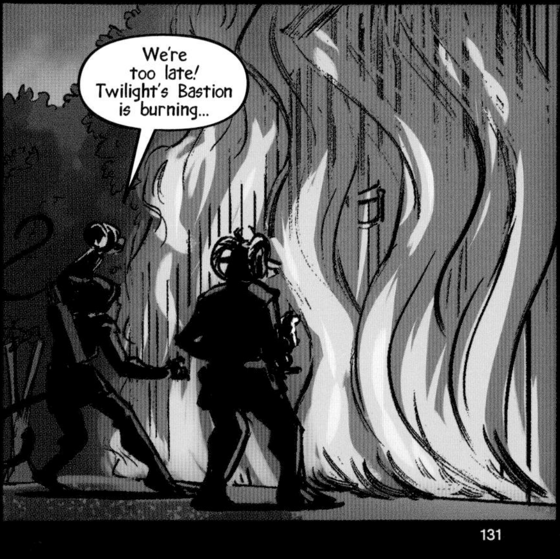
We're too late! Twilight's Bastion is burning...

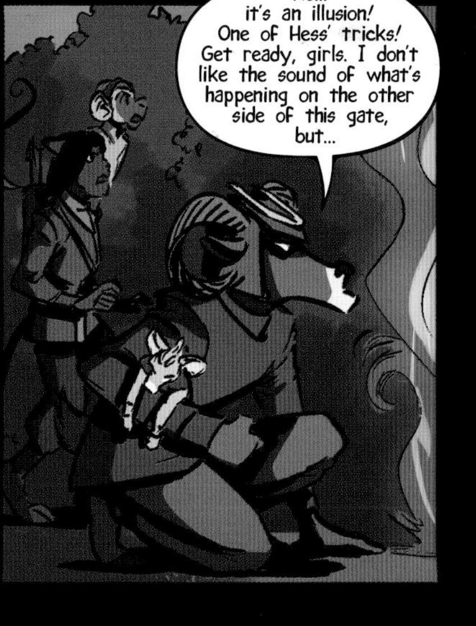
No... it's an illusion! One of Hess' tricks! Get ready, girls. I don't like the sound of what's happening on the other side of this gate, but...

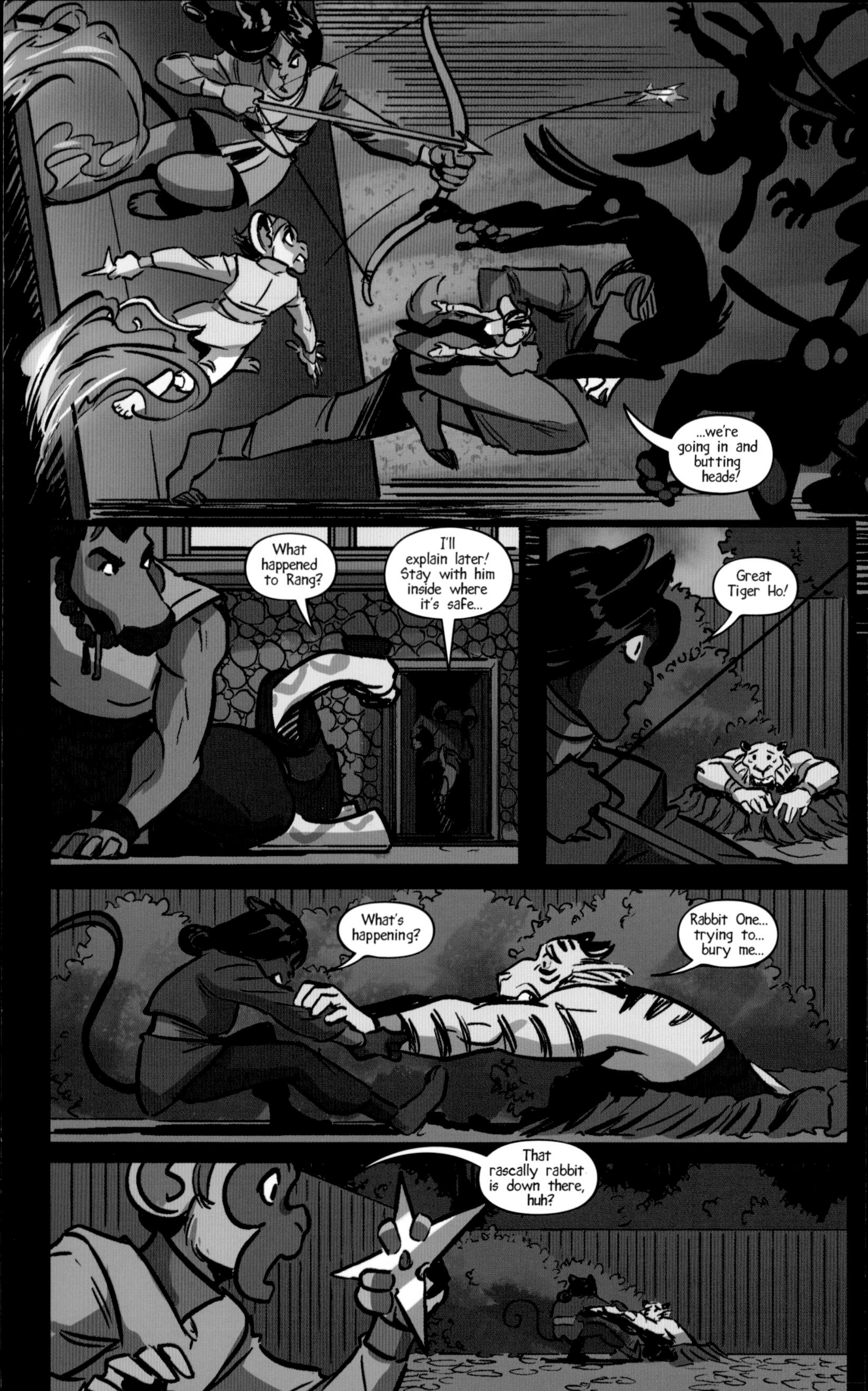
...we're going in and butting heads!
What happened to Rang?
I'll explain later! Stay with him inside where it's safe...
Great Tiger Ho!
What's happening?
Rabbit One... trying to... bury me...
That rascally rabbit is down there, huh?

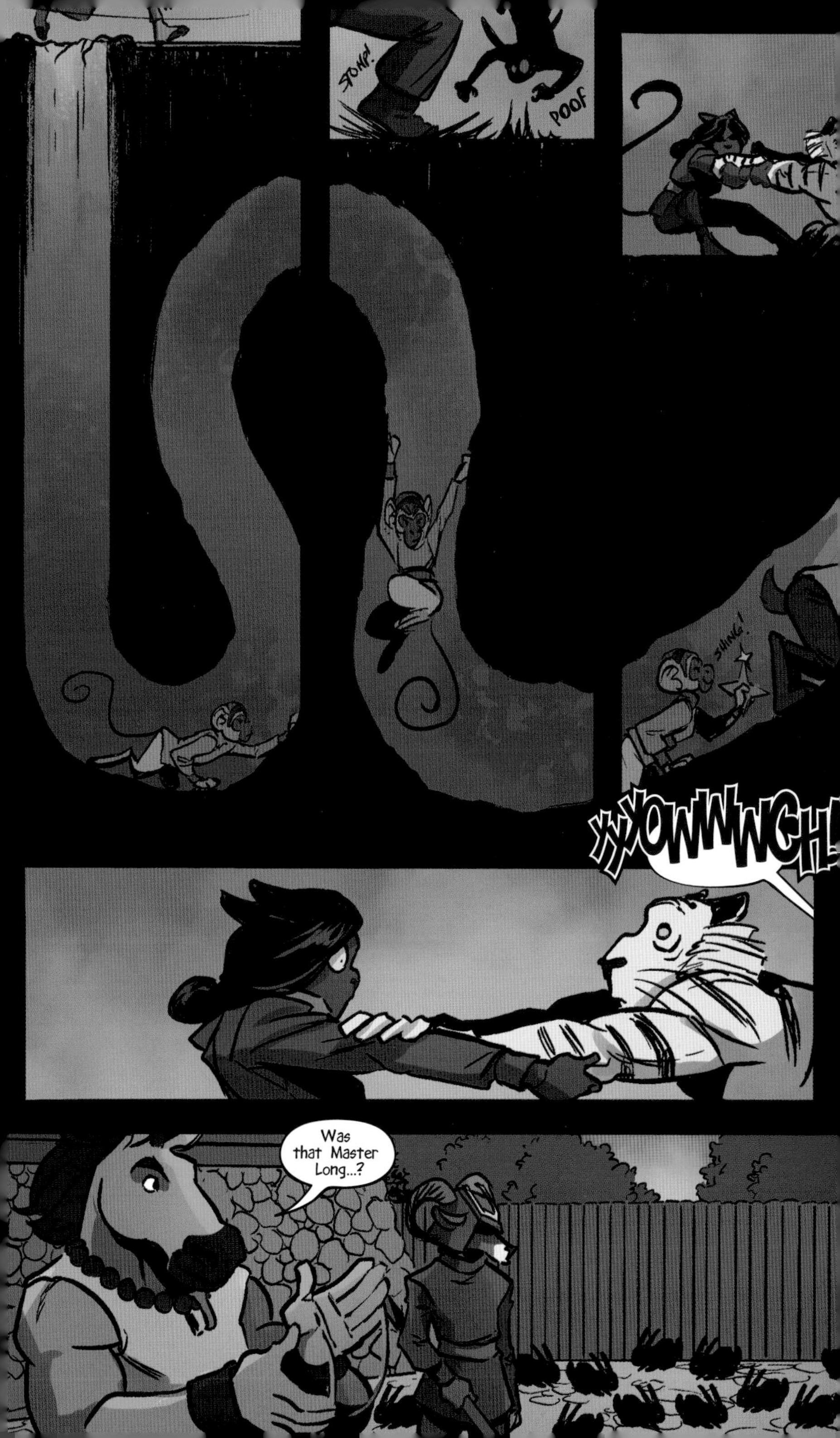
STOMP!
POOF
SHING!
YYYOWWWCH!
Was that Master Long...?

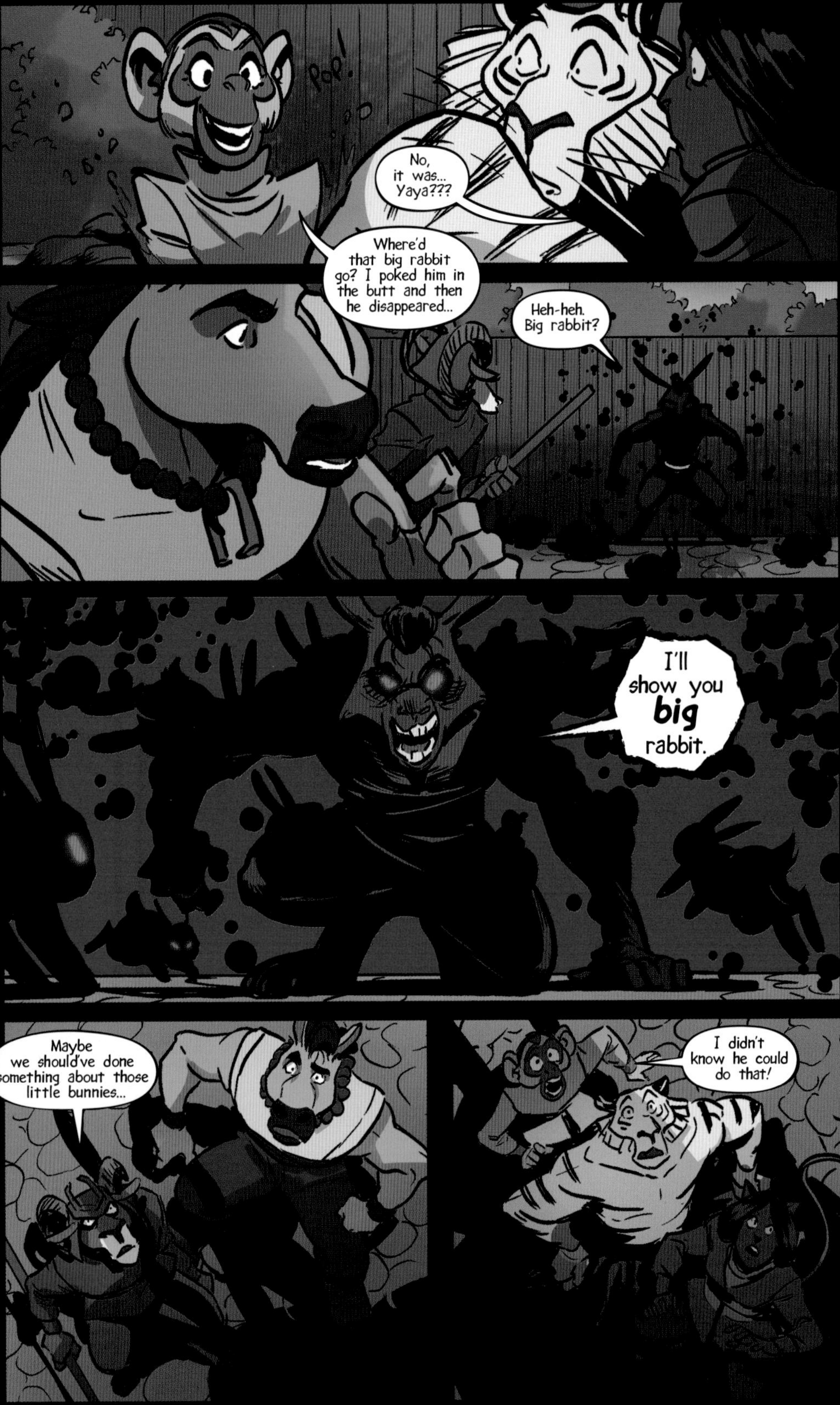
POP!
No, it was... Yaya???
Where'd that big rabbit go? I poked him in the butt and then he disappeared...
Heh-heh. Big rabbit?
I'll show you **big** rabbit.
Maybe we should've done something about those little bunnies...
I didn't know he could do that!

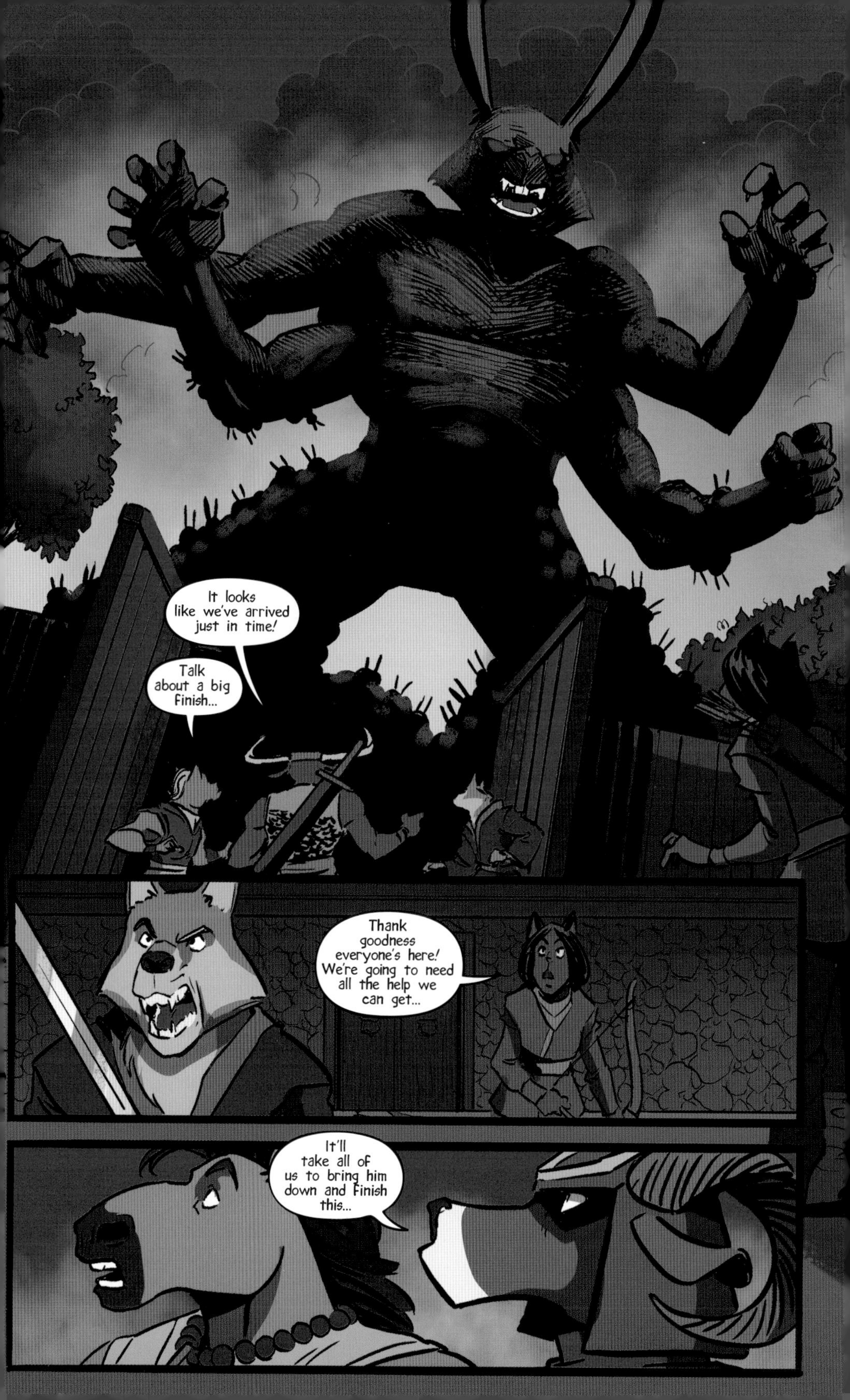
It looks like we've arrived just in time!
Talk about a big finish...
Thank goodness everyone's here! We're going to need all the help we can get...
It'll take all of us to bring him down and finish this...

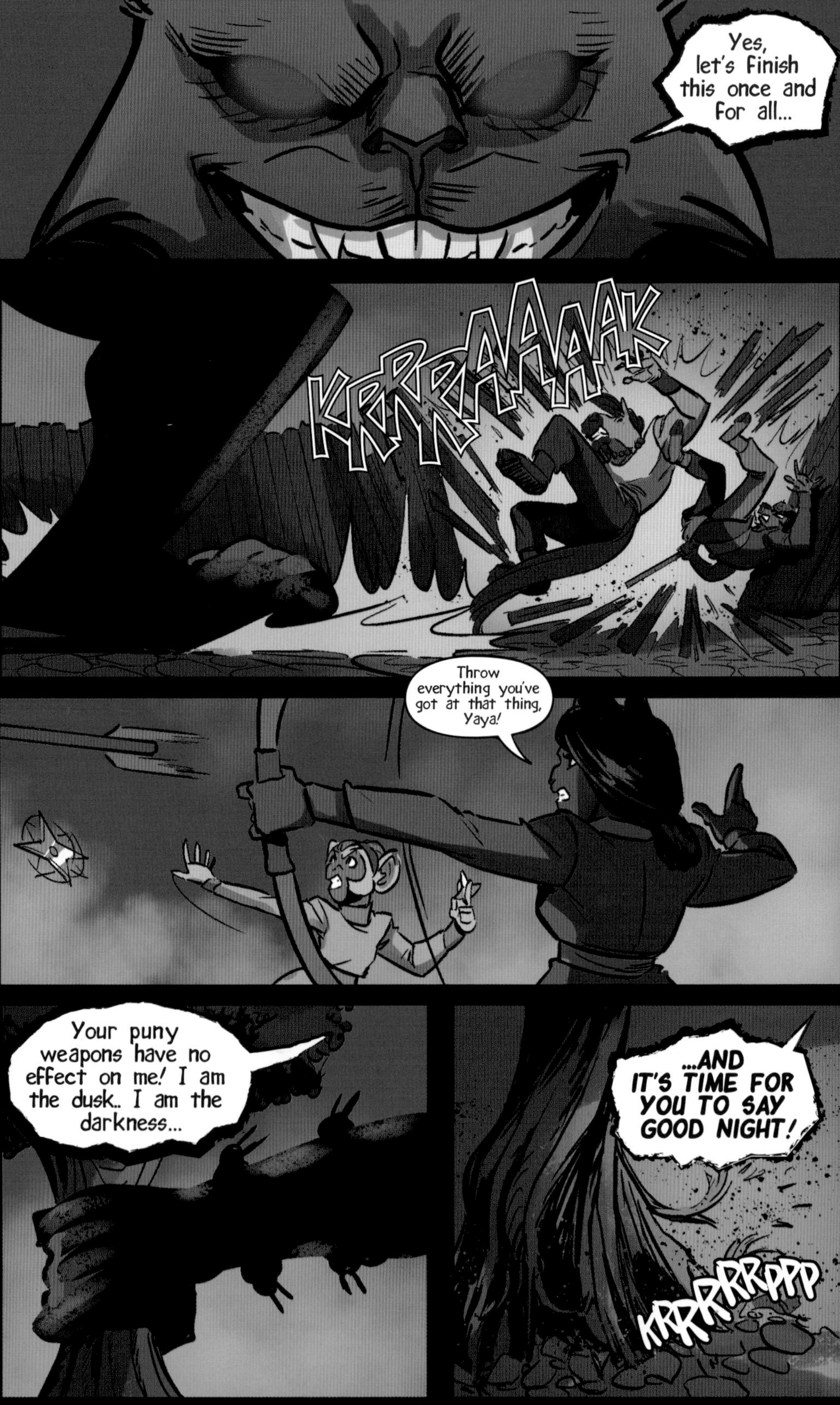
Yes, let's finish this once and for all...
KRRRAAAAAK
Throw everything you've got at that thing, Yaya!
Your puny weapons have no effect on me! I am the dusk.. I am the darkness...
...AND IT'S TIME FOR YOU TO SAY GOOD NIGHT!
KRRRRRPPP

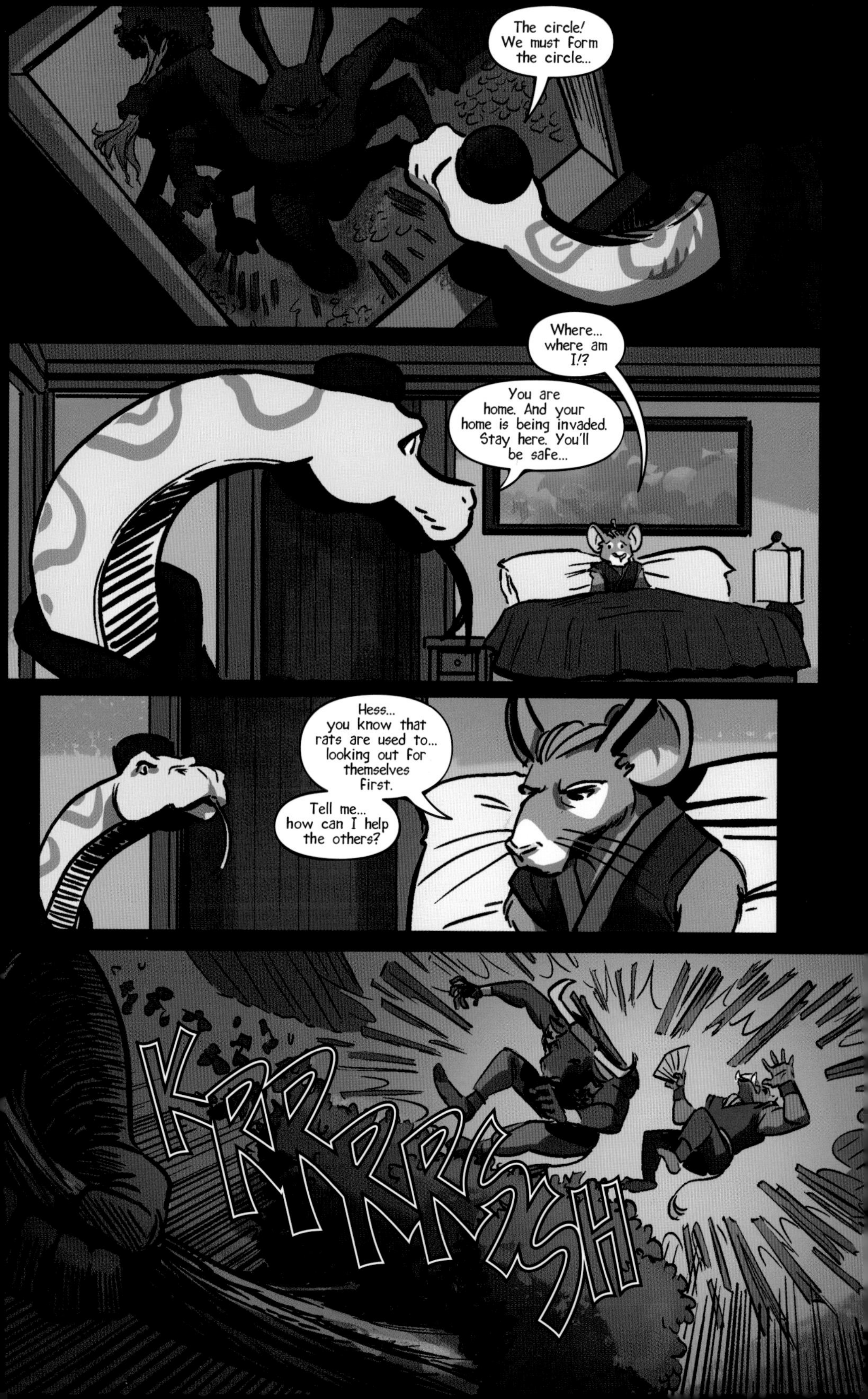
The circle! We must form the circle...
Where... where am I!?
You are home. And your home is being invaded. Stay here. You'll be safe...
Hess... you know that rats are used to... looking out for themselves first.
Tell me... how can I help the others?
KRRRRSSH

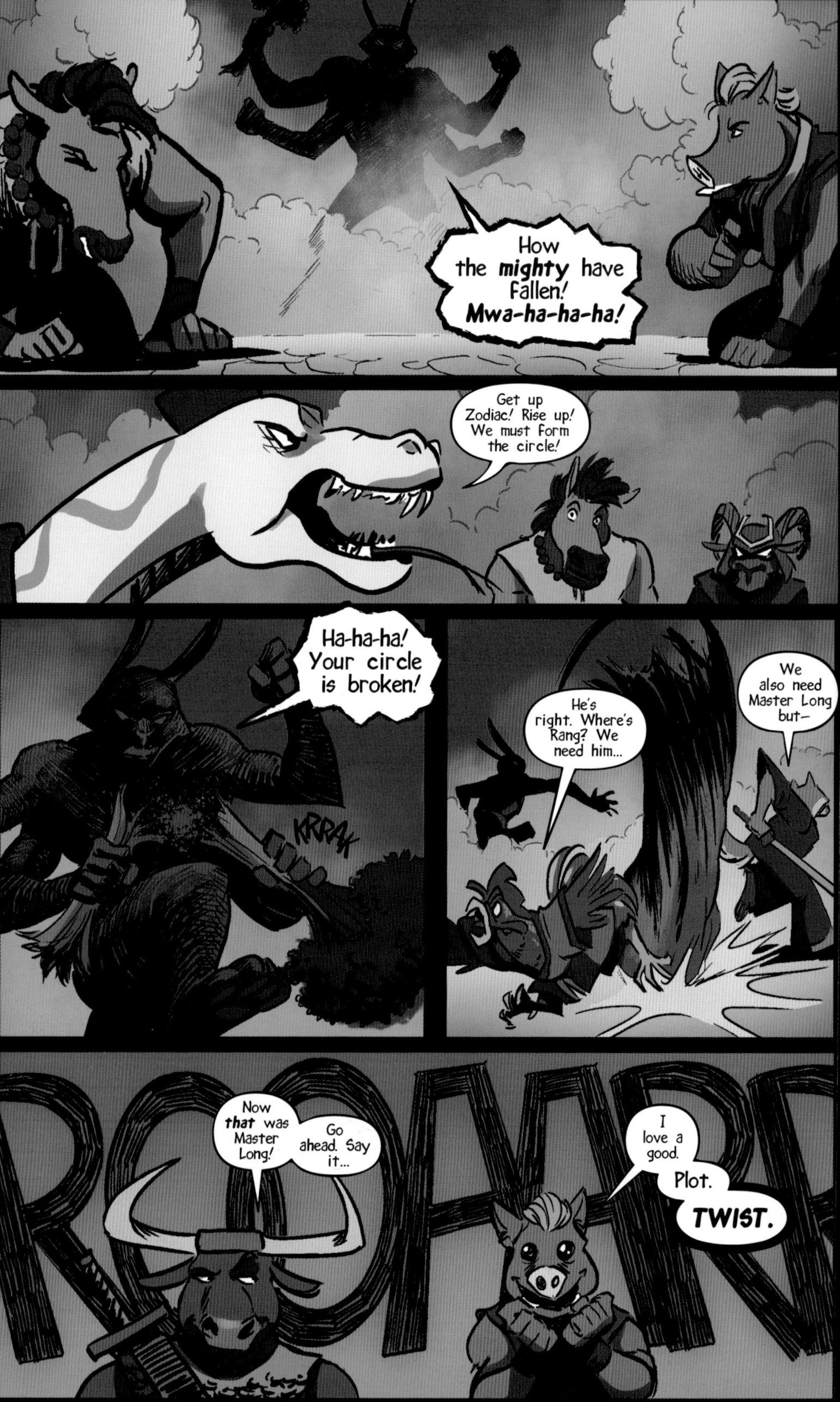
How the **mighty** have fallen! **Mwa-ha-ha-ha!**
Get up Zodiac! Rise up! We must form the circle!
Ha-ha-ha! Your circle is broken!
KRRAK
He's right. Where's Rang? We need him...
We also need Master Long but–
Now ***that*** was Master Long!
Go ahead. Say it...
I love a good.
Plot.
TWIST.

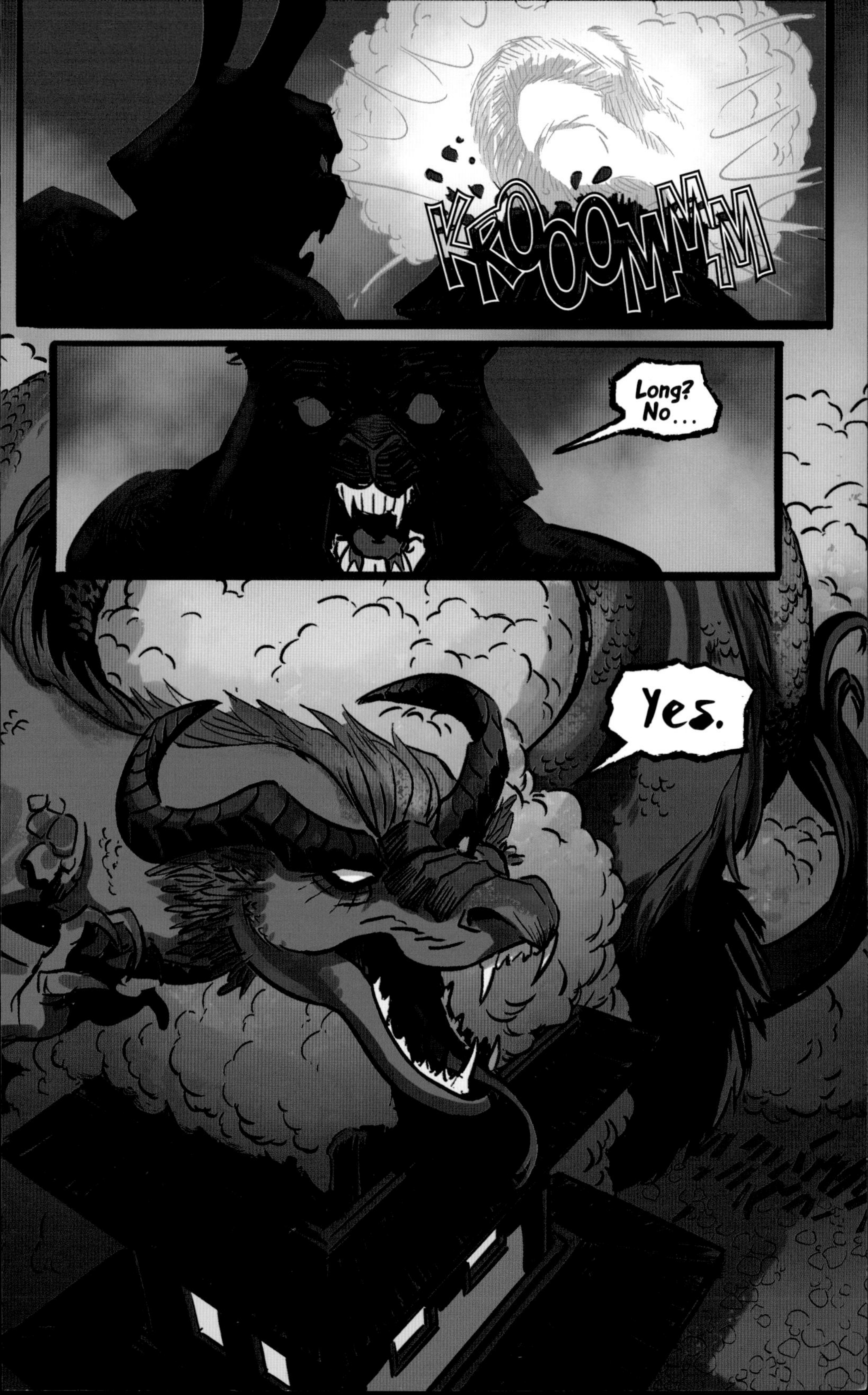
KROOOMMMM
Long? No...
Yes.

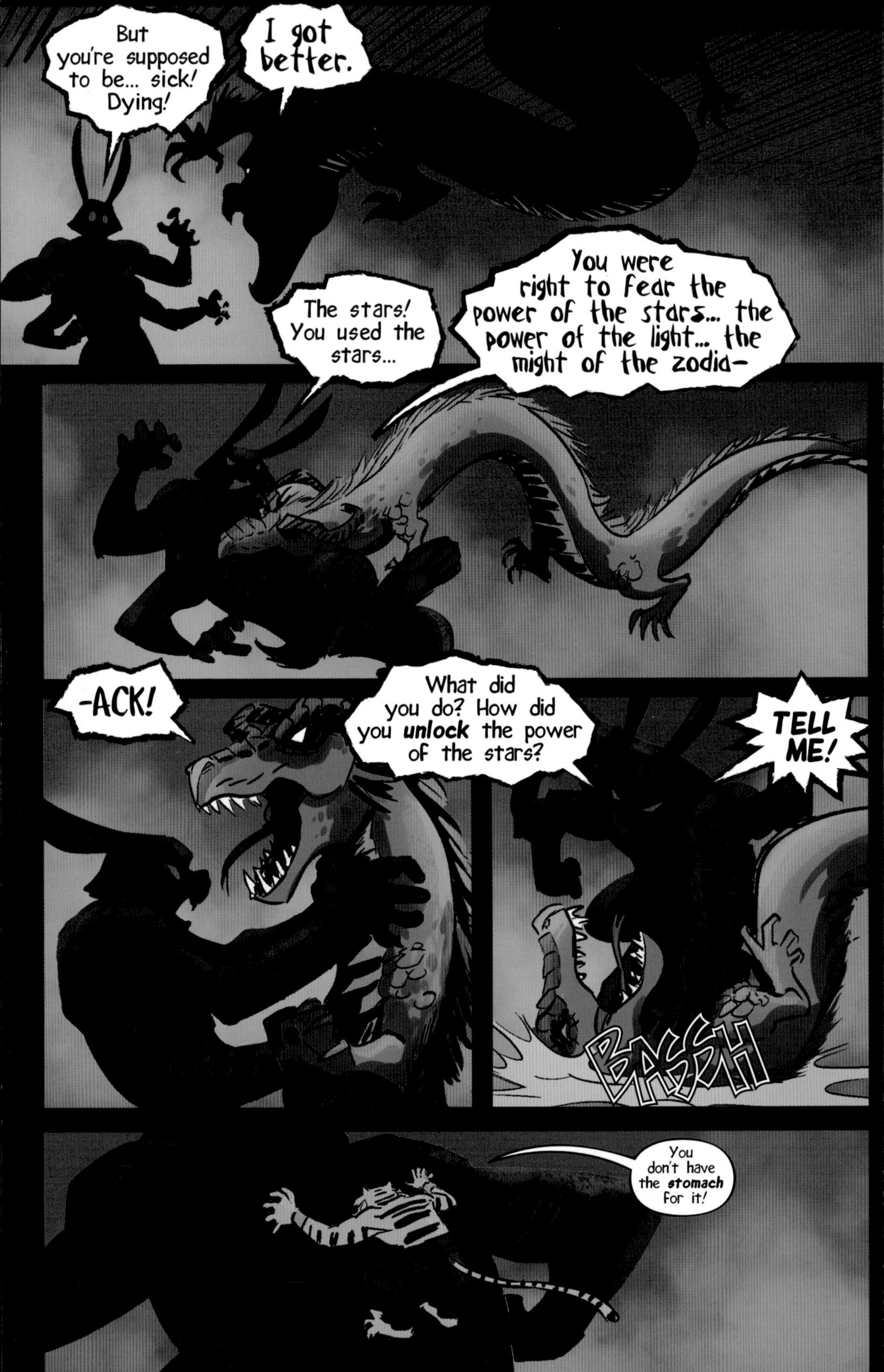
But you're supposed to be... sick! Dying!
I got better.
The stars! You used the stars...
You were right to fear the power of the stars... the power of the light... the might of the zodia-
-ACK!
What did you do? How did you **unlock** the power of the stars?
TELL ME!
BASSH
You don't have the **stomach** for it!

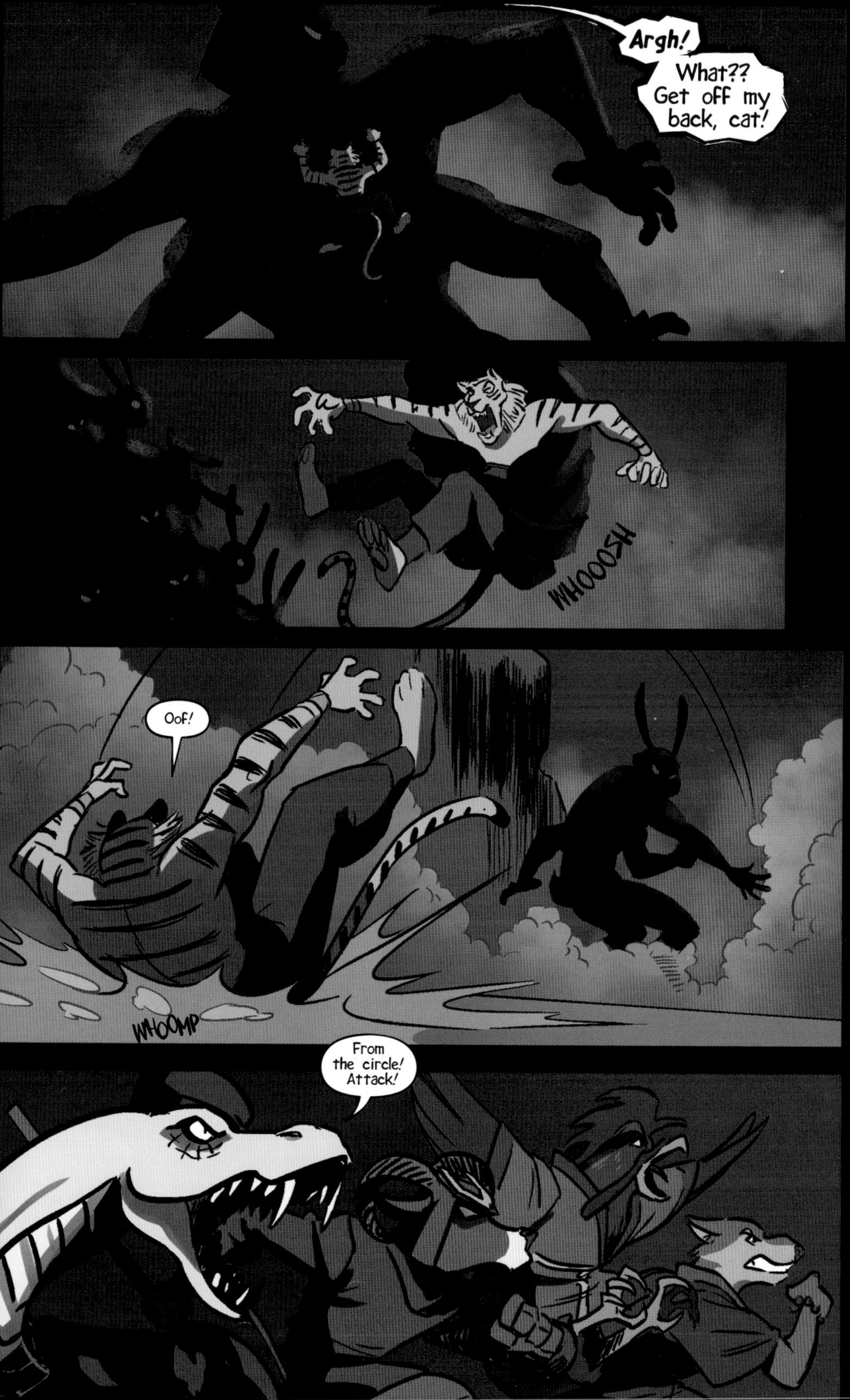
Argh!
What?? Get off my back, cat!
WHOOOSH
Oof!
WHOOMP
From the circle! Attack!

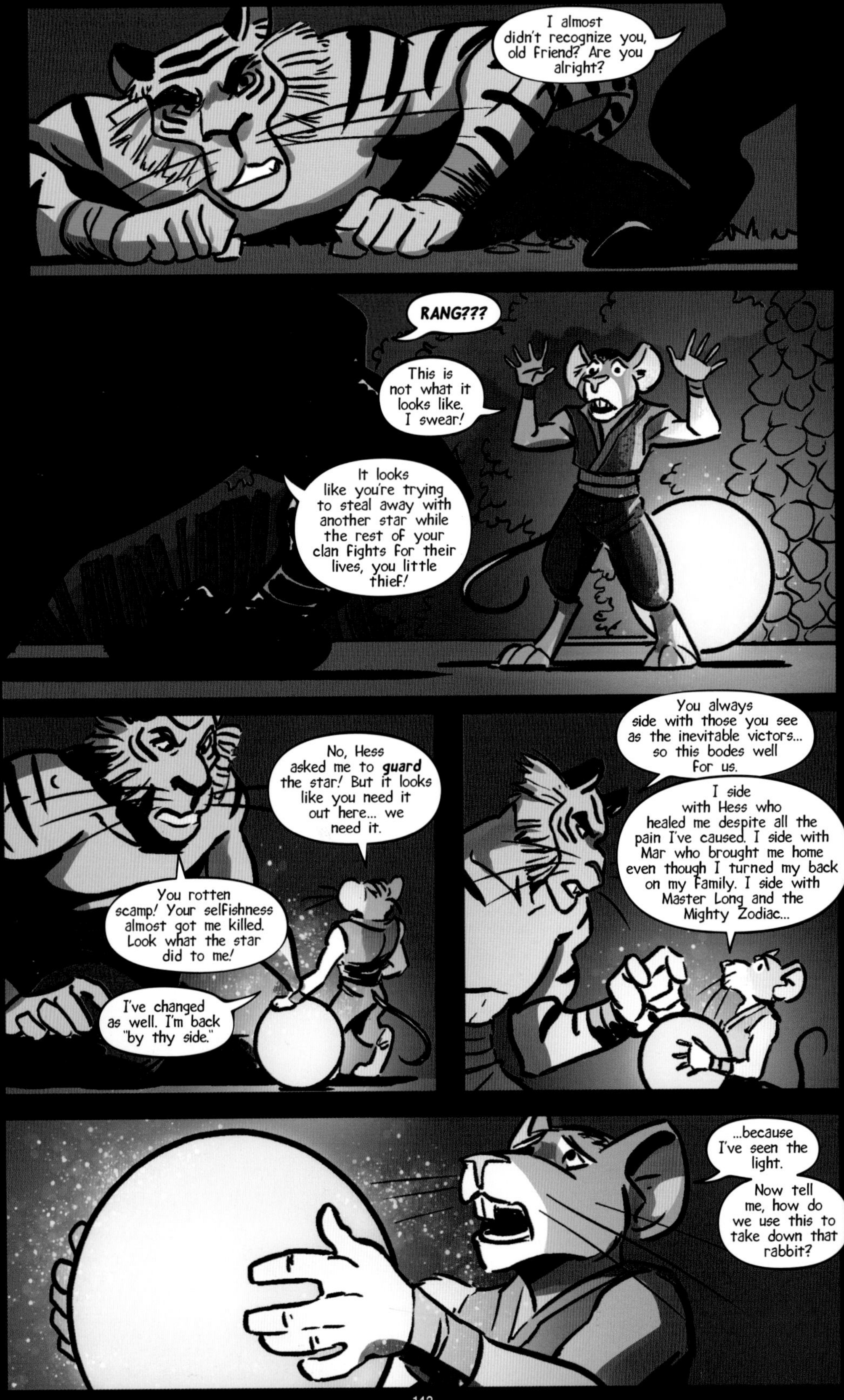

I almost didn't recognize you, old friend? Are you alright?
RANG???
This is not what it looks like. I swear!
It looks like you're trying to steal away with another star while the rest of your clan fights for their lives, you little thief!
No, Hess asked me to **guard** the star! But it looks like you need it out here... we need it.
You rotten scamp! Your selfishness almost got me killed. Look what the star did to me!
I've changed as well. I'm back "by thy side."
You always side with those you see as the inevitable victors... so this bodes well for us.
I side with Hess who healed me despite all the pain I've caused. I side with Mar who brought me home even though I turned my back on my family. I side with Master Long and the Mighty Zodiac...
...because I've seen the light.
Now tell me, how do we use this to take down that rabbit?

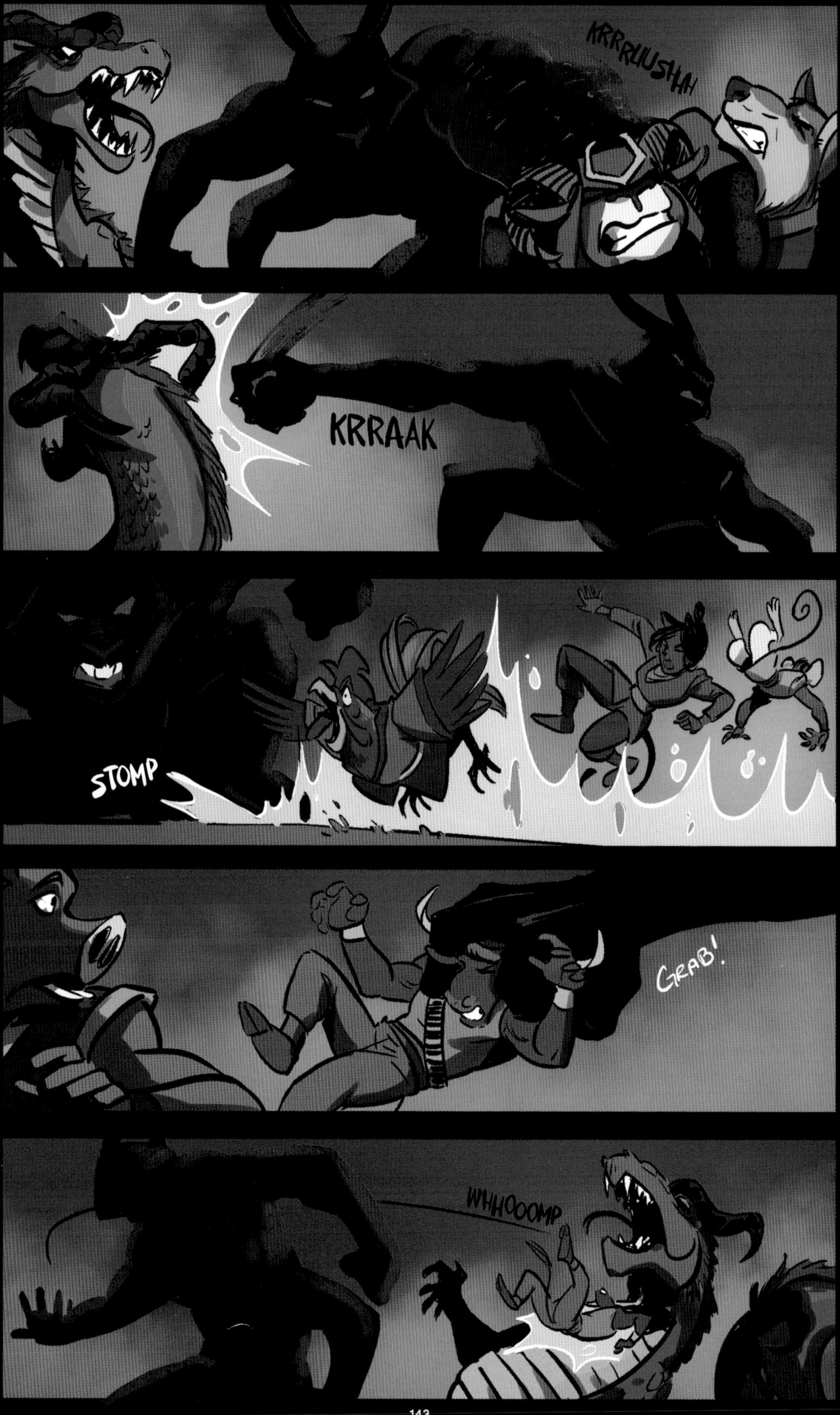
KRRRUUSHHH
KRRAAK
STOMP
GRAB!
WHHOOOMP

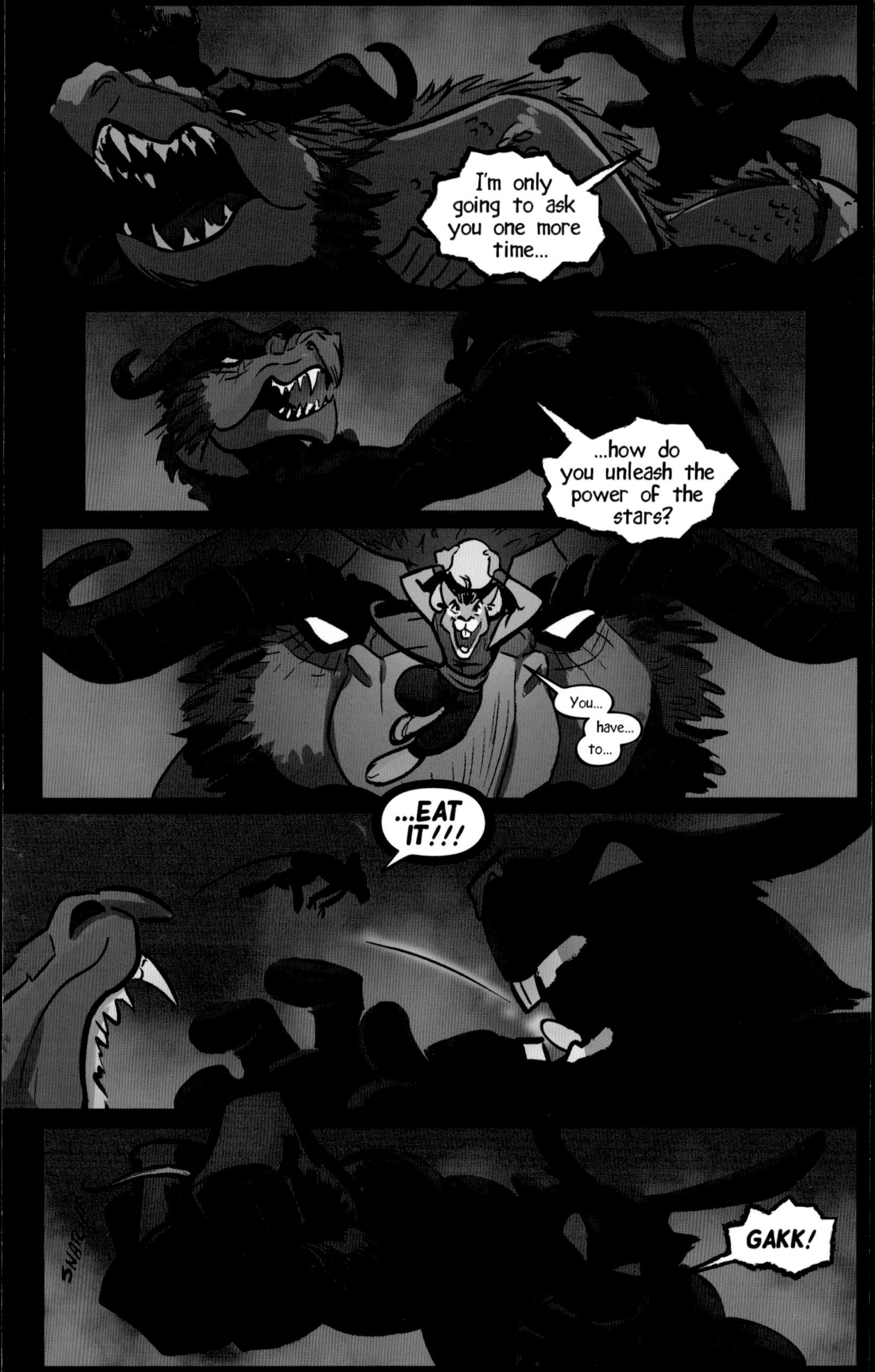
I'm only going to ask you one more time...
...how do you unleash the power of the stars?
You... have... to...
...EAT IT!!!
GAKK!

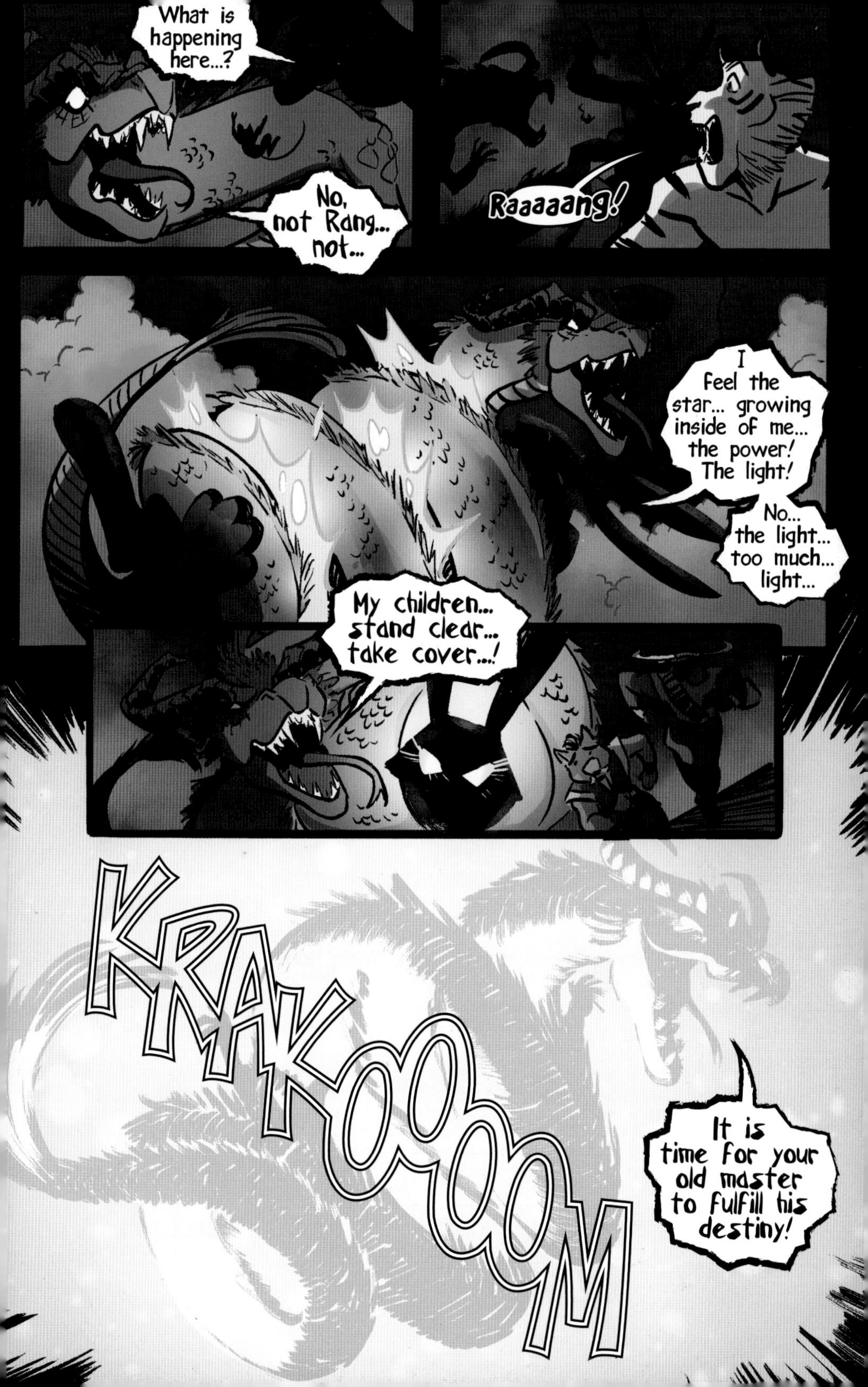
What is happening here...?
No, not Rang... not...
Raaaaang!
I feel the star... growing inside of me... the power! The light!
No... the light... too much... light...
My children... stand clear... take cover...!
KRAKOOOOOM
It is time for your old master to fulfill his destiny!

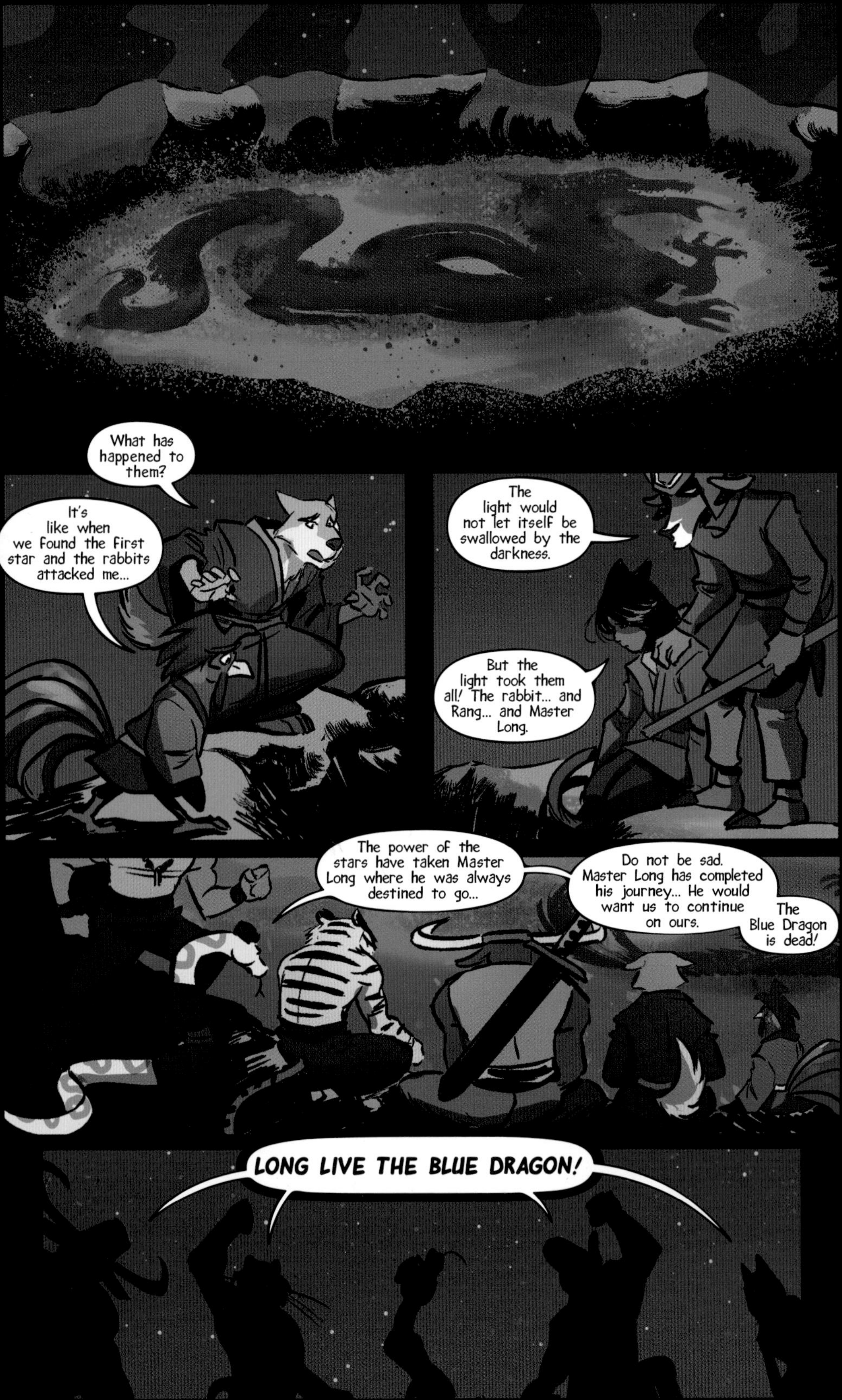
What has happened to them?
It's like when we found the first star and the rabbits attacked me...
The light would not let itself be swallowed by the darkness.
But the light took them all! The rabbit... and Rang... and Master Long.
The power of the stars have taken Master Long where he was always destined to go...
Do not be sad. Master Long has completed his journey... He would want us to continue on ours.
The Blue Dragon is dead!
LONG LIVE THE BLUE DRAGON!

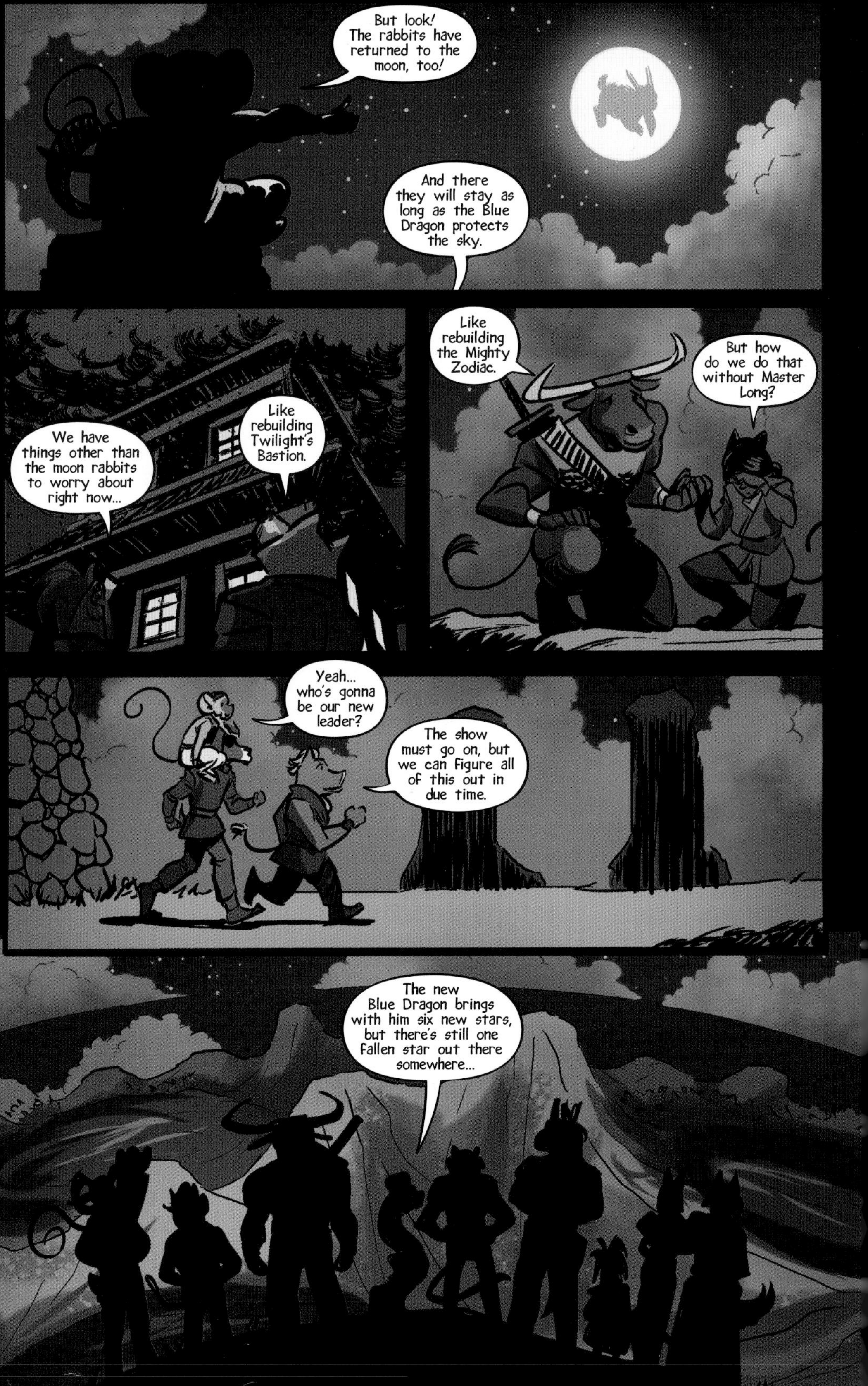
But look! The rabbits have returned to the moon, too!
And there they will stay as long as the Blue Dragon protects the sky.
We have things other than the moon rabbits to worry about right now...
Like rebuilding Twilight's Bastion.
Like rebuilding the Mighty Zodiac.
But how do we do that without Master Long?
Yeah... who's gonna be our new leader?
The show must go on, but we can figure all of this out in due time.
The new Blue Dragon brings with him six new stars, but there's still one fallen star out there somewhere...

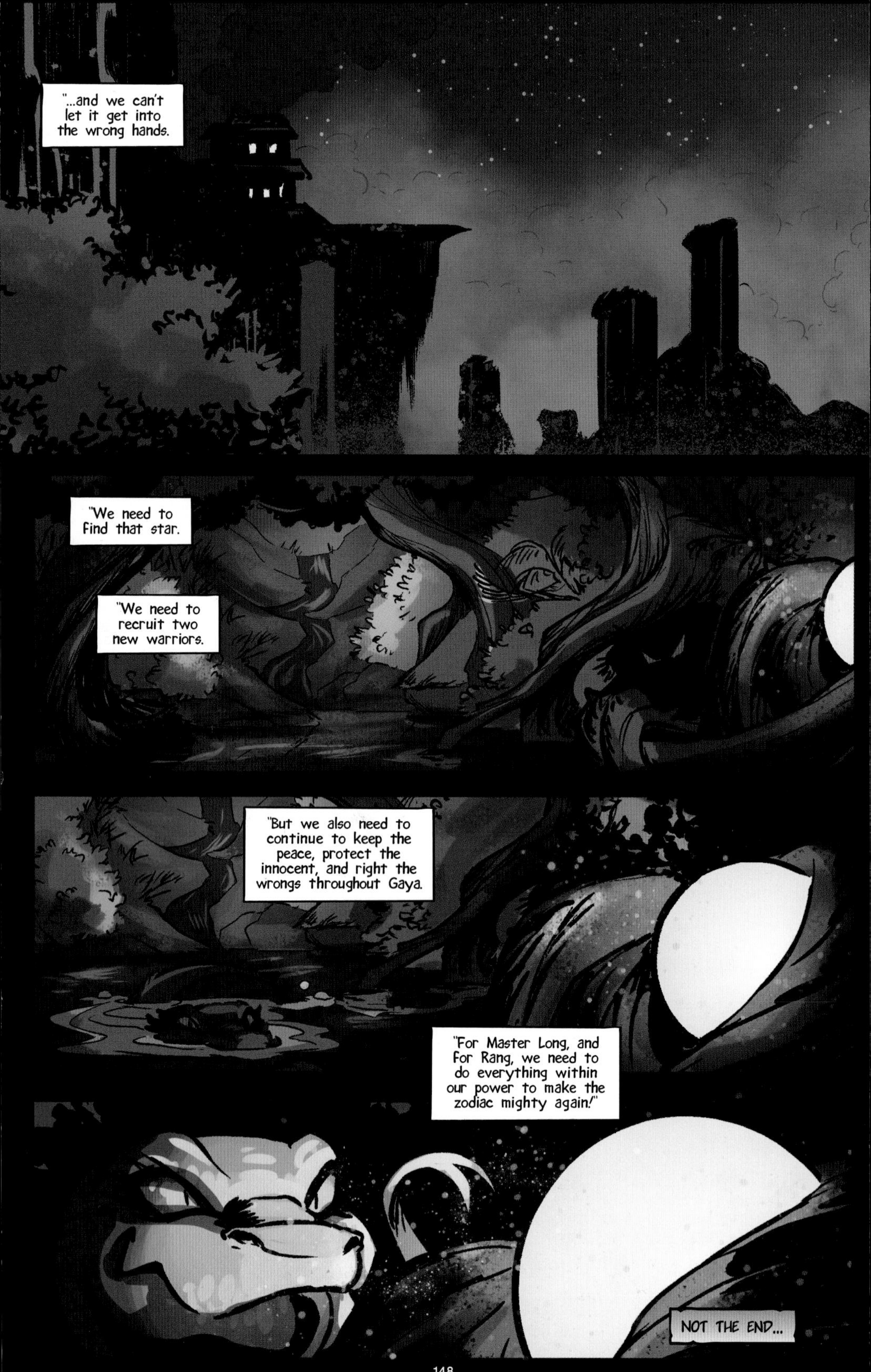
"...and we can't let it get into the wrong hands.
"We need to find that star.
"We need to recruit two new warriors.
"But we also need to continue to keep the peace, protect the innocent, and right the wrongs throughout Gaya.
"For Master Long, and for Rang, we need to do everything within our power to make the zodiac mighty again!"
NOT THE END...

SECRET ORIGIN OF THE MIGHTY ZODIAC: (PART 1)

I'm often asked where the idea for *The Mighty Zodiac* came from. The first seed for the concept was planted in my mind some ten years ago, during my first visit to Korea (where my wife is from). At a museum in Seoul, I came across these twelve stone statues of animal warriors representing the Chinese zodiac standing in a circle ("zodiac" meaning "circle of animals"). I was fascinated by these statues. I took lots of pictures. I thought that there was a story to be told here. I imagined the statues coming to life (like Disney's *Gargoyles*) and going on adventures.

A year or so later, we were visiting family in the Philippines (where I was born). We spent a few days in the countryside home of my grandmother where each morning I was prematurely awoken by the crowing of a rooster. I hated that rooster, but he reminded me of the stone rooster warrior in Seoul. The rooster is my Chinese zodiac and a symbol of the Philippines. He was also the first member of the Mighty Zodiac.

Despite being Chinese in origin, I thought it would be cool to have a more multicultural cast in this circle of animals—unlike *Kung Fu Panda* in which I presume most of not all of the animals are Chinese. And so Tan the Rooster, who I "made" a Filipino character for the reasons above, became a kind of template for the other characters in the story; I tried to base their names, dress, fighting style, and maybe even the way they spoke—much like the tribes on one of my all-time favourite animated series *Avatar: The Last Airbender*—on another nationality, ethnicity, or culture associated with that particular animal. The operative word being *try*. Sometimes it was pop culture, as is the case with Mal, a horse who walks and talks like someone from an old Hollywood Western. Or a combination of inspirations, as is the case with Mar, a ewe dressed as a ram, whose backstory is "*Mulan* set in the Rockies."

Anyway, that's how it started—with the cast. On my next trip to Korea, a few years after the first, I walked into the arrivals terminal at the airport and was greeted by six-foot tall replicas of the stone animal warriors from the museum. I guess I wasn't the only one who saw their "marketing" potential! I took it as a sign. I had my cast, for the most part, now all I needed was a story. Coming up with that took another few years, and maybe in the next volume, I'll answer the question of how I came up with "Starfall" based on a failed pitch, translating some Korean comics, and a family illness...

–J. TORRES, DECEMBER 2016

J. TORRES is an award-winning comic book writer perhaps best known for *Alison Dare, Bigfoot Boy,* and *Teen Titans Go.* His Oni Press titles include *Brobots, Do-Gooders,* and *The Mighty Zodiac.* The writer lives in Toronto, Canada with his wife and two sons.

CORIN HOWELL is an artist best known for her work on *Bat-Mite, Transformers, Back to the Future, Jem and the Holograms,* and so much more. She lives in Savannah, Georgia, with a couple of adorable cats.

MAARTA LAIHO spends her days and nights as a freelance artist and comic colorist, where her work includes *The Mighty Zodiac, Lumberjanes,* and *Adventure Time.* When she's not doing that, she can be found hoarding houseplants and talking to her cat (who quite frequently talks back). She currently lives as a hermit in the woods of Maine.

WARREN WUCINICH is an illustrator, colorist and part-time carny currently living in Durham, NC. When not making comics he can usually be found watching old *Twilight Zone* episodes and eating large amounts of pie.

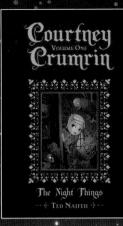

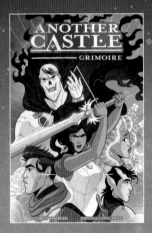